SPOTLIGHT

COSTA RICA'S CARIBBEAN COAST

Including San José

CHRISTOPHER P. BAKER

Contents

THE CARIBBEAN COAST 7

PLANNING YOUR TIME 9
SAFETY CONCERNS 11
HISTORY 11

Highway 32 to Puerto Limón 12

◖ RAINFOREST AERIAL TRAM .. 12
GUÁPILES 13
Accommodations and Food 14
Getting There 14
GUÁCIMO 15
Getting There 15
SIQUIRRES 15
◖ Veragua Rainforest
Research & Adventure Park 15
Sports and Recreation 16
Accommodations and Food 17
Getting There 17

Puerto Limón and Vicinity .. 17

PUERTO LIMÓN 17
Orientation 17
Sights 17
Entertainment and Events 19
Accommodations 19
Food 20
Information and Services 20
Getting There and Away 20
Getting Around 21
PUERTO LIMÓN TO
TORTUGUERO 21
Accommodations and Food 21

Tortuguero and Barra del Colorado 22

◖ TORTUGUERO
NATIONAL PARK 22
Turtles 24
Exploring Tortuguero 25
When to Go 26
Information and Services 26
TORTUGUERO VILLAGE
AND LAGOON 26
Sports and Recreation 27
Accommodations 28
Food 31
Information and Services 31
Getting There 32
◖ BARRA DEL COLORADO
NATIONAL WILDLIFE REFUGE .. 33
Sportfishing 34
Accommodations and Food 34
Getting There 35

South of Puerto Limón 35

PUERTO LIMÓN TO CAHUITA 35
Selva Bananito Reserve 36
Hitoy-Cerere Biological Reserve 36
Accommodations and Food 36
Getting There 37

Cahuita and Vicinity 38

◖ CAHUITA 38
Entertainment and Events 38
Sports and Recreation 39
Accommodations in Cahuita 39
Accommodations in Playa Negra 41
Food 43
Information and Services 44
Getting There 44
Getting Around 45

CAHUITA NATIONAL PARK 45
Information and Services...........45

Puerto Viejo and Vicinity....46
PUERTO VIEJO...............46
Finca la Isla Botanical Garden.......47
Keköldi Indigenous Reserve 47
Entertainment and Events..........48
Sports and Recreation.............49
Shopping 50
Accommodations 50
Food 54
Information and Services...........55
Getting There 55
Getting Around 56
PLAYA COCLES TO PUNTA UVA ..56
Sports and Recreation.............57
Accommodations 57
Food 60
Services 61

Manzanillo and Vicinity...... 61
MANZANILLO................... 61
Sports and Recreation............. 61
Accommodations and Food.......... 61
Getting There 62
**GANDOCA-MANZANILLO
NATIONAL WILDLIFE REFUGE** ..62
Turtle Patrol.....................64
Exploring the Park 64
Accommodations and Food.........64
Getting There 65

Río Sixaola Region...........65
BRIBRÍ AND VICINITY 65
Talamanca Indigenous Reserves 65
Accommodations and Food.........66
Information and Services...........66
Getting There 66
**SIXAOLA: CROSSING
INTO PANAMÁ**.................66

SAN JOSÉ.................68
PLANNING YOUR TIME 69
SAFETY CONCERNS 72
HISTORY......................72

Sights.........................73
ORIENTATION...................73
PLAZA DE LA CULTURA 73
Museo del Oro Precolumbino......80
Teatro Nacional 80
PARQUE CENTRAL..............82
Catedral Metropólitana 82
**PARQUES ESPAÑA
AND MORAZÁN**...............83
Centro Nacional de Cultura.........83
Museo de Jade................84
PLAZA DE LA DEMOCRACÍA....84
Museo de la Paz 84
Asamblea Legislativa 84
Museo Nacional...................85
PARQUE NACIONAL..........85
**BARRIO AMÓN AND
BARRIO OTOYA**...............86
Centro Costarricense de
Ciencias y Cultura 86
Parque Zoológico 86
BARRIO TOURNÓN..............86
WEST-CENTRAL DOWNTOWN....87
Mercado Central...............87
Museo Postal, Telegráfico y Filatélico..87
Parque Braulio Carrillo.............87
WEST OF DOWNTOWN 87
Cementerio General 87
Parque la Sabana 87
Pueblo Antiguo and
Parque de Diversiones..........88
SOUTH OF DOWNTOWN........88

EAST OF DOWNTOWN...........89
University of Costa Rica...........89

Entertainment and Recreation..............89

BARS 89
Downtown........................89
West of Downtown 90
East of Downtown.................90
Cigar Rooms 90
Gentlemen's Nightclubs............90

DISCOS AND NIGHTCLUBS 90

CINEMAS........................ 91

THEATER 91

LIVE MUSIC, DANCE, AND ART ..92
Folklórica 92
Classical 92
Jazz.............................92
Dance Classes 92
Peñas 92

CASINOS........................92

FESTIVALS 93

SPORTS AND RECREATION......93
Bowling.........................93
Gyms and Health Clubs 93
Skating 93
Soccer..........................94
Tennis 94

Shopping 94

BOOKS..........................94

COFFEE 94

ART, HANDICRAFTS, AND SOUVENIRS 94

CLOTHING 95

JEWELRY 95

CIGARS 95

Accommodations 96

Food...........................106

Information and Services ...114

TOURIST INFORMATION 114

TRAVEL AGENCIES 114

NEWSPAPERS AND MAGAZINES.............114

LIBRARIES......................114

MONEY.........................114

POST AND COMMUNICATIONS...114
Mail...........................114
Telephones......................114
Internet Access 115

LAUNDRIES....................115

PHOTOGRAPHY................115

MEDICAL SERVICES 115

TOILETS 116

Getting There and Around ..116

GETTING THERE 116
By Air 116
By Train 116
By Car.........................116
By Bus.........................116

GETTING AROUND..............117
Getting to and from the Airport 117
By Car.........................117
By Bus.........................117
By Train 119
By Taxi 119
By Tour........................120

COSTA RICA'S CARIBBEAN COAST

THE CARIBBEAN COAST

Costa Rica's Caribbean coast extends some 200 kilometers—from Nicaragua to Panamá. The zone—wholly within Limón Province—is divided into two distinct regions.

North of Puerto Limón, the port city midway down the coast, is a long, straight coastal strip backed by a broad alluvial plain cut through by the Tortuguero Canals, an inland waterway that parallels the coast all the way to the Nicaraguan border. Crocodiles, caimans, monkeys, sloths, and exotic birds can be seen from the tour boats that carry passengers through the jungle-lined canals and freshwater lagoons culminating in Tortuguero National Park and Barra del Colorado National Wildlife Refuge. A few roads have penetrated to the northern frontier far inland of the coast, but they are often impassable except for brief periods in the dry season. For locals, motorized canoes (*cayucos* or *canoas)* and water-taxis are the main means of getting about the swampy waterways.

South of Puerto Limón is the Talamanca coast, a narrow coastal plain broken by occasional headlands and coral reefs and backed by the looming Cordillera Talamanca. A succession of sandy shores leads the eye toward Panamá. The beaches are popular with surfers.

The coast is sparsely settled, with tiny villages spaced far apart. Except for the coastal town of Puerto Limón, what few villages lie along the coast are ramshackle, browbeaten by tropical storms and the curse of an ailing economy recently given a boost by the tourism boom. Life along the Caribbean coast of Costa Rica is fundamentally different than in the rest of the country. Life is lived at an easy

HIGHLIGHTS

◖ **Rainforest Aerial Tram:** A ride through the rainforest canopy on this "ski lift"-style tram provides a fabulous introduction to tropical ecology, while a serpentarium and other wildlife exhibits display some of the creatures you may be lucky enough to see on the ride (page 12).

◖ **Veragua Rainforest Research & Adventure Park:** Combining superb exhibits on local flora and fauna with an exhilarating tram ride, plus hiking trails, this nature facility has it all (page 15).

◖ **Tortuguero National Park:** Wildlife galore awaits in this watery world where everyone gets around by boat. The beach is a prime nesting site for marine turtles, the national park is absolute tops for birding and animal viewing, and the village is a funky charmer (page 22).

◖ **Barra del Colorado National Wildlife Refuge:** The big one that didn't get away awaits you at this prime sportfishing spot near the Nicaraguan border. Several sportfishing lodges cater to anglers keen to tackle prize tarpon and snook (page 33).

◖ **Cahuita:** Popular with the offbeat crowd, this small village has heaps of character. Several eateries serve spicy local cuisine, and Cahuita National Park offers great beaches, diverse wildlife, and a small coral reef (page 38).

◖ **Puerto Viejo:** Drawing surfers and latter-day hippies, this somnolent village has tremendous budget accommodations. Activities include horseback riding and hikes to indigenous villages, and beautiful beaches ease south for miles (page 46).

◖ **Gandoca-Manzanillo National Wildlife Refuge:** This reserve spans several ecosystems teeming with animal life, from crocodiles to monkeys to manatees. Turtles also come ashore to lay eggs (page 62).

LOOK FOR ◖ TO FIND RECOMMENDED SIGHTS, ACTIVITIES, DINING, AND LODGING.

pace. It may take you a few days to get in the groove. Don't expect things to happen at the snap of your fingers.

The black *costeños* (coast dwellers), who form approximately one-third of Limón Province's population of 220,000, have little in common with the *sponyamon*—the "Spaniard man," or highland mestizo, who represents the conservative Latin American culture. More than anywhere else in Costa Rica, the peoples of the Caribbean coast reflect a mingling of races and cultures. There are Creoles of mixed African and European descent; black Caribs, whose ancestors were African and Caribbean Indian; mestizos, of mixed Spanish and Amerindian blood; more Chinese than one might expect; and, living in the foothills of the Talamancas, approximately 5,000 Bribrí and Cabecar indigenous peoples.

The early settlers of the coast were British pirates, smugglers, log-cutters, and their slaves, who brought their own Caribbean dialects with words that are still used today. During the late 19th century, increasing numbers of English-speaking Afro-Caribbean families—predominantly from Jamaica—came to build and work the Atlantic Railroad and banana plantations, eventually settling and infusing the local dialect with lilting parochial patois phrases familiar to travelers in the West Indies. Afro-Caribbean influences are also notable in the regional cuisine.

West Indian life might be typified by the Rastafarians one meets in Cahuita and Puerto Viejo. Some of the young black males here appear sullen and lackadaisical, even antagonistic (some seem to harbor a resentment of white tourists). But most locals have hearts of gold, and there's a strong, mutually supportive community that tourists may not easily see: When a local has a need, such as medical care, locals often band together to pay the bills. (Paula Palmer's *What Happen: A Folk History of Costa Rica's Talamanca Coast* and *Wa'apin Man* provide insight into the traditional Creole culture of the area.)

The Caribbean coast is generally hot and exceedingly wet (averaging 300–500 cm of rain annually). Fortunately, light breezes blow consistently year-round. The region has no real dry season and endures a "wet season" in which the rainfall can exceed 100 centimeters per month. Rains peak May–August and again in December and January, when sudden storms blow in, bowing down the coconut palms and deluging the Talamancas.

PLANNING YOUR TIME

There are many visitors who arrive with no schedule, intent on kicking it until the money runs out or they otherwise get an urge to move on. This is particularly so of the funky, laid-back hamlets of **Cahuita** and **Puerto Viejo,** budget havens popular with surfers, the tie-dyed backpack set, and those seeking immersion in Creole culture. Most people stay at least a week to get in the groove and make the most of the southern Caribbean zone's many offbeat offerings, including **Cahuita National Park,** protecting a rainforest full of monkeys, as well as one of Costa Rica's few coral reefs. Surfers head to Puerto Viejo and the beaches that run south in a paternoster to the hamlet of **Manzanillo** and **Gandoca-Manzanillo National Wildlife Refuge.** You'll want to take horseback rides along the beach and/or a "dolphin safari" into Gandoca-Manzanillo, while experienced surfers might want to check out the Hawaiian-size waves two miles off Punta Cocles. And if you don't mind roughing it, consider an excursion into the Talamancas for an overnight at **Reserva Indígena Yorkín.**

Farther north, most travelers head to **Tortuguero National Park** for 1–3 days of viewing wildlife by rented canoe or on guided boat tours offered by nature lodges. Tortuguero is famous as the most important nesting site in the western Caribbean for the Pacific green turtle, one of four species that come ashore predictably at numerous beaches up and down this shore. Anglers favor **Barra del Colorado,** acknowledged for the best tarpon- and snook-fishing in the world; two or three days is sufficient. Tour operators and specialist lodges can make all arrangements.

You'll need to fly to Tortuguero or Barra, or take a boat. Buses serve Cahuita and Puerto

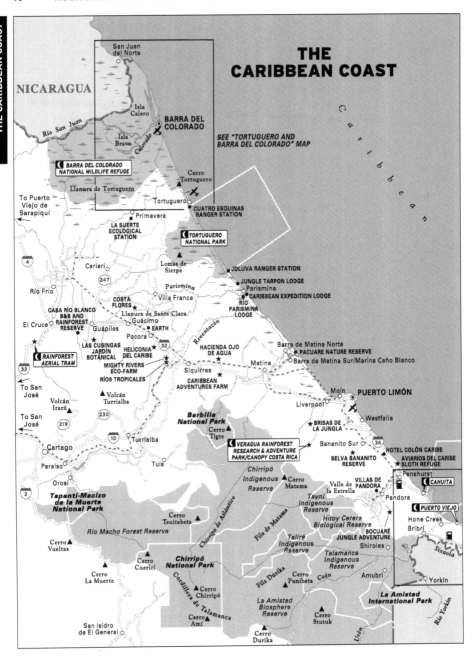

THE CARIBBEAN COAST

NICARAGUA

San Juan del Norte

Isla Calero

Río San Juan

BARRA DEL COLORADO

Isla Brava

SEE "TORTUGUERO AND BARRA DEL COLORADO" MAP

BARRA DEL COLORADO NATIONAL WILDLIFE REFUGE

Cerro Tortuguero

Llanura de Tortuguero

To Puerto Viejo de Sarapiquí

Tortuguero

CUATRO ESQUINAS RANGER STATION

Primavera

LA SUERTE ECOLOGICAL STATION

TORTUGUERO NATIONAL PARK

Cariari

Lomas de Sierpe

JOLUVA RANGER STATION

247

JUNGLE TARPON LODGE

Río Frío

Parismina

Parismina

CARIBBEAN EXPEDITION LODGE

Villa Franca

RÍO PARISMINA LODGE

COSTA FLORES

CASA RÍO BLANCO B&B AND RAINFOREST RESERVE

Llanura de Santa Clara

Guácimo

El Cruce

Guápiles

EARTH

Pocora

32

HACIENDA OJO DE AGUA

Barra de Matina Norte

PACUARE NATURE RESERVE

LAS CUSINGAS JARDÍN BOTANICAL

HELICONIA DEL CARIBE

Matina

Barra de Matina Sur/Marina Caño Blanco

RAINFOREST AERIAL TRAM

MIGHTY RIVERS ECO-FARM

Siquirres

32

RÍOS TROPICALES

CARIBBEAN ADVENTURES FARM

Moín

PUERTO LIMÓN

To San José

Volcán Irardi

Volcán Turrialba

Liverpool

Westfalia

To San José

219

230

Barbilla National Park

BRISAS DE LA JUNGLA

10

Cerro Tigre

Bananito Sur

36

Cartago

Turrialba

VERAGUA RAINFOREST RESEARCH & ADVENTURE PARK/CANOPY COSTA RICA

HOTEL COLÓN CARIBE

Paraíso

Tuis

SELVA BANANITO RESERVE

AVIARIOS DEL CARIBE SLOTH REFUGE

Orosi

2

Chirripó Indigenous Reserve

Cerro Matama

Valle de la Estrella

VILLAS DE PANDORA

Penshurst

CAHUITA

Tapantí-Macizo de la Muerte National Park

Tayni Indigenous Reserve

Pandora

PUERTO VIEJO

Cerro Vueltas

Cerro Tsuitcebeta

Río Macho Forest Reserve

Fila de Matama

Hitoy Cerere Biological Reserve

Hone Creek

Bribrí

Cerro La Muerte

Cerro Cuerici

Chirripó National Park

Teliré Indigenous Reserve

BOCUARÉ JUNGLE ADVENTURE

Shiroles

Sixaola

Cerro Chirripó

Fila Dúrika

Cerro Punibeta

Coén

Talamanca Indigenous Reserve

Yorkín

Cerro Amí

La Amistad Biosphere Reserve

Amubri

La Amistad International Park

San Isidro de El General

Cerro Durika

Cerro Stutuk

Cordillera de Talamanca

Río Yorkín

Urén

Caribbean

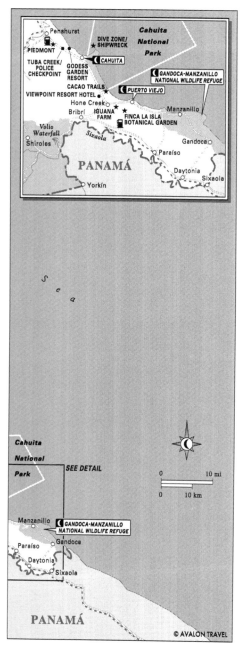

Viejo, from where tour excursions to sites of interest are offered. If you're driving along Highway 32, which connects San José to Puerto Limón, the **Rainforest Aerial Tram** makes for a rewarding stop while en route from San José to the Caribbean. And the exciting must-see **Veragua Rainforest Research & Adventure Park** opened in 2008 a short distance west of Limón.

SAFETY CONCERNS

Despite new opportunities from the tourism boom (or perhaps because of it), the region has witnessed a burgeoning drug trade, and in recent years Limón has been consumed by murderous gang wars. The southern Caribbean has also developed a reputation for crime against tourists.

On both scores, things have improved markedly in recent years, although drugs are still prevalent. (You may be pestered by young Rastas or Rasta-wannabes trying to sell you drugs.) Many undercover policemen operate locally. Hoteliers in the region claim that the bad reputation is all a sad misrepresentation, but I keep getting letters from readers who've been victims; 2005 brought reports of machete-wielding robbers around Cahuita! Don't let this put you off visiting, however—the negativity is more than counterbalanced by the scores of wonderful, welcoming souls. And local residents' associations formed by expatriate business owners have done much to eradicate crime.

Some local Afro-Caribbean men are very forward with their advances toward women, and judging from the number of young foreign women on the arms of local men, their approaches are sometimes warmly received. The "rent-a-Rasta" syndrome engendered by these foreign women with gigolos in tow has inspired a reputation for "free love" that other female travelers must contend with. Be prepared for subtle to persistent overtures.

HISTORY

In 1502, Columbus became the first European to set foot on this coast when he anchored at Isla Uvita on his fourth and last voyage to the

New World. Twenty-two years later, Hernán Cortés mapped the coast. The records the early Spaniards left tell of contact with indigenous tribes: subsistence hunters and farmers, and skilled seamen who plied the coastal waters and interior rivers in carved longboats (Cortés even mentioned Aztec traders from Mexico visiting northern Costa Rica in search of gold). The indigenous culture was quickly destroyed, however, by conquistadors. Later it was also the haunt of rumrunners, gunrunners, mahogany cutters, and pirates, mostly British, attracted by the vast riches flowing through colonial Central America. Between raids, buccaneers anchored along the wild shorelines, where they allied themselves with local native peoples. Because of them, the Caribbean coast was never effectively settled or developed by the Spanish.

Cacao was grown here in the late 17th century and was Costa Rica's first major export. Despite this, the region remained virtually uninhabited by Europeans until the Atlantic Railroad was built in the 1880s and a port at Limón was opened for coffee export. Significant numbers of Jamaican laborers were brought in.

In 1882, the government began to offer land grants to encourage cultivation of bananas. Plantations prospered until the 1930s, when banana crops were hit by disease. With the demise of the banana industry, the region went into decline. During the 1960s, plantations were revived, and the industry again dominates the region's economy.

Today, the port of Puerto Limón, along with its sister port of Moín, is the chief driving force of the urban economy. Beyond the city's hinterland, most people make their living from farming or as plantation laborers. Small-scale fishermen eke out a living from the sea, and families cling to a precarious living growing cacao (in 1979 the *Monilia* fungus wiped out most of the commercial crop). Increasingly, however, locals are being drawn into the tourism industry as guides and hotel workers.

Highway 32 to Puerto Limón

Highway 32 (the Guápiles Highway) connects San José with the Caribbean and runs east–west 104 kilometers from the foot of the Cordillera Central to Puerto Limón. Drive carefully: The heavily trafficked Highway 32 coils steeply down the mountains and is often fog-bound, landslides are frequent, and Costa Rican drivers can be exceedingly reckless—all of which makes for a white-knuckle drive. The road is frequently closed due to landslides; call the *tránsitos* (tel. 506/2268-2157) in Zurquí before setting out.

The road spills onto the northern lowlands at **El Cruce,** at the junction with Highway 4, with a gas station and **Rancho Roberto's** (tel. 506/2711-0050), a huge, modestly elegant thatched restaurant.

◖ RAINFOREST
AERIAL TRAM

The Rainforest Aerial Tram (tel. 506/2257-5961 or North America tel. 305/704-3350, www.rainforesttram.com, 6:30 A.M.–4 P.M. Tues.–Sun., 9 A.M.–4 P.M. Mon., $55 adults, $27.50 students/children), on a 475-hectare private nature reserve on the northeastern boundary of Braulio Carrillo National Park, is an unforgettable experience. Constructed at a cost of more than $2 million by Dr. Donald Perry, author of the fascinating book *Life Above the Jungle Floor,* the tram takes visitors on a guided 90-minute excursion through the rainforest canopy. The mysteries of the lush canopy unfold with each passing tree. Your ride is preceded by an instructional video. Then it's 2.6 kilometers via cable car (each car holds six people, including a naturalist guide) in the manner of a ski-lift, giving you a new vantage on the "spectacular hanging gardens of the rainforest roof." Bird excursions are also offered (bring a flashlight for nocturnal outings).

There's also a zipline with seven cables and

BANANAS . . . TURNING GREEN OR NOT?

Banana production is a monoculture that causes ecological damage. Banana plants deplete ground nutrients quickly, requiring heavy doses of fertilizer to maintain productivity. Eventually, the land is rendered useless for other agricultural activities. Fertilizers washed down by streams have been blamed for the profuse growth of water hyacinth and reed grasses that now clog the canals and wildfowl habitats, such as the estuary of the Río Estrella. And silt washing down from the plantations is acknowledged as the principal cause of the death of the coral reef within Cahuita National Park and, more recently, of Gandoca-Manzanillo.

Bananas are also prone to disease and insect assault. Pesticides such as the nematocide DBCP (banned in the United States but widely used in Costa Rica) are blamed for poisoning and sterilizing plantation workers, and for major fish kills in the Tortuguero canals.

Campaigns by local pressure groups and the threat of international boycotts have sparked a new awareness among the banana companies. A project called Banana Amigo recommends management guidelines. Companies that follow the guidelines are awarded an Eco-OK seal of approval to help them export bananas; companies continuing to clear forests are not.

Banana producers assert that the industry provides badly needed jobs. Environmentalists claim that devastating environmental effects are not worth the trade-off for a product for which demand is so fickle. The multinational corporations, too, are hardly known for philanthropy. Workers' unions, for example, have historically been pushed out of the banana fields. Some banana companies have been accused of operating plantations under virtual slave-labor conditions. The Limón government and environmentalists have also denounced British company Geest's clearcutting of forests separating Barra del Colorado and Tortuguero National Parks.

In recent years, the banana companies have scaled back due to overcapacity, and the first people to lose out have been the independent small-scale producers, many of them poor *campesinos* who had been induced to clear their forests and raise bananas for sale to the big banana companies, who are no longer buying.

six platforms ($45); several trails; an open-air serpentarium with some 20 species of snakes ($10); plus a butterfly and frog garden ($10). The fee includes all the facilities, plus as many tram rides as you wish. Expect a wait of up to one hour, as the lines are long (coffee, fruit drinks, and cookies are served). It has a restaurant and accommodations.

The tram is on Highway 32, four kilometers past the Braulio Carrillo ranger station and 15 km west of Guápiles). The parking lot is on a dangerously fast bend! The bus between San José and Guápiles will drop you off at Chichorronera la Reserva or "El Teleférico" ($1.50), but be sure to tell the driver to drop you at the entrance to the tram. Many unfortunate guests have had to trek back uphill after the driver passed the entrance and kept going!

GUÁPILES

Guápiles, 14 kilometers east of Santa Clara, is a center for the Río Frío banana region that spreads for miles to the north. It's the largest town in the Caribbean lowlands (larger by far than Limón) but there is no reason to visit.

Artist Patricia Erickson (tel./fax 506/2711-0823, patricia_erickson@amerisol.com, by appointment only) welcomes visitors to her **Gallery at Home** studio on the west bank of the Río Blanco, south of the highway, six kilometers west of town. Her vibrant paintings dance with brilliant Caribbean colors, many of them portraying her trademark faceless Limonense women of color with floating limbs. Her husband, Brian, makes fabulously creative bamboo furniture at nearby **Muebles de Bamboo** (tel. 506/2710-1958, brieri99@yahoo.com, 8 A.M.–4 P.M. Mon.–Fri., 8 A.M.–noon Sat.). He offers tours of his bamboo and sculpture garden by appointment ($25 for 1–2 people). **Las Cusingas Jardín Botánico** (Las Cusingas Botanical Garden, tel. 506/2382-5805, $5 admission), two kilometers east of Guápiles and four kilometers south by dirt road (the turn is at Soda Buenos Aires; 4WD recommended), undertakes research; raises ornamentals, medicinal plants, and fruit trees; and serves to educate visitors about tropical ecology. Trails lead into tropical forest. Horseback rides are offered. Birding is excellent. Guided two-hour tours ($5) are given.

La Suerte Biological Field Station Lodge (tel. 506/2710-8005, in North America tel. 305/666-9932, www.lasuerte.org), at La Primavera, on the banks of the Río Suerte, near the southwestern border of Barra del Colorado and 20 kilometers inland from Tortuguero National Park, has 10 kilometers of rainforest trails open to ecotourists ($8 pp day visit, including lunch). It teaches workshops in tropical ecology, from primate behavior to herpetology. It has rustic accommodations. A bus leaves Cariari, 15 kilometers north of Guápiles, at 6:30 A.M. and 10:30 A.M. daily.

Accommodations and Food

West of Guápiles, the **Hotel y Cabinas Lomas del Toro** (tel./fax 506/2710-2934, $12 s/d cold water, from $20 s/d with a/c), overlooking the Río Toro Amarillo, about two kilometers west of Guápiles, has 48 rooms with private bath. Twenty-two have cold water only and are sparsely furnished, albeit clean. Air-conditioned rooms contain modest furnishings. All rooms have a fan and cable TV. There's a swimming pool and restaurant.

I highly recommend **Casa Río Blanco Ecolodge** (tel./fax 506/2710-4124, www.casarioblanco.com, $45 s, $65 d including breakfast), on the banks of the Río Blanco, seven kilometers west of Guápiles and one kilometer south of the bridge (and only 12 kilometers from the Rainforest Aerial Tram). It has two pleasant rooms in the main lodge, plus four charming wooden cabins, all with private baths with hot water, plus orthopedic mattresses. The cabins

have one screened wall open to a spacious porch so that you can look directly into the rainforest canopy and see the river bubbling away below. They're warmly decorated with colorful spreads and pre-Colombian pottery. The delightful owners, Annette and Herbie, lead birding and nature hikes. The lodge is popular with birders and offers fantastic wildlife viewing. Vegetarian meals are served.

Continuing past Casa Río Blanco Ecolodge, David and Dalia Vaughan offer four-day, three-night rainforest adventures at **La Danta Salvaje** (tel./fax 506/2750-0012, www.ladantasalvaje.com; 4-day packages cost $210), a 410-hectare private reserve bordering Braulio Carrillo. Accommodations are in a rustic yet cozy wooden lodge. It's a tough slog by 4WD, then a stiff hike to the mountainside property (helicopter transfers are also offered). It charges $210 including lodging, meals, and guided hikes.

In Guápiles, the lively **Hotel & Country Club Suerre** (tel. 506/2710-7551, www.suerre.com, $60 s, $75 d, $120 s/d junior suite), at the east end of town, is an elegant, modern hacienda-style property with 55 spacious air-conditioned rooms appointed with hardwoods. Each has satellite TV. The hotel features an Olympic-size pool, a restaurant, two bars and a disco, and a whirlpool tub and sauna. Day guests can use the facilities for $2.50.

Alternately, the **Hotel Talamanca Pococí** (tel. 560/2710-3030), beside the gas station at the entrance to town, is an option, but traffic noise might be an issue here.

The handsome **Restaurante Río Danta** (tel. 506/2710-2626, 11 A.M.–1 P.M.), five kilometers west of Guápiles, serves *típico* lunches and has short trails leading into the adjacent private forest reserve (good for spotting poison-dart frogs).

Getting There

Empresario Guápileños (tel. 506/2222-2727) buses from San José depart the Gran Terminal del Caribe on Calle Central, Avenidas 13/15, every hour 5:30 A.M.–7 P.M. daily ($2.50). And Transportes Caribeños (tel. 506/2221-

2596) buses depart the same terminal hourly 5:30 A.M.–7 P.M., bound for Limón.

Buses depart Guápiles for Puerto Viejo de Sarapiquí seven times daily.

GUÁCIMO

Guácimo is a small town and important truck stop about 12 kilometers east of Guápiles and about 400 meters north of Highway 32. Signs point the way north to **Costa Flores** (tel. 506/2716-7645 or 506/2716-6430, costaflo@ sol.racsa.co.cr, 8 A.M.–4 P.M. $15), a tropical flower farm with more than 600 varieties of plants blossoming gloriously across 120 blazingly colorful hectares. Call ahead, as it has always been closed when I've passed by.

EARTH (Escuela de Agricultura de la Región Tropical Húmeda, tel. 506/2713-0000, www.earth.ac.cr), School of Tropical Humid Agriculture, one kilometer east of town, is a university that teaches agricultural techniques to students from Latin America. It specializes in researching ecologically sound, or sustainable, agriculture. EARTH has its own banana plantation and 400-hectare forest reserve with nature trails. Visitors are welcome. Costa Rica Expeditions (tel. 506/2257-0766, www.costarica expeditions.com) offers a full-day tour.

Getting There

Buses (tel. 506/2222-0610 and 506/2716-6037) for Guácimo leave San José from Gran Terminal del Caribe on Calle Central, Avenidas 13/15 ($2.75), at 5:30 A.M., 7 A.M., 11:30 A.M., 2 P.M., and 7 P.M. daily.

SIQUIRRES

Siquirres, 25 kilometers east of Guácimo and 49 kilometers west of Limón, is a major railroad junction, echoing to the clanging of locomotives working freight for the banana companies. One reader states, "Yuck! Don't bother" (with Siquirres). However, on Sunday at 4 P.M., head to **Finca Las Tilapias** (tel. 506/8398-1517, $12), where owner Gilberto "Chito" Sheedan swims, wrestles, and does tricks with Poncho, his one-eyed, five-meter-long crocodile.

The Standard Fruit Co. offers a tour of its **Esperanzas banana plantation** (tel. 506/2768-8683, www.bananatourcostarica.com) and packing plant. **Agritours** (tel. 506/2282-1349, www.agritourscr.com) offers 90-minute tours of Del Monte's Hacienda Ojo de Agua pineapple plantation (8 A.M.–5 P.M. Mon.–Fri., $19 adult, $8 children), 10 kilometers east of Siquirres. **Hacienda Milla 25** (tel. 506/2241-3233, www .milla25.com), at Batáan, about 10 km east of Siquirres, has horseback and wagon rides on the cattle farm, including a round-up. And **Mighty Rivers Eco-Farm** (tel. 506/2765-1116, http:// mightyrivers.net) offers tours of this sustainable dairy farm, where a medley of world-spanning cattle, from Norwegian Fjord to African Watusi, are bred and milked to produce milk and yogurt.

The town is two kilometers east of the Río Reventazón and one kilometer west of the Río Pacuare. White-water rafters traditionally take out at Siquirres.

About five kilometers east of Siquirres and 100 meters west of the Río Pacuarito, a dirt road leads south 17 kilometers to the remote 12,000-hectare **Barbilla National Park** (Parque Nacional Barbilla), on the northeast flank of the Talamanca Mountains. Its creation in the face of heavy logging is a testament to the efforts of the Fundación Nairi, which has a small field station: Estación Biológica Barbilla. The park ($6 admission) is administered by SINAC's Amistad Caribe Conservation Area office (tel. 506/2768-5341, fax 506/2768-8603, aclac@minae.go.cr) in Siquirres. The ranger station at Las Brisas del Pacuarito (10 km from the highway) has restrooms and potable water. A four-wheel-drive vehicle is required to get there.

◖ Veragua Rainforest Research & Adventure Park

This superb facility (tel. 506/2296-5056, www.veraguarainforest.com, $65 adults, $45 children half-day, $99/70 full-day), which opened in summer 2008, is the keystone of a private reserve protecting 1,300 hectares of primary and secondary rainforest at Las Brisas

the aerial tram at Veragua Rainforest Research & Adventure Park

© CHRISTOPHER P. BAKER

del Veragua; the turnoff is at Liverpool, about 12 kilometers west of Limón (4WD required). Highlights include butterfly, snake, and frog exhibits (including a walk-through nocturnal frog garden with misters) linked by elevated boardwalks over the forest. An open-air tram through the canopy whisks you steeply down to the "Trail of the Giants" riverside trail (good for spotting poison-dart frogs), which leads to a fabulous waterfall. Thoughtful education signage is a bonus. This is an active research facility also, run in collaboration with INBio; you can watch biologists at work. Even the stylishly modern yet old-fashioned urinals offer forest views! The entrance fee includes a guided tour and lunch in a lovely open-air restaurant.

Sports and Recreation

The **Original Canopy Tour** (tel. 506/2291-4465, www.canopytour.com, $45 adult, $35 student, $25 child), at Veragua Rainforest Research & Adventure Park, offers a thrilling zipline adventure through the rainforest canopy. On the access road to Veragua, **Brisas de la Jungla** (tel. 506/2797-1291,

Veragua Rainforest Research & Adventure Park

© CHRISTOPHER P. BAKER

www.junglebreeze.com) competes with a 13-platform zipline tour ($45 adults, $35 children), plus horseback rides, and a trail.

Caribbean Adventures Farm (tel. 506/2765-9912, www.caribbeanadventuresfarm.com), eight kilometers east of Siquirres, offers horseback riding, waterfall rappelling, river floats, and hikes.

Accommodations and Food

In Siquirres, the **Hotel Alcema** (tel. 506/2768-6004, $10 pp shared bath, $20 s/d private bath), two blocks north and two east of the plaza, has 23 small and simply furnished but clean rooms with fans and shared bath with cold water. Six newer cabins to the rear have TV and private bath. There's a TV lounge and a small restaurant.

Of the several simple hotels along the main highway, **Cabinas Don Quito** (tel. 506/2765-8076), five kilometers east of town, is one of the better options.

Getting There

Buses (tel. 506/2222-0610 or 506/2768-9484) for Siquirres leave San José from Gran Terminal del Caribe on Calle Central, Avenidas 13/15, at 6:30 A.M. and 9:30 A.M., then hourly 10 A.M.–6 P.M. daily ($2.75). Buses from Siquirres depart hourly for Guápiles, Puerto Limón, and San José from the bus terminal on the main street, 50 meters north of the plaza.

Puerto Limón and Vicinity

PUERTO LIMÓN

Puerto Limón (pop. 65,000) is an important maritime port and gateway to all other points on the Caribbean. The harbor handles most of the sea trade for Costa Rica. Trucks hauling containers rumble along the main road day and night. A new cruise port (tel. 506/2799-0215) draws cruise ships. However, except for Carnival, when it gets in the groove, Puerto Limón is merely a jumping-off point for most travelers as there is little of interest to see.

The earthquake of April 22, 1991, dealt Puerto Limón a serious blow. The city has come a long way since, as reflected in the razing of decrepit buildings and a sense of newfound prosperity.

The city has a bad reputation among Ticos and is often referred to as Piedropolis (Crack City). You should beware of pickpockets by day and muggings at night, and gang violence has recently consumed the city.

Orientation

Highway 32 from San José enters town from the west and becomes Avenida 1, paralleling the railway track that runs to the cruise port. The *avenidas* (east–west) are aligned north of Avenida 1 in sequential order. The *calles* (north–south) are numbered sequentially and run westward from the waterfront. The street signs are not to be trusted. Most addresses and directions are given in direction and distance from the market or Parque Vargas.

The road leading south from the junction of Avenida 1 and Calle 9 leads to Cahuita and Puerto Viejo. Avenida 6 leads out of town to Moín and the JAPDEVA dock, where boats can be hired for the trip to Tortuguero.

Sights

There's not much to hold you in town, although the **Mercado Central** (Avenidas Central/2, Calles 3/4), at the heart of town, is worth a browse. The unremarkable **Parque Vargas,** at the east end of Avenidas 1 and 2, is literally an urban jungle, with palm promenades and a crumbling bandstand amid a tangle of vines. On the north side, a fading mural shows life in Limón since pre-Columbian days. A bronze bust of Christopher Columbus, erected in 1990 for the 500th anniversary of his party's landing, faces the sea. On the west side of the park is the stucco **Town Hall** (Alcadía), a fine example of tropical architecture.

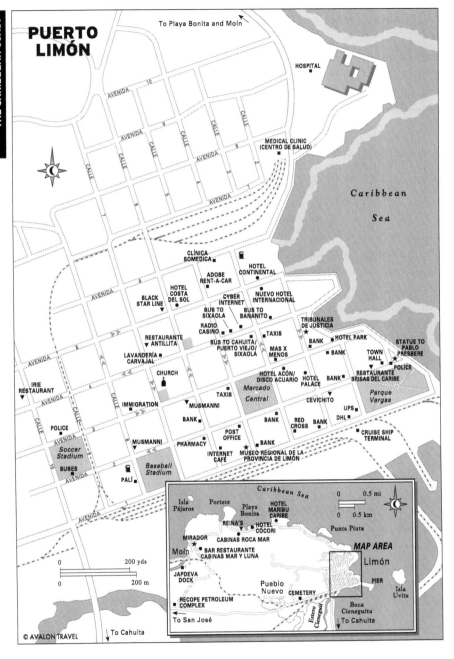

PUERTO LIMÓN

To Playa Bonita and Moín

AVENIDA 10

CALLE

CALLE

CALLE

CALLE

AVENIDA

AVENIDA

AVENIDA

HOSPITAL

MEDICAL CLINIC
(CENTRO DE SALUD)

Caribbean

Sea

CLÍNICA SOMEDICA
HOTEL CONTINENTAL
ADOBE RENT-A-CAR
HOTEL COSTA DEL SOL
BLACK STAR LINE
CYBER INTERNET
NUEVO HOTEL INTERNACIONAL
BUS TO SIXAOLA
BUS TO BANANITO
RADIO CASINO
TRIBUNALES DE JUSTICIA
RESTAURANTE ANTILLITA
BUS TO CAHUITA/ PUERTO VIEJO/ SIXAOLA
TAXIS
BANK
HOTEL PARK
STATUE TO PABLO PRESBERE
LAVANDERÍA CARVAJAL
MAS X MENOS
BANK
TOWN HALL
POLICE
CHURCH
HOTEL ACÓN/ DISCO ACUARIO
HOTEL PALACE
BANK
RESTAURANTE BRISAS DEL CARIBE
IRIE RESTAURANT
AVENIDA
Mercado Central
CEVICHITO
Parque Vargas
TAXIS
IMMIGRATION
MUSMANNI
UPS
BANK
BANK
RED CROSS
BANK
DHL
POLICE
MUSMANNI
PHARMACY
POST OFFICE
BANK
CRUISE SHIP TERMINAL
Soccer Stadium
BUSES
INTERNET CAFÉ
MUSEO REGIONAL DE LA PROVINCIA DE LIMÓN
PALÍ
Baseball Stadium

AVENIDA 6

AVENIDA 5

AVENIDA 4

AVENIDA 3

AVENIDA

AVENIDA

0   200 yds
0   200 m

To Cahuita

Caribbean Sea

Isla Pájaros
Portete
Playa Bonita
HOTEL MARIBU CARIBE
REINA'S
HOTEL COCORI
MIRADOR
CABINAS ROCA MAR
Moín
BAR RESTAURANTE CABINAS MAR Y LUNA
JAPDEVA DOCK
Pueblo Nuevo
CEMETERY
RECOPE PETROLEUM COMPLEX
To San José

Punta Piuta

MAP AREA

Limón

PIER

Isla Uvita

Boca Cieneguita
To Cahuita

Estero Cieneguit

0   0.5 mi
0   0.5 km

© AVALON TRAVEL

The oldest building in town, the **Black Star Line** (Avenida 5, Calle 6, tel. 506/2798-1948), was built in 1922 as Liberty Hall, former headquarters of Jamaican black activist Marcus Garvey's Black Star Line Steamship Company.

The **Museo Regional de la Provincia de Puerto Limón** (Calle 4, Avenidas 1/2, tel. 506/2758-2130, 9 A.M.–noon and 1–4 P.M. Mon.–Fri., free) displays artifacts, photography, and exhibits tracing the culture and history of the region.

Craggy **Isla Uvita** lies one kilometer offshore. Columbus supposedly landed on the islet in 1502; it is now a national landmark park.

Playa Bonita, four kilometers north of Puerto Limón, boasts a golden beach popular with Limonenses. Swimming is safe only at the northern end. The surf is good, but unreliable.

The port of **Moín,** six kilometers north of Puerto Limón, is where Costa Rica's crude oil is received for processing (RECOPE has its main refinery here) and bananas are loaded for shipment to Europe and North America. The only reason to visit Moín is to catch a boat to Tortuguero from the dock north of the railway tracks. However, boat captains here offer one-hour tours of the local mangroves ($10 pp), good for spotting sloths and other wildlife.

Entertainment and Events

The **Black Culture Festival** is hosted in late August and early September, with domino and oratory contests, music, and art. Contact the Black Star Line (Avenida 5, Calle 6, tel. 506/2798-1948), which has a legendary social club upstairs and also hosts an annual "Lady Black Beauty" contest for women over 35.

Each October 12, Puerto Limón explodes in a bacchanal. The annual Columbus Day **Carnival** is celebrated with a fervor akin to the bump-and-grind style of Trinidad, with street bands, floats, and every ounce of Mardi Gras passion, though in a more makeshift fashion. The weeklong event attracts people from all over the country, and getting a hotel room is virtually impossible. The celebrations include a Dance Festival—a rare opportunity to see dances from indigenous tribes, Afro-Caribbeans, and the Chinese communities—plus bands from throughout the Caribbean and Latin America, as well as beauty contests, crafts stalls, fireworks, theater, and calypso contests.

Most bars have a raffish quality. An exception is **Cevichito** (Avenida 2, Calles 2/3, tel. 506/2758-4976, from 10 A.M. daily). This tremendous bar, decorated with flags of the world, has a large-screen TV and one-armed bandits, plus groovy music.

The weekend **Disco Acuario** in the Hotel Acón is jam-packed and sweaty, with a pulsing Latin beat ($5, including a beer; free to hotel guests).

Accommodations
IN LIMÓN

It's not safe to park outside anywhere in Puerto Limón at night; your car will probably be broken into. The Hotel Acón, Hotel Park, and Hotel International have secure parking.

A stand-out among the budget options is **Hotel Continental** (Avenida 5, Calles 2/3, tel. 506/2798-0532, $10 s, $15 d), with 12 simple but spacious rooms with fans and private baths with hot water. It's spotlessly clean and offers secure parking. The same owners run the **Nuevo Hotel Internacional** (tel. 506/2758-0434, $10 s or $15 d with fans, $12 s or $18 d with a/c) across the road; it has 22 tiled rooms of a similar standard to the Continental.

Likewise, the **Hotel Costa del Sol** (Avenida 5, Calle 5, tel. 506/2798-0808, grupodelso@racsa.co.cr, $12 s, $20 d), offers clean rooms with modest, modern furnishings, fans, and private baths with hot water. It has secure parking.

The best bet in town is the **Hotel Park** (Avenida 3, Calle 1, tel. 506/2758-3476, fax 506/2758-4364, parkhotellimon@ice.co.cr, $38 s or $50 d standard, $40 s or $55 d ocean view with balcony), with 32 air-conditioned rooms featuring TVs and private baths with hot water. Prices vary according to room standard and view. It has a nice restaurant, plus secure parking.

Slightly less appealing is the four-story **Hotel Acón** (Avenida 3, Calles 2/3, tel. 506/2758-1010, fax 506/2758-2924, hotel acon@racsa.co.cr, $32 s, $38 d), with 39 air-conditioned rooms. The hotel has a reasonable restaurant. Take a top-floor room away from the noise of the second-floor disco.

OUTSIDE LIMÓN

At Playa Bonita, **Hotel Cocori** (tel. 506/2798-1670, fax 506/2758-2930, $40 s, $50 d) is a modern clifftop complex with a pleasing ocean-view terrace restaurant open to the breezes. It fills with Ticos on weekends, when the disco could wake the dead. It has 25 simple but pleasing air-conditioned rooms with cable TV and private bathrooms with hot water. Rates include breakfast.

Hotel Maribu Caribe (tel. 506/2795-2543, fax 506/2795-3541, maribucaribe@hotmail.com, $70 s or $82 d standard, $120 family suite), at the south end of Playa Bonita, has a scenic setting above the ocean. The simple, uninspired resort, which caters mostly to Ticos, is centered on a swimming pool. It has two restaurants and offers 17 round, thatched, African-style bungalows and 50 rooms, each with air-conditioning, telephone, and private bath. Rooms have narrow beds and unappealing decor. Roomy showers make amends with piping hot water.

At Moín, **Hotel Mar y Luna** (tel. 506/2795-1132, fax 506/2795-4828, $20 pp) sits atop the hill above the dock to Tortuguero. It has 14 modestly appointed air-conditioned rooms with TV and hot water. There's secure parking and a clean restaurant that has karaoke.

Food

You can sample local Caribbean dishes at the open-air *sodas* around the Mercado Central, good for filling *casados* (set lunches, $2).

I also recommend the modestly upscale, air-conditioned **Restaurante Brisas del Caribe** (Avenida 2, tel. 506/2758-0138, 9 A.M.–11 P.M. Mon.–Fri., 11 A.M.–11 P.M. Sat.–Sun.), on the north side of Park Vargas, serving an excellent, bargain-priced set buffet of *típico* dishes.

The clean, air-conditioned restaurant in the **Hotel Park** (6:30 A.M.–midnight daily) is also recommended; it serves soups, salads, shrimp cocktail ($8), lobster ($16), sea bass in garlic ($8), pastas, and cheesecake.

For Caribbean dishes, head to the **Black Star Line** (Calle 5, Avenida 5, tel. 506/2798-1948, 7:30 A.M.–10 P.M. Mon.–Sat., 11 A.M.–5 P.M. Sun., *casado* $3), in an old wooden structure where locals gather to play dominoes and socialize; or the simple **Irie Restaurant** (Calle 9, Avenidas 4/5, tel. 506/2758-3668, $2–12), serving I-tal (Rastafarian) health foods and Jamaican fare, with seating on a small balcony.

At Playa Bonita, the open-air beachfront **Reina's** (tel. 506/2795-0879, 10 A.M.–11 P.M. Mon.–Thurs., 8 A.M.–1 A.M. Fri.–Sun.) is the hip spot hereabouts and draws the party crowd on weekends. It's a good place to hang and watch the surf pump ashore while savoring a shrimp cocktail ($9), ceviche ($6), snapper ($10), or rice and beans Caribbean-style ($6).

Information and Services

The **Hospital Tony Facio** (tel. 506/2758-2222; for emergencies, tel. 506/2758-0580) is on the seafront *malecón*, reached via Avenida 6. For private service, head to **Clínica Somedica** (Avenida 6, Calle 4, tel. 506/2798-4004, www.somedicacr.com). The **Red Cross** (tel. 506/2758-0125) is at Avenida 1, Calle 4.

The **police station** is on the northwest corner of Avenida 3, Calle 8. Criminal investigation is handled by the OIJ (tel. 506/2799-1437).

The **post office** is at Calle 4, Avenida 2. The best Internet café is **Cyber Internet** (Avenida 4, Calle 4, tel. 506/2758-5061).

Immigration (Dirección de Migración y Extranjerá) is on Avenida 3, Calles 6/7.

Getting There and Away

Nature Air and **SANSA** offer regular service to the airport (tel. 506/2758-1379) two kilometers south of Limón.

Transportes Caribeños (tel. 506/2221-2596) double-decker buses depart the Gran Terminal del Caribe, on Calle Central, Avenidas 13/15 in San José hourly 5 A.M.–7 P.M. daily. The buses continue to Cahuita, Puerto Viejo, Bribrí, and Sixaola. Buses to San José depart Puerto Limón from Calle 2, Avenida 2 ($4).

Local buses depart Limón for Cahuita ($1.25), Puerto Viejo ($2), and Sixaola ($3.50) from opposite Radio Casino on Avenida 4 eight times daily (5 A.M.–6 P.M.). Buses for Manzanillo ($2) leave at 6 A.M., 2:30 P.M., and 6 P.M. daily. Buy tickets in advance at the *soda* beside the bus stop, as buses get crowded. Around the corner on Calle 4 to the north is the bus stop for Playa Bonita and Moín.

Getting Around

From Puerto Limón, the bus to Playa Bonita, Portrete, and Moín operates hourly from Calle 4, Avenida 4, opposite Radio Casino.

Taxis await customers on the south side of the market.

PUERTO LIMÓN TO TORTUGUERO

Lagoons and swamps dominate the coastal plains north of Limón. Many rivers meander through this region, carrying silt that the coastal tides conjure into long, straight, brownsand beaches. The only community along the canals is **Parismina,** on the Oceanside spit at the mouth of the Río Parismina, 45 kilometers north of Moín. It is popular year-round with anglers.

Sea turtles come ashore to nest all along the shore, notably at **Barra de Matina,** midway between Moín and Parismina (see www.costaricaturtles.com). Here, the **Pacuare Nature Reserve** (tel. 506/2719-7702, www .parisminaturtles.org) exists primarily to protect the eggs of leatherback turtles from poachers during the nesting season. The reserve is run in conjunction with Rainforest Concern (in the U.K., 8 Glanricarde Gardens, London W2 4NA, tel. 020/7229-2093, www.rainforest concern.org) and is open to visitors March 25–August 15. Volunteers are needed to join biologists and hired guards to patrol the beach, tag and measure turtles, and relocate nests; contact c.fernandez@turtleprotection.org. There is a one-week minimum stay. Conselvatur (tel./ fax 506/2253-8118, www.conselvatur.com) offers an eight-day Sea Turtle Research and Rainforest Exploration trip that features Reserva Pacuare.

The reserves can be accessed by road via **Matina,** a banana town on the banks of the Río Matina four kilometers north of Highway 32 (the turnoff is at Bristol, about 28 kilometers east of Siquirres); and by boat from Moín ($20 pp) or **Caño Blanco Marina** (tel. 506/2710-1299, or tel. 506/2206-5138 in San José), near Barra de Matina Sur.

Accommodations and Food

In Parismina, **Carefree Ranch** (tel. 506/2798-0839, $10 pp including breakfast), set in a landscaped garden, has nine rooms along a porch

---

COSTA RICA'S AQUATIC COASTAL HIGHWAY

During the Trejos administration (1966-1970) four canals were dug from solid ground to link the natural channels and lagoons stretching north of Moín to Tortuguero and the Río Colorado. Today these canals form a connected "highway" – virtually the only means of getting around along the coast. One can now travel from Siquirres eastward along the Río Pacuare, then northward to Tortuguero, and from there to the Río Colorado, which in turn connects with the Río San Juan, which will take you westward to Puerto Viejo de Sarapiquí.

The waterway is lined with rainforest vegetation in a thousand shades of green, making for a fascinating journey. Noisy flocks of parrots speed by doing barrel rolls in tight formation. Several species of kingfishers patrol the banks. In places the canopy arches over the canal, and howler monkeys sounding like rowdy teenagers may protest your passing. Keep a sharp eye out, too, for mud turtles and caimans absorbing the sun's rays on logs.

with decorative *carretas* (oxcarts). They're simply appointed, cross-lit, and have fans and somewhat basic private bathrooms. The restaurant appeals. And it rents kayaks.

Nearby, and also set in a lovely garden, is **Iguana Verde** (tel. 506/2710-1528, $10 pp with fan, $20 pp with a/c), with three clean rooms with private bath. It has a café and grocery. The neighboring **Carablanco Lodge** (tel. 506/2710-1161, $8 pp with fan, $12 pp with a/c) has 10 clean rooms with private baths, plus an open-air restaurant (9 A.M.–9 P.M.)

serving Caribbean fare; its bar draws locals for dancing.

Sportfishing enthusiasts are catered to at three dedicated sportfishing lodges at Parismina: **Caribbean Expedition Lodge** (tel./fax 506/2232-8118, www.costaricasportfishing.com); **Río Parismina Lodge** (tel. 506/2229-7597, in North America tel. 800/338-5688, www.riop.com); and **Jungle Tarpon Lodge** (U.S. tel. 800/544-2261, www.jungletarpon.com). All offer fishing packages and take in guests on an ad-hoc basis.

Tortuguero and Barra del Colorado

◖ TORTUGUERO NATIONAL PARK

Parque Nacional Tortuguero extends north along the coast for 22 kilometers from Jaloba, six kilometers north of Parismina, to Tortuguero village. The 19,000-hectare park is a mosaic of deltas on an alluvial plain nestled between the Caribbean coast on the east and the low-lying volcanic hills. The park protects the nesting beach of the green turtle, the offshore waters to a distance of 30 kilometers, and the wetland forests extending inland for about 15 kilometers.

The park—one of the most varied within the park system—has 11 ecological habitats, from high rainforest to herbaceous marsh communities. Fronting the sea is the seemingly endless expanse of beach. Behind that is a narrow canal, connected to the sea at one end and fed by a river at the other; it parallels the beach for its full 35-kilometer length. Back of the canal (and the lagoon to its north) is a coastal rainforest and swamp complex threaded by an infinite maze of serpentine channels and streams.

Tortuguero shelters more than 300 bird species, among them toucans, aricaris, oropendolas, herons, kingfishers, anhingas, jacanas, and the great green macaw; 57 species of amphibians and 111 of reptiles, including three species of marine turtles; and 60 mammal species, including jaguars, tapirs, ocelots, cougars, river

otters, and manatees. Tortuguero's fragile manatee population was thought to be extinct until a population was found in remote lagoons. A decade ago a study indicated that about 100 manatees inhabited the area. The population seems to be growing, as indicated by an increase in the number of collisions with boats

VOLUNTEERS FOR CONSERVATION

The **Caribbean Conservation Corps** (CCC, tel. 506/2224-9215 or 506/2238-8069, fax 506/2225-7516, baulas@racsa.co.cr; in the U.S., 4424 NW 13th St. Suite #A1, Gainesville, FL 32609, tel. 352/373-6441 or 800/678-7853; www.cccturtle.org) needs volunteers to assist in research, including during its twice-yearly turtle tagging and monitoring programs.

The CCC also invites volunteers to join its fall and spring bird-research projects at Tortuguero. No experience is needed. The fieldwork is complemented by guided hikes, boat tours, and other activities.

The numerous other organizations that seek volunteers for environmental, social, and developmental work include **Planet Conservation** (UK tel. 7878-055265, www.planetconservation.net).

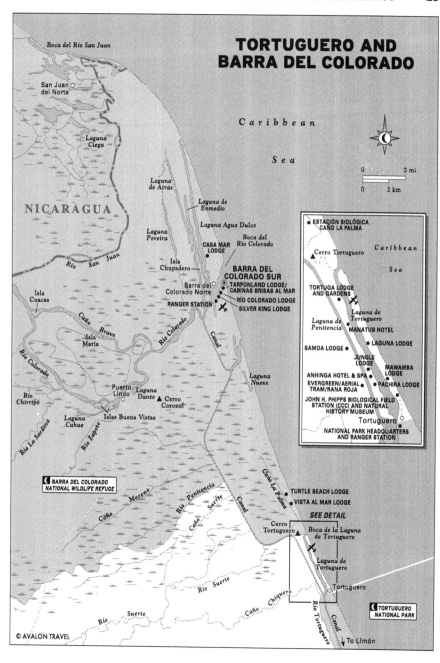

TORTUGUERO AND BARRA DEL COLORADO

Boca del Río San Juan

San Juan del Norte

Laguna Ciega

Caribbean

Laguna de Atras

Sea

Laguna de Enmedio

NICARAGUA

Laguna Pereira

Laguna Agua Dulce

Boca del Río Colorado

CASA MAR LODGE

Río San Juan

Isla Chupadero

BARRA DEL COLORADO SUR

Isla Cuacas

Barra del Colorado Norte

TARPONLAND LODGE/ CABINAS BRISAS AL MAR

RANGER STATION

RÍO COLORADO LODGE

SILVER KING LODGE

Caño Bravo

Isla María

Río Colorado

Río Colorado

Laguna Nueve

Río Chirripó

Puerto Lindo

Laguna Danto

Cerro Coronel

Islas Buena Vistas

Laguna Cahue

Río La Sardina

Río Zapat

BARRA DEL COLORADO NATIONAL WILDLIFE REFUGE

Caño

Moreno

Río Penitencia

Caño Suerte

Caño La Palma

Canal

TURTLE BEACH LODGE

VISTA AL MAR LODGE

SEE DETAIL

Cerro Tortuguero

Boca de la Laguna de Tortuguero

Laguna de Tortuguero

Río Suerte

Tortuguero

Río Suerte

Caño Chiquero

Río Tortuguero

Canal

TORTUGUERO NATIONAL PARK

To Limón

© AVALON TRAVEL

0 ___ 2 mi
0 ___ 2 km

Detail inset

■ ESTACIÓN BIOLÓGICA CAÑO LA PALMA

▲ Cerro Tortuguero

Caribbean

Sea

TORTUGA LODGE AND GARDENS

Laguna de Tortuguero

Laguna de Penitencia

MANATUS HOTEL

SAMOA LODGE ●

● LAGUNA LODGE

JUNGLE LODGE

MAWAMBA LODGE

ANHINGA HOTEL & SPA ●

EVERGREEN/AERIAL TRAM/RANA ROJA

● PACHIRA LODGE

JOHN H. PHIPPS BIOLOGICAL FIELD STATION (CCC) AND NATURAL HISTORY MUSEUM

Tortuguero

NATIONAL PARK HEADQUARTERS AND RANGER STATION

© CHRISTOPHER P. BAKER

boat speeding on Laguna Penitencia

(in 2005, several "manatee sanctuaries" were created, where boats are prohibited or velocity is restricted, although boat captains still whiz through these zones at high speed).

The wide-open canals are superb for spotting crocodiles, giant iguanas, basilisk lizards, and caimans luxuriating on the fallen raffia palm branches. At night you might even spy bulldog bats skimming the water and scooping up fish right on cue. Amazing!

The western half of the park is under great stress from logging and hunting, which have increased in recent years as roads intrude. The local community is battling a proposed highway sponsored by banana and logging interests. Rubbish disposal is a problem: leave no trash.

Turtles

The park protects a vital nesting ground for green sea turtles, which find their way onto the brown-sand beaches every year June–October (the greatest numbers arrive in September). Mid-February–July, giant leatherback turtles arrive (with greatest frequency Apr.–May), followed by female hawksbill turtles in July.

Tortuguero is the most important green-turtle hatchery in the western Caribbean; annually as many as 30,000 greens swim from their feeding grounds as far away as the Gulf of Mexico and Venezuela to lay their eggs on the beach. Each female arrives 2–6 times, at 10- to 14-day intervals, and waits two or three years before nesting again. The number of green turtles nesting has quadrupled during the last 25 years; that of leatherbacks continues to decline.

During the 1950s, the Tortuguero nesting colony came to the attention of biologist-writer Archie Carr, a lifelong student of sea turtles. His lobby—originally called the Brotherhood of the Green Turtle—worked with the Costa Rican government to establish Tortuguero as a sanctuary where the endangered turtles could nest unmolested. The sanctuary was established in 1963 and the area was named a national park in 1970.

Local guides escort **Turtle Walks** at 8–10 P.M. and 10 P.M.–midnight each evening in turtle-nesting season ($10, including guide, who alone can buy tickets to access the beach at night). *No one is allowed on the 22-mile nesting*

Don't Bother Turtles sign in Tortuguero

sector *without a guide after 6 P.M.* (10 people maximum per guide per night). Each of the five sectors has a guard post. No cameras or flashlights are permitted. Keep quiet, as the slightest noise can send the turtle hurrying back to sea, and keep a discreet distance. *You are asked to report any guide who digs up turtle hatchlings to show you—this is absolutely prohibited.*

Exploring Tortuguero

Trails into the forests—frequently waterlogged—also begin at the park stations at both ends of the park; the number of people permitted at any one time is limited. The two-kilometer-long **El Gavilán Trail** leads south from the Cuatro Esquinas ranger station south of Tortuguero village and takes in both beach and rainforest. Rubber boots are compulsory in wet season, when the trail is often closed due to flooding (you can rent boots at Ernesto Tours, tel. 506/2709-8070, $1). A two-kilometer section of **Sendero Jaguar** is accessible with a guide; the other 16 km is accessible at night for turtle viewing.

Outside the park, but within Barra del Colorado Wildlife Refuge, a trail (in terrible condition at last visit) that begins north of Tortuga Lodge leads two kilometers to **Cerro Tortuguero** (119 meters), the highest point for miles around, offering a superb perspective over the swamps and coastline. Officially, the trail is closed.

You can hire dugout canoes (*cayucas* or *botes*) in Tortuguero village ($6 pp the first hour, $3 each additional hour, without a guide). Check on local currents and directions, as the former can be quite strong and it's easy to lose your bearings amid the maze of waterways. Skippered *pangas* (flat-bottomed boats with outboard motors) and *lanchas* (with inboard motor) can also be rented; try to rent one with an electric or non-polluting four-stroke motor. And don't forget to pay your park entrance fee before entering Tortuguero National Park.

If you want to see wildlife you *absolutely* need a guide. The local guides—there are about 40 trained guides organized into a local cooperative—have binocular eyes; in even the darkest shadows, they can spot caimans, birds, crocodiles, and other animals you will most

caiman at Turtle Beach Lodge

likely miss. You can hire local guides in the village for about $10 per person per hour (go only with a certified guide, such as Daryl Loth at Tortuguero Safaris). The best guides are employed by the local lodges.

You can also book guided trips at any of the lodges or through tour companies in San José and Tortuguero village. **Costa Rica Expeditions** (tel. 506/2257-0766, www.costaricaexpeditions.com) is recommended.

When to Go
Rain falls year-round. The three wettest months are January, June, and July. The three driest are February, April, and November. Monsoon-type storms can lash the region at any time. The interior of the park is hot, humid, and windless. Bring good raingear, and it can be cool enough for a windbreaker or sweater while speeding upriver. Take insect repellent—the mosquitoes and no-see-ums can be fierce.

Information and Services
The park ($10 entrance) is open 6 A.M.–6 P.M. daily; last entry is at 5 P.M.; admission also includes access to Caúa de Palma, in Barra del Colorado Wildlife Refuge. The fee is payable at the **Cuatro Esquinas** ranger station (tel./fax 506/2709-8086), at the southern end of Tortuguero village, or at **Estación Jalova,** at the park's southern end (45 minutes by boat from Tortuguero village). No fee applies if you're in transit. The ranger station has an excellent information center. You can camp ($2 pp) at Jalova, with outside showers and toilets. (Crocodiles are often seen sunning on the mud banks immediately south of the Jalova station.)

TORTUGUERO VILLAGE AND LAGOON
Somnolent, funky Tortuguero Village (pop. 550), on the northern boundary of Tortuguero National Park, sprawls over a thin strip of land at the northern end of the **Canal de Tortuguero** and the southern end of **Laguna del Tortuguero,** at the junction with **Laguna Penitencia,** a canal that leads to Barra del Colorado. Laguna del Tortuguero extends north six kilometers to the ocean, where the

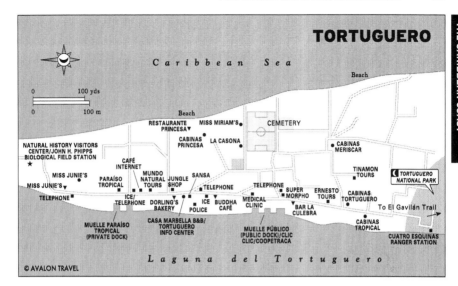

© AVALON TRAVEL

tannin-stained freshwater pours into the Caribbean; it is lined with nature lodges.

It's an 80-kilometer, three-hour journey along the Canal de Tortuguero from Moín; by small plane from San José, it's a 30-minute flight that sets you down on a thin strip of land with the ocean crashing on one side and the lagoon and the jungle on the other (the ocean here is not safe for swimming because of rip currents and the large number of sharks).

The higgledy-piggledy village comprises a warren of narrow sandy trails (there are no roads) lined by rickety wooden houses and, increasingly, more substantial buildings spawned by the tourism boom. The south end of the village is best avoided after dark.

The **John H. Phipps Biological Field Station** (tel. 506/2709-8125, www.cccturtle.org), about 500 meters north of the village, can be accessed by boat or via a trail behind the beach. It features a must-see **Natural History Visitor's Center** (tel. 506/2709-8091, 10 A.M.–noon and 2–5 P.M. Mon.–Sat., 2– P.M. Sun., $1) with turtle exhibits and educational presentations on rainforest ecology, including a video about turtle ecology, and life-size models of turtles hatching and another of a female laying eggs.

Sports and Recreation

The most reputable tour operator in the village is **Tortuguero Wildlife Tours,** based out of Casa Marbella B&B (tel. 506/2709-8011, http://casamarbella.tripod.com), run by Daryl Loth, a multilingual Canadian naturalist, who offers canal trips ($15 pp for up to three hours), turtle-watching trips ($10), rainforest hikes ($15 two hours), and kayak rental ($10). Also recommended is multilingual German biologist and guide, Barbara Hartung. Her **Tinamon Tours** (tel. 506/2709-8004, www.tinamontours.de) offers canoe tours, turtle-watching, and medicinal plant tours. **Mundo Natural Tours** (tel. 506/2709-8159, mundonaturaltours@hotmail.com) and **Caiman Tours** (tel. 506/8814-7403) have similar programs.

Eddie Brown Sportfishing (c/o Costa Rica Expeditions, tel. 506/2257-0766, www.costaricaexpeditions.com) operates from Tortuga Lodge using 26- and 28-foot boats with Bimini tops. Rates of $320–395 per fishing day include lodging, all meals, and open bar. He also offers fishing by the hour ($50). **Caribbean Fishing** (tel. 506/2709-82113) and **Caribeño Fishing Tours** (tel. 506/2709-8026) also arrange fishing trips.

Tortuguero village map

Yes, even Tortuguero has a zipline! **Aerial Trails Tortuguero Canopy** (tel. 506/2223-6200), at Evergreen, has eight platforms and 11 suspension bridges and offers zipline tours at 11:30 A.M. and 2:30 P.M. daily ($25, including transfers). You need to reserve 24 hours ahead.

You can rent hydrabikes (floating pedalbikes) at Manatu Hotel ($10 for two hours). **Tortuguero Jungle Spa** (tel. 506/2256-7080, info@pachiralodge.ca), at Pachira Lodge, offers massage and a delectable chocolate body treatment ($95).

Accommodations
IN THE VILLAGE

Tortuguero sometimes fills up; if you arrive without reservations, make it a priority to secure accommodations immediately. Many of the accommodations listed here are profiled at www.tortuguerovillage.com.

You have two dozen options in the budget bracket. The **John H. Phipps Biological Field Station** (tel. 506/2709-8125, www.ccc turtle.org) has dormitory accommodations with communal kitchen and bathroom for researchers, students, and volunteers only.

A good backpackers' option is **Cabinas Meriscar** (tel. 506/2709-8202, cabinas meriscar@rocketmail.com, $7 pp shared bath, $9 pp private bath), with 18 simply appointed rooms with fans and hot water. Owner (and local baker) Dorling plans to upgrade and turn it into a classic bed-and-breakfast. And **Mundo Natural Tours** ($20 s, $30 d) has two charming cabins with colorful decor, ceiling fans, heaps of light, and modern bathrooms.

Cabinas Tortuguero (tel. 506/2709-8114, $10 s, $16 d shared bath year-round; $15 s, $20 d private bath low season; $20 s, $25 d private bath high season), toward the southern end of the village, is run by friendly Italian Borghi Morena. It has 11 simple rooms, each with three single beds, ceiling fan, and baths with hot water.

Cabinas Miriam (tel. 506/2709-8002, $15 pp), on the north side of the soccer field, has six simple rooms with fans and private bathroom with hot water. You should stay here for Miss Miriam's restaurant.

© CHRISTOPHER P. BAKER

Miss Junie's Hotel in Tortuguero village

I also like **La Casona** (tel. 506/2709-8092, $15 s, $20 d), on the west side of the soccer field. It has nice cabins with modern bathrooms in a garden; the rustic restaurant with sand floor is a charmer; there's an Internet café here; and Andres is a licensed tour guide. And the **Cabinas Tropical Lodge** (tel. 506/2709-8110, $10 pp) has charming, simple cabins that are a worthy alternative.

Miss Junie's (tel. 506/2709-8102, www .iguanaverdetours.com, $40 s/d downstairs, $60 s/d upstairs, including breakfast), at the north end of the village, has parlayed its international fame into exorbitant rates for what you get: 12 clean and simply furnished rooms in a two-story unit, each with tiled floor, ceiling fan, screened windows, and modern bathroom with hot water.

One of the nicest options is **Casa Marbella B&B** (tel. 506/2709-8011, http://casa marbella.tripod.com, $30 s or $35 d low season, $35 s or $40 d high season), a bed-and-breakfast with five airy, clean, delightfully simple bedrooms with terra-cotta floors, high ceilings with fans, and clinically clean and spacious bathrooms with tiled showers and hot water. You can settle down in a common room to watch TV or enjoy games when rain strikes, plus there's a communal kitchen and a dock with hammocks. Rates include a hearty Costa Rican breakfast.

For a beachfront locale, opt for **Cabinas Princesa** (tel. 506/2709-8131, $15 pp). This two-story wooden structure has 12 no-frills but clean rooms with private bathrooms; they open to a breeze-swept veranda. It has a restaurant serving seafood and Caribbean dishes.

ALONG THE LAGOONS

Most nature lodges offer multi-day packages, with meals, transfers, and tours included in the rates below.

The **Canadian Organization for Tropical Education and Rainforest Conservation** (COTERC, P.O. Box 335, Pickering, Ont. L1V 2R6, tel. 905/831-8809, www.coterc.org, $40 pp) has a research field station, Estación Biológica at Caño Palma, a dead-end channel about eight kilometers north of Tortuguero. A dorm has bunk beds. You may also camp or sleep in hammocks. Rates include all meals and a guided walk on trails into the rainforest and swamps.

I'm fond of **Turtle Beach Lodge** (tel. 506/2248-0707, www.turtlebeachlodge.com, from $245 s, $410 d for one-night/two-day packages), also at Caño Palma. It has 25 spacious, simply furnished cabins raised on stilts, with fans, porches, and modern bathrooms. Meals are served in an airy thatched restaurant, and you can relax in the hammock hut or take a cooling dip in the turtle-shaped pool with sundeck. It has the advantage of both beach and lagoon location.

Nearby, the almost identical **Vista al Mar Lodge** (tel. 506/2709-8180, www.vistaalmarlodge.com) is also a pleasant option.

Mawamba Lodge (tel. 506/2293-8181, www.grupomawamba.com, from $240 s or $396 d low season, $289 s or $506 d high season, for one-night/two-day packages, including transport and meals), about 800 meters north of Tortuguero on the east side of Laguna del Tortuguero, has 36 attractive all-wood rooms reached by canopied walkways. There's an airy family-style restaurant and bar, a lovely swimming pool and sun deck, plus a whirlpool tub, game room, and nature trail. Nearby, almost identical and with identical pricing, the **Laguna Lodge** (tel. 506/2709-8082, www.laguna tortuguero.com), sprawls amid spacious landscaped grounds. It has 52 modestly elegant rooms in eight hardwood bungalows, plus a swimming pool, and a hip riverside *ranchito* restaurant and bar.

Set in lush grounds, **Pachira Lodge** (tel. 506/2256-7080, www.pachiralodge.com, from $249 s, $418 d for a two-day, one-night package), on the west side of the lagoon, has 34 attractively furnished thatched cabins. A handsome dining room serves buffet meals, and there's a gift store, bar, and turtle-shaped pool. The owners of Pachira Lodge also operate **Anhinga Hotel & Spa,** a more upscale option in the same style, using 32 A-frame stilt cabins connected by raised boardwalks; the aesthetic is lovely and they get heaps of light. It has a large turtle-shaped pool and whirlpool tub, and

an open-air, full-service spa with steam baths. Monkeys abound at this property, in the thick of the forest. And Pachira also has an annex—**Evergreen** (www.evergreentortuguero.com)—on the west bank of Laguna Penitencia. Actually, it's divided into **Evergreen I** and **Evergreen II.** Together they have 36 handsome stilt-legged A-frame cabins (some in a riverside clearing; some in the forest) and rooms with wrought-iron furniture. There's a pool in a raised sundeck, plus a nice restaurant, and the Aerial Trails Canopy Tour.

Squeezed between the two Evergreens, and sharing its pool (yet independently owned), is **Rana Roja** (tel. 506/2709-8211, www.tortuguerocabinasranaroja.com), with identical units to Evergreen I.

Two similar options are the **Jungle Lodge** (tel. 506/2223-1200, www.grupopapagayo.com), 400 meters north of Pachira Lodge; and, on Laguna Penitencia, **Samoa Lodge** (tel. 506/2258-5790, www.samoalodge.com).

Manatus Hotel (tel. 506/2709-8197, www.manatuscostarica.com, from $300 s or $540 d low season, $355 s or $640 d high season for a one-night/two-day package) is the snazziest show in Tortuguero. The reception lobby has a pool table, a small gym, and Internet. The 12 air-conditioned rooms with glazed hardwood floors are beautifully appointed with canopy beds, cable TV, and spacious modern bathrooms with both indoor and outdoor showers (the latter in their own garden patios). Sheltered raised pathways connect the units. Kayaks and aquabikes are available for guests, and a nice pool and the finest restaurant for miles round out this winner. A potential downside: All the glass and the TVs potentially divorce you from the nature experience.

I still prefer 🅒 **Tortuga Lodge and Gardens** (tel. 506/2257-0766, www.costarica expeditions.com, $118 s/d standard low season, $208 d penthouse low season; $128 s/d standard high season, $218 s/d penthouse high season; rates include guided tours and tax), operated by Costa Rica Expeditions and offering the best food, the best guides, and the best overall experience. The eco-sensitive lodge, facing the airstrip four kilometers north of town, upgraded in 2008 with a sophisticated lounge bar and gourmet nouvelle Costa Rican cuisine in its torch-lit waterfront restaurant. It has 24 spacious riverfront rooms (each with ceiling fans plus fully equipped bathrooms with heaps of solar-heated water; telephones were to be added) fronted by wide verandas with leather rockers. Each has queen-size beds, huge screened windows, ceiling fans, and modern bathrooms. The lovely two-bathroom penthouse suite has king-size *and* queen-size beds! A stone-lined, gradual-entry swimming pool shines beside the river, where a sun deck has lounge chairs. It's set amid 20 hectares of landscaped grounds and forest; a short (albeit muddy) nature trail offers good sightings of poison-dart frogs and other wildlife. Service is exemplary. It's also the only fishing lodge in Tortuguero and also offers hikes, turtle walks, plus multi-day packages. Guests arriving by boat are greeted with a gourmet picnic lunch mid-way, and staff gather to wave as guests arrive and depart. Nice!

© CHRISTOPHER P. BAKER

Tortuga Lodge's gourmet lunch at Jalova ranger station

Food

Not to be missed for local fare is **⟨ Miss Junie's** (tel. 506/2709-8102, 7:30 A.M.–2:30 P.M. and 6:30–9:30 P.M. daily), where $10 will buy you a platter of fish, chicken, or steak, with rice and beans simmered in coconut milk, plus fruit juice and dessert. Reservations are needed. For better or worse, Miss Junie's has enclosed her restaurant in glass; the funky charm has been replaced with air-conditioned elegance. **Miss Miriam's** (7:30 A.M.–9 P.M. daily), on the north side of the soccer field, offers a similar experience and cuisine.

The colorful, thatched **Buddha Café** (tel. 506/2709-8084, 11 A.M.–10:30 P.M. daily, below $8), riverside in the village center, serves Italian cuisine that includes crepes and lasagna.

La Casona (tel. 506/2709-8092, 7:30–11:30 A.M. and 1–9 P.M. daily), on the north side of the soccer field, serves pancakes with bananas, plus omelettes, lasagna, and *casados*. I recommend the chicken in coconut ($6).

At **Dorling's Bakery** (tel. 506/2709-8132,

5 A.M.–9 P.M. daily), gracious Nicaraguan Dorling bakes delicious *empanadas,* cakes, apple pie, and cheesecakes. You've got to try the raspberry truffle brownie! Dorling also has hearty breakfasts (including omelettes and granola with fruit and yogurt), plus cappuccinos, milk shakes, and cheap lunches, including pizza.

To splurge, catch a ride to **Manatus Hotel** (7–9 A.M., noon–2 P.M. and 6:30–8:30 P.M. daily), offering romantic candlelit settings and a three-course prix fixe dinner ($25) for nonguests by reservation. The menu is gourmet—think hearts of palm sushi with avocado spinach appetizer, and vegetable penne pasta with herb pesto and stuffed roasted tomato, eggplant, and cheese.

Information and Services

Daryl Loth mans the **Tortuguero Information Center** at Casa Marbella B&B (tel. 506/2709-8011, http://casamarbella.tripod.com) and is by far the best source of information. **Jungle Shop** (tel. 506/2709-8072, jungle@racsa.co.cr), in the village center, and **Paraíso Tropical** (tel.

506/2709-8095), 50 meters farther north by the main dock, also offer tourist information services. Both sell souvenirs and telephone cards. The **medical clinic,** facing the dock, is open 8 A.M.–4 P.M. Tuesday and Wednesday. There's a **pharmacy** 100 meters farther south, near the **police station** (public tel. 506/2709-8188). There's a **Café Internet** (tel. 506/2709-8058, 9 A.M.–9 P.M. daily) on the waterfront path. **Mundo National Tours** (tel. 506/2709-8159, 7 A.M.–7 P.M. Mon.–Sat.) also has Internet service.

Getting There

BY AIR

Both **Nature Air** and **SANSA** operate scheduled daily flights between San José and the landing strip four kilometers north of Tortuguero village. SANSA offers a boat transfer to the village.

   Costa Rica Expeditions (tel. 506/2257-0766, www.costaricaexpeditions.com) and other tour operators with lodges in Tortuguero operate private charter service; tour members get priority, but you may be able to get a spare seat (about $75 one-way). You can arrange charter flights for about $500 per plane, one-way.

BY BOAT

Locals prefer to use public *lanchas* (tel./fax 506/2709-8005 in Tortuguero) that leave from **La Pavona marina**. To get there, take the 9 A.M. Empresario Guápileño (tel. 506/222-2727 or 2710-7780) bus to Cariari (15 km northeast of Guápiles) from San José's Gran Caribe bus terminal. Buses also depart at 6:30 P.M., 10:30 A.M., 1 P.M., 3 P.M., 4:30 P.M., 6 P.M., and 7 P.M.; buy your ticket in the Guápiles booth. A Coopetraca bus leaves Cariari for La Pavona from the local bus station, five blocks north of the San José terminal in Cariari at noon (and 6 A.M. and 3 P.M.), arriving at La Pavona (29 km from Cariari) in time for the early afternoon boat departures. Buy your boat ticket at La Pavona dock (which has secure parking, $10 nightly) rather than prepaid at the bus station. Several boat companies compete and touts are known to direct

you to specific businesses for commission; their information cannot be trusted! **Clic Clic** is the most trustworthy boat company: Its boats leave at 8 A.M., 1 P.M., and 4 P.M. daily ($10 pp each way for bus-and-boat); return boats depart Tortuguero for La Pavona at 6 A.M., 11:30 A.M., and 3 P.M. The route follows the Río Suerte through Tortuguero National Park and can be impassable in extreme high and low waters; you might even have to get out and help push the boat over sandbars—a good reason to choose the *least* full boat at La Pavona. The quickest way back to San José is to take the early boat, then a direct bus to Guápiles, then a bus to San José.

   An alternative to La Pavona is to take a bus from Cariari to La Geest dock; the banana company requires passengers to get off the bus and walk through a mold poison. And private cars may not enter. Most locals avoid this route. *Lanchas* operated by Empresarios de Transportes Acuático Tortuguero (tel. 506/2709-8005, www.tortuguero-costa rica.com), the boatmen's cooperative, depart Geest for Tortuguero at 3 A.M. and 1:30 P.M.; return boats depart Tortuguero at 7 A.M. and 11 A.M. ($10 pp).

   Private water-taxis also serve Tortuguero from the JAPDEVA dock in Moín (public tel. 506/2795-0066), including the **Riverboat Francesca** (tel. 506/2226-0986, www.tortu guerocanals.com). Prices are negotiable. Expect to pay $60–80 pp for four people round-trip ($220 for one or two people). *Warning:* Some boat captains work in union with touts in Tortuguero to steer you toward specific lodgings and guides. Most cannot be relied upon.

   Private boats for package tour groups serve Tortuguero from **Caño Blanco Marina** (tel. 506/2710-1299, or tel. 506/2206-5138 in San José), near Barra de Matina Sur. Tour operators in San José will accept reservations for these boat transfers on a space-available basis. A private skipper willing to take individuals without pre-booked group boat transfers can usually also be found here; a private charter to Tortuguero costs about $100 one-way, $180

© CHRISTOPHER P. BAKER

children playing at Barra del Colorado

round-trip. To get to the marina from San José, take a 9 A.M. bus (buses run 5 A.M.–7 P.M.) from San José's Gran Caribe bus terminal and get off at Siquirres, from where buses depart for Caño Blanco Marina at 4:30 A.M. and 1 P.M. Monday–Friday and at 7:30 A.M. and 3 P.M. Saturday and Sunday (return buses depart Caño Blanco at 6 A.M. and 3 P.M. Mon.–Fri. and 9 A.M. and 5 P.M. Sat.–Sun.). Caño Blanco Marina has secure parking, 10 simple cabins with fans ($25 s/d with fan, $30 s/d with a/c), plus a restaurant.

◖ BARRA DEL COLORADO NATIONAL WILDLIFE REFUGE

Refugio Nacional de Vida Silvestre Barra del Colorado (91,200 hectares) protects the vast rainforests and wetlands extending north from the estuary of Lagunas del Tortuguero to the Río San Juan, the international border with Nicaragua. About 30 kilometers from the sea, the Río San Juan divides, with the San Juan flowing northeast and the main branch—the Río Colorado—flowing southeast to the sea

through the center of the reserve. Dozens of tributaries form a labyrinth of permanent sloughs and ephemeral waterways that have made the region inaccessible to all but boat traffic.

Barra del Colorado is a replica of Tortuguero National Park—to which it is linked by canal—on a larger scale, and it protects a similar panoply of wildlife. Great green macaws wing screeching over the canopy, mixed flocks of antbirds follow advancing columns of army ants, and jabiru storks with two-meter wingspans circle above. Large crocodiles inhabit the rivers and can be seen basking on mud banks. However, there are virtually no facilities for exploring, and no ranger station.

Unexciting and ramshackle Barra del Colorado village sits astride the mouth of the 600-meter-wide Río Colorado. **Barra del Norte,** on the north side of the river, has no roads (just dirt paths littered with trash and a broken concrete walkway down its center between cabins made of corrugated tin and wooden crates). The slightly more salubrious **Barra del Sur** has an airstrip and most of the hamlet's few services. The village once prospered as a lumber center but went into decline during two decades of Nicaraguan conflict, when the village became a haven for Nicaraguan refugees. Locals mainly rely on fishing or serve as guides for the half dozen sportfishing lodges, but drug trafficking is also entrenched.

Despite the end to the conflicts, tensions with Nicaragua run high. Nicaragua disputes Costa Rica's territorial rights to land north of the Río Colorado. The Río San Juan is entirely Nicaraguan territory (when you are on the water you are inside Nicaragua). Costa Ricans have right of use. Nicaraguan authorities charge foreigners for use of the Río San Juan ($5 pp, plus $7 per boat); you must carry your passport on the river.

Local expat resident Diana Graves at **CyD Souvenirs** (tel. 506/2794-0152, 8 A.M.–9 P.M. daily) is the best source of tourist information; she has an Internet café.

Sportfishing

The rivers are famous for their game fishing; all of the lodges specialize in sportfishing. Local tarpon are so abundant that a two-meter whopper might well jump into your boat. Gar—with an ancestry dating back 90 million years—is also common; growing up to two meters long, these bony-scaled fish have long, narrow, crocodile-like snouts full of vicious teeth.

Accommodations and Food

The sportfishing lodges rely on group business. When there are no groups, they can be lonely places. All offer multi-day packages.

Hardy budget travelers might try the dingy **Tarponland Lodge** (tel. 506/2710-2141, $15 pp), in Barra del Sur; at least it has reasonable local fare.

Far nicer is **Cabinas Brisas del Mar** (tel. 506/2794-116, $30 pp including three meals), on the east side of the airstrip and run by a pleasant Tico couple. It has two rooms upstairs (with carpets) and two below, all with screened windows, local TV, ceiling fans, and clean bathrooms with hot water. Seafood, Chinese, and local dishes are served in a simple thatched *soda*.

Casa Mar Fishing Lodge (tel. 506/8381-1380 or U.S. tels. 714/578-1881 or 800/543-0282, www.casamarlodge.com; fishing packages from $2,495 pp for five nights), on Laguna Agua Dulce, about two kilometers north of Barra, offers 12 rustic, comfortable, and spacious thatched duplex cabins set in attractive landscaped grounds. Each has shining hardwoods, screened windows, fans, clean bathrooms, and wooden canoes that serve as planters. There's a tackle shop, a handsome restaurant, and a bar with leather Sarchí rockers, a dartboard, and large-screen TV with VCR.

The venerable **Río Colorado Lodge** (tel. 506/2232-4063 or U.S. tels. 813/931-4849 or 800/243-9777, www.riocoloradolodge.com, $505 s, $950 d all-inclusive of meals and fishing, $120 for non-fishing guests) at Barra del Sur has 18 rather spartan air-conditioned rooms open to the breeze; all have no-frills baths, hot showers, and electric fans. The rooms and public areas are connected by covered walkways perched on stilts (when the river rises, the lodge extends only a few inches above the water). There's an open-air restaurant, TV and VCR room, bar, game room, whirlpool tub, and tackle shop. The lodge offers five-, six-, and seven-night packages.

More salubrious, **Silver King Lodge** (tel. 506/8381-1403, or U.S. tel. 800/847-3474, www.silverkinglodge.net, call for rates), 300 meters upriver, offers 10 spacious, modestly furnished duplexes linked by covered catwalks. All have queen-size beds with orthopedic mattresses, ceiling fans, coffeemakers, plus private baths with their own water heaters and large showers. Other features include a small swimming pool and sundeck with hammocks, a masseuse, a huge colonial-tiled indoor whirlpool tub, tackle shop, a restaurant serving all-you-can-eat buffets, and a bar with widescreen TV and VCR. A heavy-duty offshore craft permits deep-sea fishing. The lodge closes mid-June–August and in December. Rates include meals.

Food is available at all of the lodges listed in this section.

© CHRISTOPHER P. BAKER

Río Colorado Lodge, Barra del Colorado

Getting There

Both **SANSA** and **Nature Air** fly daily from San José if they get two or more passengers. You can also charter a light plane from San José.

A rough road leads from Puerto Viejo de Sarapiquí to Pavas (at the juncture of the Ríos Toro and Sarapiquí), where you can also charter a boat.

Water-taxis serve Barra del Colorado from the dock at La Pavona. Lodge boats will also pick you up by prior arrangement.

South of Puerto Limón

PUERTO LIMÓN TO CAHUITA

South of Puerto Limón, the shore is lined by brown-sand beaches fringed by palms. About 30 kilometers south of Limón the road crosses the Río Estrella a few kilometers north of the village of **Penshurst,** where a branch road leads into the Valle del Río Estrella.

The Valle del Río Estrella is blanketed by banana plantations of the Dole Standard Fruit Company, headquartered at **Pandora,** about six kilometers inland of Penshurst. The Río Estrella is spawned in the foothills of the steep-sided, heavily forested Talamanca massif, and it irrigates the banana plantations as it crosses the broad plains in search of the Caribbean. The river estuary forms a dense network of channels and lagoons that shelter birds, including great flocks of snow-white cattle egrets.

At **Piedmont** (tel. 506/2750-0789, orchid pierrre@yahoo.com, 9 A.M.–3 P.M. daily, $10), about 500 meters south of the gas station in Penshurst, Pierre Dubois welcomes visitors to his organic fruit farm. Here you can even cut banana stems and taste homemade chocolate.

Unfortunately, the **Aviarios del Caribe**

Sloth Refuge (tel. 506/2750-0775, www.sloth rescue.org, $30 by reservation only), one kilometer north of the Río Estrella, has become focused on cruise-ship business and less welcoming to individual visitors; complaints about owner Luis's cranky attitude continue to trickle in (be sure to visit when his amiable wife, Judy, is available). It has a "slothpital" where injured sloths are cared for, plus a learning center.

Bocuare Jungle Adventure (tel. 506/2759-0122, www.bocuarejungle.com), 14 km inland of Penshurst, is a lodge and ecological plantation on the edge of the rainforest. It has a frog garden and butterfly garden and offers horseback rides, river tubing, birding, and guided hikes to local indigenous communities. It didn't overly impress me.

Selva Bananito Reserve

This 950-hectare private reserve (Conselvatur, tel. 506/2253-8118, www.selvabananito.com), 15 kilometers inland from Bananito (five kilometers inland from the coast road), protects primary rainforest on the slopes of the Talamancas. Two-thirds is rainforest; the rest is devoted to low-impact agriculture and cattle management. Activities from birding and nature hikes to horseback riding and waterfall rappels are offered, as is a trip to a Dole banana packing plant.

The reserve is tough to get to; a high-clearance four-wheel-drive vehicle is absolutely essential for the muddy track churned into an assault course by logging trucks. Ask in the village of Bananito, where you cross the railway lines and keep going straight; take the right fork at the Y junction. Eventually you'll get to a metal gate with a sign reading "No entrance. Private Property." You've arrived. There are two more barbed wire gates to pass through, then you have to drive along a riverbed to cross to the lodge (or you can park at the farm facing the lodge).

Hitoy-Cerere Biological Reserve

Undeveloped and off the beaten track, the 9,050-hectare Reserva Biológica Hitoy-Cerere (tel. 506/2798-3170, www.sinac.go.cr, 8 A.M.–5 P.M. daily, $10), part of the Parque Internacional La Amistad, is one of the nation's least-visited parks. It is surrounded by three indigenous reservations—Talamanca, Telire, and Estrella. Dense evergreen forests are watered by innumerable rivers.

Take your pick of arduous trails or moderately easy walks from the ranger station along the deep valley of the Río Hitoy-Cerere to waterfalls with natural swimming holes. The park is a starting point for trans-Talamanca journeys to the Pacific via a trail that leads south to the village of San José Cabecar and up the valley of the Río Coén and across the saddle between Cerro Betsú (2,500 meters) and Cerro Arbolado (2,626 meters) to Ujarrás, in the Valle de El General. Large sections have not been explored, and trails into the interior are overgrown, unmarked, and challenging (indigenous guides are available for local hikes).

Rainfall is prodigious: seven meters a year is not unknown (March, September, and October are usually the driest months). The result: one of the best specimens of wet tropical forest in the country. Large cats are found throughout the reserve, as well as margays, tapirs, peccaries, agoutis, pacas, otters, monkeys, and harpy eagles.

You can reserve basic lodging at the ranger station; researchers get priority. Camping is permitted; there are basic showers and toilets.

The park is signed from Pandora. You'll need a four-wheel-drive vehicle if driving.

Accommodations and Food

Hotel Colón Caribe (tel. 506/2256-5520, www.coloncaribe.com, $78 pp low season, $87 pp high season), 22 kilometers south of Puerto Limón and 200 meters from a lonesome beach that seems to stretch to eternity, is an attractive resort. The lobby provides a touch of Tahiti with its soaring *palenque* roof and bamboo furnishings in bright floral prints. Choose from 32 air-conditioned *cabinas* or 11 standard rooms set amid shade trees and boasting cable TVs, and private bathrooms with hot water. There's a swimming pool, plus tennis court and volleyball. It also offers all-inclusive options with meals, well drinks, and entertainment. Rates include tax.

© CHRISTOPHER P. BAKER

ranger station at Hitoy-Cerere Biological Reserve

Selva Bananito Lodge (Conselvatur, tel. 506/2253-8118, www.selvabananito.com, $152 s, $260 d standard, $172 s, $280 d superior) is on a 950-hectare private reserve, 15 kilometers inland from Bananito (five kilometers inland from the coast road), and has 11 elegant wooden cabins on stilts on a ridge. Each has a queen- and full-size bed, tiled bathroom and solar-heated water (there's no electricity), and deck with hammocks for enjoying the splendid views. More spacious superior cabins have terra-cotta floors, fold-away doors opening to verandas with hammocks, plus bathrooms with high-tech fittings and picture windows. Dining is family style (I've received complaints about food quality). It offers various packages, with a two-night minimum.

Bocuare Jungle Adventure (tel. 506/2759-0122, www.bocuarejungle.com), 14 kilometers inland of Penshurst, offers rustic accommodations in cozy wooden cabins. More salubrious digs are available at **Villas de Pandora** (tel. 506/2759-0440, www.banana tourcostarica.com, $50 for up to five people), 10 km inland of Penshurst, at the Dole

headquarters. Here, five former managers' duplex bungalows have metamorphosed into tourist villas pleasantly furnished with colorful fabrics, cable TV, and simple but full kitchens. Packages include a plantation tour, meals, and activities such as horseback riding. The huge employees' club has a game room and kids' playground, and there's tennis and a swimming pool.

Getting There

Cahuita-bound Transportes Mepe (tel. 506/2257-8129) buses depart the Gran Caribe terminal in San José at 6 A.M., 10 A.M., 1:30 P.M., and 3:30 P.M., all stopping in Estrella en route.

Local buses depart Puerto Limón (Calles 3/4, Avenida 4) for Pandora and the Dole banana plantation (10 kilometers from the Hitoy-Cerere park entrance) every two hours 5 A.M.–6 P.M. daily. Jeep-taxis from Finca 6 in the Estrella Valley cost about $15 one-way. Jeep-taxis from Cahuita cost about $50 each way (you will need to arrange your return trip in advance if you stay overnight in the park).

Cahuita and Vicinity

◀ CAHUITA

This offbeat village (pop. 3,000), 45 kilometers south of Puerto Limón and one kilometer east of Highway 36, is an in-vogue destination for the young backpacking crowd and others for whom an escapist vacation means back to basics. Cahuita is no more than two parallel dirt streets crossed by four rutted streets overgrown with grass, with ramshackle houses spread apart. The village is totally laid-back and not for those seeking luxuries. What you get is golden- and black-sand beaches backed by coconut palms, an offshore coral reef (now severely depleted), and an immersion in Creole culture, including Rastafarians, with their dreadlocks and a lifestyle that revolves around reggae, Rasta, and—discreetly—reefer. Bob Marley is God in Cahuita.

Cahuita has struggled to recover from a lingering negative perception fed by high crime (and the surly attitude displayed by many local Afro-Caribbeans). The bad publicity stuck; for several years, tourists and Ticos shunned Cahuita. The police force has been beefed up (there's even a police checkpoint on the main road north of Cahuita; every vehicle is searched). Cahuita has regained its popularity, and locals now run a committee to police the community, keep the beaches clean, and generally foster improvements. Crime is no more prevalent here than on the Pacific beaches.

In 2006, the first shopping mall and bank arrived, but Cahuita thus far seems immune to the boom in nearby Puerto Viejo and to the upscale boutique revolution sweeping the rest of the country.

North of Cahuita village is a black-sand beach, **Playa Negra,** which runs for several miles. Cahuita's more famous beach, **Playa Blanca,** is a two-kilometer-long scimitar of golden sand that stretches south from the village along the shore of the national park. Beware riptides! A second pale-sand beach lies farther along, beyond the rocky headland of Punta Cahuita; it is protected by an offshore coral reef and provides safer swimming in

calmer waters. Theft is a problem on the beach; do not leave possessions unattended.

Entertainment and Events

Cahuita hosts a five-day mini-Carnival—Carnavalitos Cahuita—in early December, when theater comes to town, the calypso and reggae is cranked up, and everyone lets their hair down. At other times, there's plenty of night action in Cahuita, though it's an almost exclusively male affair (as far as locals go).

The class act is **Café Cocorico** (50 meters north of the plaza, tel. 506/2755-0324, 7 A.M.–2 P.M. and 5 P.M.–midnight Wed.–Mon.), which shows free movies nightly while you sip killer cocktails.

Coco's Bar (tel. 506/2755-0437), across the street from Cocorico, is the livelier spot. Formerly a laid-back reggae bar that drew dreadlocked Rastas (plus a few drug dealers and leeches hitting up the clientele for drinks),

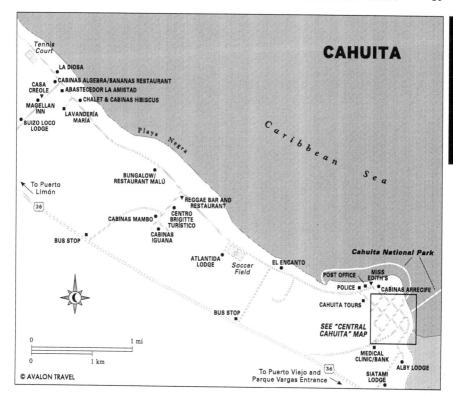

CAHUITA

Tennis Court

LA DIOSA

CASA CREOLE
MAGELLAN INN
SUIZO LOCO LODGE

CABINAS ALGEBRA/BANANAS RESTAURANT
ABASTECEDOR LA AMISTAD
CHALET & CABINAS HIBISCUS

LAVANDERÍA MARÍA

Playa Negra

Caribbean Sea

To Puerto Limón

BUNGALOW/ RESTAURANT MALÚ

REGGAE BAR AND RESTAURANT

CABINAS MAMBO
CENTRO BRIGITTE TURÍSTICO
CABINAS IGUANA

BUS STOP

ATLANTIDA LODGE
Soccer Field
EL ENCANTO

Cahuita National Park

POST OFFICE
MISS EDITH'S
POLICE
CABINAS ARRECIFE

CAHUITA TOURS

BUS STOP

SEE "CENTRAL CAHUITA" MAP

0   1 mi
0   1 km

© AVALON TRAVEL

MEDICAL CLINIC/BANK
ALBY LODGE

To Puerto Viejo and Parque Vargas Entrance
SIATAMI LODGE

it has cleaned up its act and is now preferred by the Latin set for salsa.

Sports and Recreation

Turística Cahuita (tel. 506/2755-0071, dltacb@racsa.co.cr), **Cahuita Tours** (tel. 506/2755-0000, www.cahuitatours.com), and **Willie's Tours** (tel. 506/2755-0267, www.willies -costarica-tours.com), in the village center, offer a panoply of tours and activities, including snorkeling trips, bird-watching, fishing, dolphin-watching, horseback rides, and trips farther afield. Cahuita Tours even has a full-day manatee-spotting tour to the San San Wetlands, in Panama ($95).

Mister Big J's (tel. 506/2755-0353) offers fishing and horseback rides. Cabinas Brigitte also offers guided horseback rides.

Hotel National Park specializes in snorkeling tours of the national park reefs ($25 pp), as does **Snorkeling House** (tel. 506/2755-0248, www.snorkelinghouse.com), with tours at 9 A.M. and 1 P.M.

Accommodations in Cahuita

Cahuita offers lots of options; most are in the budget category. Hustlers hang around the bus stop with the intent of guiding you to a hotel where they receive commission; they're not above lying (such as telling you that your preferred hotel has closed or is full). Many hoteliers are as laid back as their clientele, and don't expect Wi-Fi. There are many more options than listed here.

UNDER $25

In the village, **Cabinas Palmer** (tel. 506/2755-0046, fax 506/2755-0340, $15 s, $20 d) has 20

© CHRISTOPHER P. BAKER

Cabinas Jenny, Cahuita

rooms (13 with hot water); they're mainly small but clean, and include fans. The friendly owner Rene accepts credit cards. There's parking, and a sunny garden out back.

Cabinas Smith (tel. 506/2755-0157, $12 s, $16 d) offers a similar bargain, is nicely kept, and has secure parking. And **Cabinas Jenny** (tel. 506/2755-0256, www.cabinasjenny.com, $25 s/d downstairs, $35 s/d upstairs) has two simple downstairs cabins with ceiling fans and small, hot-water bathrooms; and four larger, nicer, cross-ventilated upstairs rooms with balconies with hammocks.

$25-50

A good option is the **Hotel National Park** (tel. 506/2755-0244, www.cahuitanational parkhotel.com, $40 s, $45 d), directly in front of the park entrance. The 20 pleasant air-conditioned rooms are clean and bright, with cable TV, safes, and private baths and hot water. Oceanview rooms have larger beds and more facilities. An Internet café was being added.

On the east side of the village are several reasonable options beginning with **Cabinas Arrecife** (tel./fax 506/2755-0081, $25 s or $30 d standard, $35 s/d larger units), whose 11 rooms have breezy verandas and are clean and roomy, if gloomy. Bathrooms have hot water. Newer wood-paneled units are larger and have shady verandas with swing chairs. There's a delightful open-air dining area and small pool.

The simple **Hotel Belle Fleur** (tel./fax 506/2755-0283, hotelbellefleur@hotmail.com, $15 s or $20 d rooms, $30 s/d cabins low season; $25 s or $35 d rooms, $45 s/d cabins high season) offers cross-ventilated, wood-paneled rooms with small modern bathrooms above Super Vaz, and colorful cabins in the garden. It also has two air-conditioned suites with cable TV. It has secure parking.

Seeking self-catering? **Apartmento Angela** (tel. 506/2755-0319, lizchacon42@ hotmail.com, $40 s/d) offers humongous octagonal units in a four-story tower beside the shore. All have wraparound glass walls with veranda and simple wooden furnishings. Two-week rentals are the norm.

© CHRISTOPHER P. BAKER

beach cruiser in Cahuita

$50-100

I like **Kelly Creek Cabins & Restaurant** (tel. 506/2755-0007, www.hotelkellycreek.com, $45 s/d low season, $55 s/d high season) for its location beside the park entrance. Run by a Spanish couple, it has four large, simply furnished rooms in a single, handsome, all-hardwood, Thai-style structure with heaps of light pouring in through tall louvered windows. Each has two double beds with cheap mattresses, and uninspired bathrooms and dribbling hot water. A restaurant serves Spanish cuisine. Past guests report that this hotel has a habit of not honoring reservations.

A romantic gem, the private and peaceful Austrian-run **Alby Lodge** (tel./fax 506/2755-0031, www.albylodge.com, $50 s/d) has four beautiful, thatched, Thai-style cabins sitting on stilts amid lawns and hibiscus. All have tons of character, with high-pitched roofs, screened and louvered windows, hardwood floors, bamboo furnishings, mosquito nets, nice bathrooms with hot water, safes, fans, Wi-Fi, and private patios with hammocks and marvelous tables hewn from logs. There's a common

kitchen, and a natural pond attracts frogs. Rates include tax.

Nearby, the "quaint" description fits Cahuita Tours' pastel-hued, gingerbread, air-conditioned cabins at **Ciudad Perdida Ecolodge** (tel. 506/2755-0303, www.ciudadperdida ecolodge.com, call for rates), 600 meters inland of Kelly Creek. Each has mod cons such as ceiling fans, safes, and cable TV.

In 2008, Cahuita acquired its first real two-story modern hotel, the Italian-owned **La Casa de las Flores Hotel** (tel. 506/2755-0326, www.lacasadelasfloreshotel.com, $70 s/d low season, $80 s/d high season). This handsome complex centered on a garden courtyard makes good use of hardwoods and ocher color schemes and is the class act in town. The lovely air-conditioned rooms have platform beds and contemporary bathrooms with small, hot-water showers. Flat-screen TVs were to be added. One room has a full kitchen.

Accommodations in Playa Negra
UNDER $25
On the shorefront road about three kilometers

north of the village is **Cabinas Algebra** (tel./ fax 506/2755-0057, www.cabinasalgebra.com, $18–30 s/d), run by a German named Alfred and his charming wife, Andrea; they offer three double cabins with hot water, and a four-person unit with kitchen. I enjoyed a tasty, wholesome meal in the offbeat restaurant.

$25-50

The **Chalet & Cabinas Hibiscus** (tel. 506/2755-0021, www.hotels.co.cr/hibiscus .html, from $40 s/d, $50–100 chalets low season; $50 s/d, $60–120 chalets high season) is one of the best places in Cahuita, with five pleasing *cabinas* plus four chalets for 3–10 people. There's no restaurant, but the units have kitchens, plus ceiling fans and hot water. Chalets have a spiral staircase up to the second floor, where rockers and hammocks allow a balcony siesta. There's a swimming pool, volleyball court, and game room.

The Swiss-run **Bungalow Malú** (tel. 506/2255-0114, bungalowmalu@gmail.com, $30 s or $35 d standard, $40 s or $45 d with a/c, $50 s or $55 d with kitchen) offers five exquisite, thatched octagonal cabins in landscaped grounds. They're spacious and have refrigerator, fans, Guatemalan bedspreads, and quaint stone-floored bathrooms with hot water, plus stone balconies. One unit has a kitchen. The restaurant offers fine Italian fare.

Farther south, a dirt road leads inland 50 meters to **Centro Turístico Brigitte** (tel. 506/2755-0053, www.brigittecahuita.com, $20 s or $25 d without kitchen, $30 s or $35 d with kitchen), run by Swiss-born Brigitte. She has two simple cabins with hot water. Meals are served in a charming little restaurant, and Brigitte offers horseback tours ($45, half-day). Brigitte also rents houses.

Cabinas Iguana (tel. 506/2755-0005, www.cabinas-iguana.com, $20 s/d rooms, $35–70 bungalows low season; $25 s/d rooms, $40–78 bungalows high season), still farther south, is also run by a Swiss couple. They offer a large wooden house with rooms for six people, a smaller house for three people, and a bungalow (without kitchen) with bunks and

a double bed. All have hot water, plus verandas with hammocks. There's a small, attractive pool and sundeck with cascade, and trails lead through the expansive grounds.

$50-100

I recommend **El Encanto Bed & Breakfast Inn** (tel. 506/2755-0113, www.elencantobed andbreakfast.com, $55 s or $60 d low season, $60 s or $70 d high season), a splendid and fully equipped two-story bed-and-breakfast run by French-Canadians. They offer three rooms in the main building, with queen-size orthopedic mattresses and Guatemalan bed covers, Oriental carvings, ceiling fans, and pleasant bathrooms. They also have cabins in the well-maintained garden, plus a small but exquisite patio restaurant and secure parking. It has a yoga center and oozes tranquility. Rates include breakfast (and taxes in low season).

The romantic **Magellan Inn** (tel./fax 506/2755-0035, www.magellaninn.com, $69 s/d standard, $89 s/d with a/c low season; $79 s/d standard, $99 s/d with a/c high season, including continental breakfast) is set in lush landscaped grounds. Six spacious, sparsely furnished rooms are done up in mauves, with plentiful hardwoods (and musty carpets), and bathrooms with piping hot water. French doors open onto private patios. All rooms have Wi-Fi. The lounge, with Oriental rugs and sofas, is an atmospheric place to relax. A sunken swimming pool is cut into a coral reef. Alas, its Casa Creole restaurant has closed.

Claiming its own little beach, **La Diosa** (tel. 506/2755-0055, www.hotelladiosa.net, $50–75 s, $65–95 d low season; $55–85 s, $65–95 d high season) is one of the most inviting lodgings in Cahuita. Adorned with river stones, the four lovely rooms and six inviting bungalows are painted in lively canary yellow and tropical blues, with divinely comfortable double beds (with batik spreads) on poured concrete platforms, plus spacious modern bathrooms. Two cabins have whirlpool tubs in raised platforms. It has a small pool and a lovely yoga space adorned with Asian art. The owner was due to open the **Goddess Garden Eco-Resort**

© CHRISTOPHER P. BAKER

restaurant sign, Cahuita

& Spa (tel. 506/2755-0444, www.thegoddess
garden.com) amid rainforest at Tuba Creek,
one kilometer north of Playa Negra. Intended
as a spiritual retreat, it will have 12 rooms, a
restaurant, and conference center, plus a huge
yoga center.

Suizo Loco Lodge & Resort (tel. 506/2755-
0349, www.suizolocolodge.com, $55–95 s,
$76–95 d low season; $63–99 s, $89–110 d
high season), inland at the north end of Playa
Negra, is a tropics-meets-Alps lodge with 10
cozy if meagerly appointed cabins in landscaped
grounds. The highlight is the romantic thatched
restaurant overlooking a figure-eight pool.

Competing in the same price range and
with similar ambience and facilities is the
French-Canadian–run **Atlantida Lodge** (tel.
506/2755-0115, fax 506/2755-0213), closer to
the village.

Food

There's excellent eating in Cahuita, but the
scene is ever-changing. Some places are only
open in season (Dec.–May), and most accept
cash only.

In Playa Negra, **Bananas Restaurant**
(7 A.M.–10 P.M.), at Cabinas Algebra, is recommended for breakfasts, and at lunch and dinner serves salads, burgers, and a choice of fish,
chicken, or steak with rice and beans and coconut sauce (from $5). It occasionally has live
music at night. My preferred breakfast spot in
the village is **100 percent Natural Chocolate**
(tel. 506/2755-0311, 6:30 A.M.–4 P.M. daily), a
delightful, airy café with split-tree-trunk ta-
bles. It serves omelettes, plus burritos, sandwiches, and veggie plates.

The renowned **⟨ Miss Edith's** (tel.
506/2755-0248, 11:30 A.M.–10 P.M. Mon.–
Sat., noon–10 P.M. Sun., $6–10), 50 meters
east of the police station, is a homey place that
offers aromatic Caribbean specialties such as
"rundown" (a spiced stew of fish, meat, and
vegetables simmered in coconut milk), or lobster with curry and coconut milk ($15). Miss
Edith also offers a vegetarian menu.

Otherwise the best dining in town is the
open-air **Cha Cha Cha** (tel. 506/2755-0476,
noon–10 P.M. daily, $5–15), an unpreten-
tious place where Chef Bertrand Fleury serves

CARIBBEAN SPICY

One of the pleasures of the Caribbean coast is the uniquely spicy local cuisine, which owes much to the populace's Jamaican heritage. The seductive flavors are lent predominantly by coconut, ginger, chiles, and black pepper. Breadfruit, used throughout the Caribbean isles but relatively unknown elsewhere in Costa Rica, is a staple, as are various tropical roots.

You'll even find ackee and saltfish (one of my favorite breakfasts), made of ackee fruit and resembling scrambled eggs in texture and color. It is often served with johnnycakes, fried sponge dumplings that make great fillers to accompany escoveitched (pickled) fish, or "rundown," mackerel cooked in coconut milk. You must try highly spiced jerk chicken, fish, or pork, smoked at open-air grills and lent added flavor by tongue-searing pepper marinade.

Desserts include ginger cakes, puddin', *pan bon* (a kind of bread laced with caramelized sugar), banana brownies, and ice cream flavored with fresh fruits.

superb "cuisine of the world" with such appetizers as tapenade ($6) and grilled calamari salad ($7.50) and such entrées as curried chicken ($10), followed by banana flambé, all artfully presently on chic oversize plates. The rustic decor is romantic by candlelight, while world music adds just the right note. Kitchen service is excruciatingly slow and, alas, smoking is permitted.

Also for romantic atmosphere, head to **Café Cocorico** (50 meters north of the plaza, tel. 506/2755-0324, 7 a.m.–2 p.m. and 5 p.m.–midnight Wed.–Mon.) for its colorful decor and Arabian-style ceiling drapes. An Italian chef conjures gnocchi, pizzas, and homemade ice cream. All dishes are less than $10. Nearby, the lively **Ristorante Corleone** (tel. 506/2755-0341, noon–10 p.m. Sat.–Wed., 5–10 p.m. Fri.) competes with Italian fare such as carpaccio

($7) and pasta pomodoro ($6.50), plus two dozen types of pizza.

The **Kelly Creek Cabins & Restaurant** (6:30 p.m.–10 p.m. Mon.–Sat., $3–15) is a winner with its paella and sangria, to be enjoyed on an open deck facing the beach.

Information and Services

Cahuita Tours (tel. 506/2755-0000, www.cahuitatours.com) acts as an informal tourist information office. So, too, **Mister Big J's** (tel. 506/2755-0353, 8 a.m.–6 p.m. daily) which does laundry ($7 for a full basket) and has a book exchange in addition to fishing and horseback tours. **Centro Turístico Brigitte** also offers laundry ($8 a basket).

MINAE (tel. 506/2755-0060, 8 a.m.–4 p.m. Mon.–Fri.) has a National Parks Service office in the village.

There's a government **medical center** at the entrance to town, on the main road from Highway 36. There is a private clinic (tel. 506/2755-0345, cell 506/8352-6981) at Suizo Loco Lodge.

The **post office** (tel. 506/2755-0096, 8 a.m.–noon and 1:30–5:30 p.m. Mon.–Fri.) is three blocks north of the plaza. The **police station** (Guardia Rural, tel. 506/2755-0217 or 911) is next door.

The **bank** (tel. 506/2284-6600) is open 8 a.m.–4 p.m. Monday–Friday.

Centro Turístico Brigitte has Internet service (7 a.m.–7 p.m. daily) for $1 per 30 minutes, as does **Willie's Tours** (tel. 506/2755-0267, www.willies-costarica-tours.com, 8:30 a.m.–12:30 p.m. and 2–8 p.m. Mon.–Sat., 4–8 p.m. Sun.), in the village center.

Getting There

Transportes Mepe (tel. 506/2257-8129) buses depart the Gran Caribe terminal in San José for Cahuita ($8) at 6 a.m., 10 a.m., 1:30 p.m., and 3:30 p.m. They continue to Puerto Viejo and Sixaola. Local buses depart Puerto Limón (tel. 506/2758-1572) from Avenida 4, Calles 3/4, hourly 5 a.m.–6 p.m. daily (one hour, $1.25).

Buses depart Cahuita (from 50 meters southwest of Coco Bar) for San José at 8 a.m.,

9:30 A.M., 11:30 A.M., and 4:30 P.M.; and for Limón hourly 6:30 A.M.–8 P.M. The ticket office is open 7 A.M.–5 P.M. daily.

The nearest gas stations are at Penshurst and about 15 kilometers southeast of Bribrí. Several locals sell gas (petrol) from jerry cans.

Getting Around

For a taxi, call 506/2755-0435, or contact Cabinas Palmas (tel. 506/2755-0046) and Cahuita Tours (tel. 506/2755-0000, www .cahuitatours.com). Mister Big J's (tel. 506/2755-0353) arranges car rental.

Centro Turístico Brigitte also rents bicycles ($6 daily).

CAHUITA NATIONAL PARK

Cahuita's 14 kilometers of beaches are shaded by palm trees, lush forests, marshlands, and mangroves. Together they make up Cahuita National Park (1,067 hectares), created in 1970 to protect the 240 hectares of offshore coral reef that distinguish this park from its siblings. Animal life abounds in the diverse habitats—an ideal place to catch a glimpse of tamanduas, pacas, coatis, raccoons, sloths, agoutis, armadillos, iguanas, and troops of howler and capuchin monkeys, and to focus your binoculars on ibis, rufous kingfisher, toucans, and parrots (and even, Dec.–Feb., macaws). Cahuita's freshwater rivers and estuaries are also good places to spot caimans.

The offshore reef lies between Puerto Vargas and Punta Cahuita. Smooth water here provides good swimming; it's possible to wade out to the edge of the coral with the water only at knee level. At the southern end of the park, beyond the reef, huge waves lunge onto the beach—a nesting site for three species of turtles—where tidepools form at low tide. Check with rangers about currents and where you can walk or snorkel safely. Snorkelers can try their luck near Punta Cahuita or Punta Vargas (you must enter the water from the beach on the Punta Vargas side and swim out to the reef). *Snorkeling is only permitted with a guide or organized snorkeling tour.* Up to 500 species of fish gambol among the much-diminished reefs.

sign at entrance to Cahuita National Park
© CHRISTOPHER P. BAKER

Besides what remains of the coral, there are two old shipwrecks about seven meters below the surface, both with visible ballast and cannons; one wreck has two cannons, and the second, a more exposed site, has 13. The average depth is six meters. The best time for diving and snorkeling is during the dry season, February–April; water clarity during the rest of year is not good because of silt brought by rivers emptying from the Talamanca mountains.

Gangs of capuchin monkeys may beg for tidbits, often aggressively. Many folks have been bitten. Feeding wild monkeys with human foodstuffs alters their habits and can adversely affect their health. *Don't feed the monkeys!*

Information and Services

A footbridge leads into the park from the **Kelly Creek Ranger Station** (tel. 506/2755-0461, 6 A.M.–5 P.M. daily, entry by donation) at the southern end of Cahuita village. A shady seven-kilometer nature trail leads from the Kelly Creek Ranger Station to the **Puerto Vargas Ranger Station** (tel. 506/2755-0302, 8 A.M.–4 P.M. Mon.–Fri., 7 A.M.–5 P.M. Sun.,

THE DESTRUCTION OF CAHUITA'S CORAL REEFS

Corals are soft-bodied animals that secrete calcium carbonate to form an external skeleton that is built upon and multiplied over thousands of generations to form fabulous and massive reef structures. The secret to coral growth is the symbiotic relationship with single-celled algae – zooxanthellae – that grow inside the cells of coral polyps and photosynthetically produce oxygen and nutrients, which are released as a kind of rent directly into the coral tissues. Coral flourishes close to the surface in clear, well-circulated tropical seawater warmed to a temperature of between 21° and 27°C.

Twenty years ago, Cahuita had a superb fringing reef – an aquatic version of the Hanging Gardens of Babylon. Today, much of it is dead following uplift during the 1991 earthquake and silt washing down from mainland rivers. Coral growth is hampered by freshwater runoff and by turbidity from land-generated sediments, which clog their pores so that zooxanthellae can no longer breathe. Along almost the entire Talamanca coast and the interior, trees are being logged, exposing the topsoil to the gnawing effects of tropical rains. The rivers bring agricultural runoff, too – poisonous pesticides used in the banana plantations and fertilizers ideal for the proliferation of seabed grasses and algae that starve coral of vital oxygen. It is only a matter of time before the reef is completely gone.

Prospects for the reef at Gandoca-Manzanillo are equally grim.

entry costs $10), three kilometers south of Cahuita midway along the park; the trail takes about two hours with time to stop for a swim. You must wade the Perozoso (Sloth) River just west of Punta Cahuita.

The main park entrance is about 400 meters west of Highway 36, about three kilometers south of Cahuita (the Sixaola-bound bus will drop you off near the entrance). You can drive to Puerto Vargas from here; the entrance gate is locked after hours.

Camping is not permitted.

Puerto Viejo and Vicinity

◖ PUERTO VIEJO

About 13 kilometers south of Cahuita, the road forks just after Hone Creek (also spelled Home Creek). The main road turns east toward Bribrí; a spur leads three kilometers to Playa Negra, a black-sand beach that curls east to Puerto Viejo, enclosing a small bay with a capsized barge in its center. The tiny headland of Punta Pirikiki at its eastern end separates Puerto Viejo from the sweep of beaches—Playa Pirikiki, Playa Chiquita, and others—that run all the way to Manzanillo and Panamá. You can walk along the beach from Cahuita at low tide.

Puerto Viejo is one of the most happenin' spots in Costa Rica. The discos are hopping, and, on peak weekends, you can't find a room to save your soul. Nonetheless, it is low-key and funky. The surfer, backpacker, and counterculture crowds are firmly rooted here and dominate the scene, having settled and established bistros and restaurants alongside the locals. Drugs traded up the coast from Colombia find their way here, and the whiff of ganja (marijuana) drifts on the air. Violent crime has risen accordingly.

The first deluxe hotels, however, have opened. Malls have arrived. And a huge 398-slip marina was proposed but was killed in 2008 due to local opposition.

The overpriced **Caribe Butterfly Garden** (8 A.M.–4 P.M. daily, $5), at Cabinas Calalú east of town, has a netted garden with about

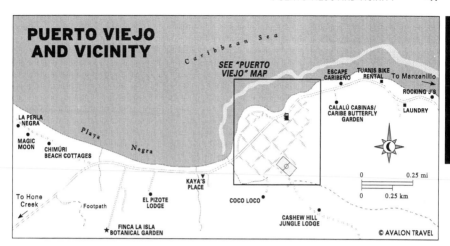

PUERTO VIEJO AND VICINITY

Caribbean Sea

SEE "PUERTO VIEJO" MAP

ESCAPE CARIBEÑO
TUANIS BIKE RENTAL
To Manzanillo

ROCKING J'S

CALALÚ CABINAS/ CARIBE BUTTERFLY GARDEN
LAUNDRY

LA PERLA NEGRA

MAGIC MOON
CHIMÚRI BEACH COTTAGES

Playa

Negra

KAYA'S PLACE

To Hone Creek
Footpath
EL PIZOTE LODGE
COCO LOCO

FINCA LA ISLA BOTANICAL GARDEN
CASHEW HILL JUNGLE LODGE

0   0.25 mi
0   0.25 km

© AVALON TRAVEL

20 species of butterflies. Also overpriced is **Cacao Trails** (tel. 506/2756-8186, www.cacaotrails.com, $25), at Hone Creek. This cacao farm with a tiny "chocolate museum" also has crocodiles, a snake exhibit, a museum on indigenous culture, and a botanical garden, plus canoeing ($25) on canals through the cacao plantation. Stay a while and enjoy a meal at the thatched restaurant.

Viewpoint Resort Hotel (tel. 560/2750-8038, www.viewpoint-resorthotel.com), a private 30-acre nature park about four kilometers south of Cahuita, midway between Cahuita and Hone Creek, offers magnificent views up and down the coast from a hilltop *mirador* amid forest; it's a stiff hike uphill. Day guests get use of a small swimming pool and sundeck, an oversize chess game under a shade canopy, and hiking trails that lead into the forest. It has a shuttle service. Day use costs $3, or $5 including the swimming pool.

Finca la Isla Botanical Garden

This five-hectare botanical garden and farm (tel. 506/2750-0046, jardbot@racsa.co.cr, 10 A.M.–4 P.M. Fri.–Mon., $5 admission, $10 with guided tour for three people or more), one kilometer west of town, is a treat for anyone interested in nature. Here, Lindy and Peter Kring grow spices, exotic fruits, and ornamental

plants for sale. You can sample the fruits and even learn about chocolate production. There's also a self-guided booklet. Toucans and sloths are commonly seen, and poison-dart frogs make their homes in the bromeliads grown for sale. You're virtually guaranteed to see them hopping around underfoot even as you step from your car! The *finca* is 400 meters from the road (200 meters west of El Pizote Lodge) and is signed. Lunches are offered by arrangement.

Keköldi Indigenous Reserve

The 3,547-hectare Reserva Indígena Keköldi, in the hills immediately west of Puerto Viejo, extends south to the borders of the Gandoca-Manzanillo refuge. It is home to some 200 Bribrís and Cabecar people. Reforestation and other conservation projects are ongoing. Gloria Mayorga, coauthor of *Taking Care of Sibo's Gift,* educates tourists on indigenous history and ways.

You can visit the **Iguana Farm** ($1.50) where green iguanas are raised; the turnoff is 400 meters south of Hone Creek, beside Abastacedor El Cruce, then 200 meters along the dirt road.

The **Talamanca Association for Ecotourism and Conservation** (ATEC, tel./fax 506/2750-0191 www.ateccr.org, 8 A.M.–9 P.M. Mon.–Sat. and 10 A.M.–6 P.M. Sun.) arranges tours (from $20 half day, $35 full day). The

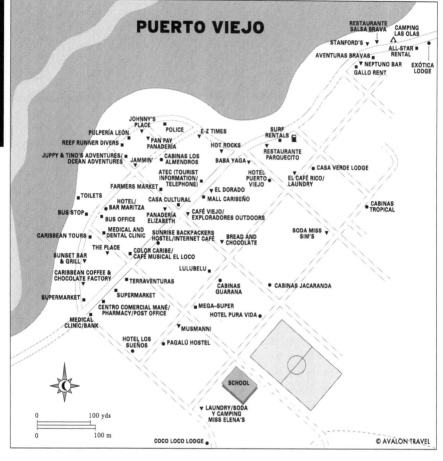

PUERTO VIEJO

RESTAURANTE SALSA BRAVA
CAMPING LAS OLAS
STANFORD'S
ALL-STAR RENTAL
AVENTURAS BRAVAS
NEPTUNO BAR
EXÓTICA LODGE
GALLO RENT

JOHNNY'S PLACE
POLICE
E-Z TIMES
SURF RENTALS
PULPERÍA LEÓN
REEF RUNNER DIVERS
PAN PAY PANADERIA
HOT ROCKS
JUPPY & TINO'S ADVENTURES/ OCEAN ADVENTURES
JAMMIN'
CABINAS LOS ALMENDROS
BABA YAGA
RESTAURANTE PARQUECITO
CASA VERDE LODGE
ATEC (TOURIST INFORMATION/ TELEPHONE)
HOTEL PUERTO VIEJO
EL CAFÉ RICO/ LAUNDRY
FARMERS MARKET
EL DORADO
TOILETS
HOTEL/ BAR MARITZA
CASA CULTURAL
MALL CARIBEÑO
CABINAS TROPICAL
BUS STOP
CAFÉ VIEJO/ EXPLORADORES OUTDOORS
BUS OFFICE
PANADERÍA ELIZABETH
MEDICAL AND DENTAL CLINIC
SODA MISS SIM'S
CARIBBEAN TOURS
SUNRISE BACKPACKERS HOSTEL/INTERNET CAFÉ
BREAD AND CHOCOLATE
THE PLACE
COLOR CARIBE/ CAFÉ MUSICAL EL LOCO
SUNSET BAR & GRILL
LULUBELU
CARIBBEAN COFFEE & CHOCOLATE FACTORY
TERRAVENTURAS
CABINAS GUARANA
CABINAS JACARANDA
SUPERMARKET
SUPERMARKET
CENTRO COMERCIAL MANÉ/ PHARMACY/POST OFFICE
MEGA-SUPER
HOTEL PURA VIDA
MEDICAL CLINIC/BANK
MUSMANNI
HOTEL LOS SUEÑOS
PAGALÚ HOSTEL
SCHOOL
LAUNDRY/SODA Y CAMPING MISS ELENA'S
0   100 yds
0   100 m
COCO LOCO LODGE
© AVALON TRAVEL

Costa Rican Association of Community-Based Rural Tourism

(tel. 506/2248-9470, www.actuarcostarica.com) also offers tours.

The **Kéköldi Scientific Center** (tel. 506/2756-8136, www.kekoldi.org) works to safeguard the local environment through research projects. It welcomes volunteers and offers dorm accommodation ($20 per night including meals). Ad you can donate to **The Bridge** (tel. 506/2750-0524, www.elpuente -thebridge.org), a community assistance organization that works to help indigenous communities help themselves.

Entertainment and Events

Puerto Viejo is known for its lively bars and discos, and folks travel from as far afield as Limón to bop. The prize dance spots are **Stanford's** (tel. 506/2750-0016, 9 P.M.–2 A.M. Wed.–Sun.) for reggae! reggae! reggae!; and **Johnny's Place** (tel. 506/2750-0445, 6 P.M.–2:30 A.M. Mon., noon–2:30 A.M. Tues.–Sat.), where a bonfire draws patrons to dance in the sand.

The happenin' bar at last visit was the **Hot Rocks Bar** (6 P.M. until the last guest staggers home), which shows open-air movies nightly and epitomizes Puerto Viejo's laid-back

© CHRISTOPHER P. BAKER

girl with dog on the beach at Puerto Viejo

philosophy; its cocktail list runs from mojitos to *orgasmos*.

Baba Yaga (tel. 506/2750-0587) is the hot spot on Sunday and Monday nights, with reggae, while **Bar Maritza** (tel. 506/2750-0003), on the waterfront, also packs 'em in Fri.–Sun. nights. Also on Fridays, DJ Dodo spins at **Sunset Bar & Grill** (no tel.), 100 meters south of Maritza.

El Dorado (tel. 506/2750-0604, 8 A.M.–midnight daily), on the main drag, has a bar, pool table, board games, and movies on a TV.

The **ArteViva Festival** (www.arteviva-puertoviejo.com), each fall, features fireworks, live music, and art exhibits.

Sports and Recreation

The local community organization **ATEC** (tel./fax 506/2750-0191 www.ateccr.org, 8 A.M.–9 P.M. Mon.–Sat. and 10 A.M.–6 P.M. Sun.) offers hiking and nature excursions, including into the Keköldi reserve. Hiking and horseback trips into Keköldi are also offered by Mauricio Salazar from Beach Cottages Chimúri (seven hours, $25 pp, including box lunch and a contribution to the Indian Association). Three-day trips cost $140, including overnight stays with the locals.

Caribbean Tours (tel. 506/2750-0306, www.ptoviejotours.com) offers a range of tours from local jungle hikes to tours to Boca del Toro, in Panamá. **Terraventuras** (tel. 506/2750-0750, www.terraventuras.com) offers similar trips.

Rolf, of **Bushmaster Expeditions** (tel./fax 506/2750-0283, www.cabinas-tropical.com), offers nature tours to Gandoca ($40).

All-Star Rental (tel. 506/2750-0511) rents snorkeling gear ($15 half day, $20 all day), sea kayaks ($25 half day, $40 full day), and Jet Skis.

Puerto Viejo is legendary among the surfing crowd. November through April, especially, the village is crowded with surfers, who come for a killer six-meter, storm-generated wave called La Salsa Brava. Beach Break, at Playa Cocles, about three kilometers south of Puerto Viejo, is good for novices and intermediates. Snorkelers should use extreme caution in these waters, and never snorkel during rough weather; at least two snorkelers drowned in 2008.

© CHRISTOPHER P. BAKER

Salsa Brava beach, Puerto Viejo

Reef Runner Divers (tel. 506/2750-0480, www.reefrunnerdivers.com) offers guided dive tours ($50 one tank, $80 two tanks, $60 night dive), PADI certification ($325), and dolphin and snorkeling tours. **Juppy & Tino Adventures** (tel. 506/2750-0621) rents kayaks, boogie boards, and snorkeling and surfing gear; it also has kayak tours to Gandoca. **Aventuras Bravas** (tel. 506/2750-2000, junglejamjohn@mail.com) also has kayak tours, shuttles to Boca del Toro (in Panamá), and a surf school that guarantees you'll get standing on a board.

Shopping
Color Caribe (tel. 506/2750-0075, 9 A.M.– 8 P.M. daily), on the main drag, stocks a great selection of clothing, jewelry, and souvenirs, including hand-painted and silk-screened clothing, plus hammocks and colorful wind chimes. **LuluBelu** (tel. 506/2750-0394, 9 A.M.–9 P.M. daily), one block east of the main drag, sells an original range of ceramics, jewelry, and miscellany.

Accommodations
Demand is high; make your reservation in advance or secure a room as soon as you arrive. Beware touts who await as the bus arrives and try to entice you to specific lodgings—they're known to tell lies to dissuade you from any specific place you may already have in mind. The following are the best of dozens of options.

CAMPING
The beachfront **Camping Las Olas** (tel. 506/2750-0424, $5 pp low season, $8 pp high season), on the east side of town, is well run and has large tents under metal shade platforms. It has basic toilets and showers. **Soda y Camping Miss Elena** (tel. 506/2750-0580), on the southwest side of the village, charges $5 per person low season, $10 high season with your own tent ($2 pp extra for tent and cushion rental). Miss Elena is a charmer and offers storage, baths, hammocks, parking, and American breakfasts.

UNDER $25
Backpackers have two great options. The first is **◖ Rocking J's** (tel. 506/2750-0665,

ATEC: GRASSROOTS ECOTOURISM

The grassroots **Asociación Talamanca de Ecoturismo y Conservación** (ATEC, tel./fax 506/2750-0191, www.ateccr.org, 8 A.M.–9 P.M. Mon.-Sat. and 10 A.M.–6 P.M. Sun.), in Puerto Viejo, trains locals as approved guides and sponsors environmental and cultural tours of the Talamanca coast (from $20 half day, $35 full day).

Options include "African-Caribbean Culture and Nature Walks," trips to the Kéköldi and other indigenous reserves, rainforest hikes, snorkeling and fishing, bird and night walks, overnight "Adventure Treks" into the Gandoca-Manzanillo reserve, and an arduous eight-day trek over the Talamancas. Trips are limited to six people.

www.rockingjs.com, $5 hammocks, $6 tents, $7 pp dorm, $20 private room, $25 tree house, $50–60 suites, $350 house), a splendid and well-run backpackers' haven landscaped with ceramics and seats roughly hewn from tree trunks. You can pitch your tent at one of the sheltered campsites beneath shade eaves, or sleep outside at the "hammock hotel," with hammocks under shade canopies. It also has two dorm rooms, plus private rooms in varying configurations with lofty bunks and desks below; rooms share two solar-heated showers and five cold-water showers. Other accommodation options here include a tree house, suites, and a three-story house. Guests can use a community kitchen, plus there's laundry, grill, and secure parking, and an upstairs bar with live music midweek. Kayaks and bicycles are available for rent.

Opened in August 2008, the German-run ◖ **Pagalú Hostel** (tel. 506/2750-1930, www.pagalu.com, $9 pp dorm, $20 s or $22 d shared bathroom, $25 s or $28 d private bathroom) elevated the concept of hostel accommodation to a whole new level with its beautiful contemporary design. It makes great use of space, with a huge open-air lounge with kitchen. All rooms have ceiling fans, super clean and tasteful bathrooms with glass-brick walls and plenty of real hot water, plus thoughtful extras such as bedside halogen reading lights and shelving. One room is wheelchair equipped, and there's secure parking.

Sunrise Backpackers Hostel (tel. 506/2750-0028, sunrisebackpackers@hotmail .es, $14 s/d shared bathroom, $25 s/d private

bathroom) has an upstairs tent deck, plus a dorm and 13 private rooms (some are singles, others are doubles), all spartan and with particle-board walls. It has a pleasant café and Internet café.

Less appealing, but still popular with surfers is the venerable **Hotel Puerto Viejo** (tel. 506/2750-0620, $5–8 pp shared bath, $10 pp private). It has 72 small, spartan rooms with fans, mosquito nets, and shared, tiled bathrooms (upstairs rooms are preferable). Larger, more appealing cabins are at the rear. It has a community kitchen and surf school.

$25-50

The **Hotel Maritza** (tel. 506/2750-0003, fax 506/2750-0313, $35 s, $40 d *cabinas*), on the beachfront, has 14 clean rooms with ceiling fans, double and single beds, and private baths with hot water. On weekends, the bar and disco make the walls throb. There's parking.

I love **Cabinas Jacaranda** (tel./fax 506/2750-0069, www.cabinasjacaranda.net, from $20 s or $28 d low season, from $25 s or $32 d high season), with 14 cabins set in an exquisite garden, all with private bathroom and hot water. Furnishings are basic but delightful, with subdued tropical walls and colorful mosaic floors throughout. Japanese paper lanterns, mats, Guatemalan bedspreads, hammocks, and mosquito nets are nice touches. A garden massage is offered, and there's a communal kitchen.

For heartfelt hospitality and positive vibes, I recommend **Kaya's Place** (tel. 506/2750-0690, www.kayasplace.com, $14 s or $21 d

© CHRISTOPHER P. BAKER

Sunrise Backpackers Hostel

shared bath, $20–55 s, $30–65 d private low season; $19 s or $27 d shared bath, $25–60 s, $35–70 d private high season), a two-story stone-and-timber lodge supported by tree trunks washed up from the beach. It has 26 rooms of varying sizes and types, all charmingly if simply furnished with hardwood beds and furniture, screened windows, and walls in Caribbean pastels (however, dust from the road is a problem). Some rooms have huge double bunks. It has an Internet café and Wi-Fi. Parking, a swimming pool, and a sunset *mirador* (lookout) were planned.

For out-of-town seclusion I like **Chimúri Beach Cottages** (tel./fax 506/2750-0119, www.chimuribeach.com, $29–55 s/d), west of town, with three nice log-and-thatch cabins set on pleasant grounds. Each is a different size; one, in Caribbean style, has a colorful gingerbread motif and a loft bedroom plus kitchenette and hot water. A three-person unit also has a loft bedroom. Two have kitchens. Owner Mauricio Salazar, a generous, genteel host, offers guided day trips into the Keköldi Indigenous Reserve. Low-season rates are variable.

In the village, the delightful, bargain-priced, Italian-run **Cabinas Guarana** (tel. 506/2750-0244, www.hotelguarana.com, $25 s or $30 d low season, $30 s or $37 d high season) is entered by a charming lobby with bar. It has 12 simple but clean and tastefully decorated rooms with colorful sponge-washed walls and tasteful ethnic fabrics, plus fans, tile floors, mosquito nets, and private bath with hot water. Larger cabins have louvered windows and patios with hammocks. They're set in a lush garden with a tree house. Guests get use of a kitchen, and there's a laundry and secure parking.

One of the nicest options, and a superb bargain, is the clinically clean, Swiss-run (**Casa Verde Lodge** (tel. 506/2750-0015, www .cabinascasaverde.com, $28–42 s, $30–48 d low season; $32–48 s, $34–62 d high season). It has six cabins, five double rooms, and two single rooms, each with ceiling fans, mosquito nets, and lots of light, plus hot water in spotlessly clean showers and bathrooms. Wide balconies have hammocks. There's also a small bungalow, romantic as all get out, plus Casa Topo. Features include a gift store, a laundry,

© CHRISTOPHER P. BAKER

Pagalú Hostel

secure parking, a tour booth, a lovely café, and a beautiful landscaped swimming pool with raised whirlpool tub. The lush garden includes a poison-frog garden. At last visit, there were plans to open a dorm as well.

Nearby, the German-run **Cabinas Tropical** (tel. 506/2750-0645, www.cabinas-tropical .com, $30 s or $35 d low season, $35 s or $40 d high season) has eight pleasing rooms: clean and airy, with ceiling fans, huge showers with hot water, mosquito nets, and wide French doors opening onto little verandas. Smaller single rooms are dingy; three newer rooms are larger and have refrigerators and balconies. It's quiet and secure. There's also parking.

I always enjoy resting my head at **Coco Loco** (tel./fax 506/2750-0281, www.cocoloco lodge.com, $30–45 s/d low season, $35–50 s/d high season), where eight handsome Polynesian-style *cabinas* are raised on stilts amid lawns. The log-and-thatch huts are simply furnished but crafted with exquisite care. They have mosquito nets over the beds and hammocks on the porches. Simple breakfasts are served on a raised deck. Two two-room

bungalows with kitchen are also available. The Austrian owners offer tours.

East of the village, **Calalú Cabinas** (tel. 506/2750-0042, www.bungalowscalalu.com, $28–45 s, $36–45 d) has five handsome little A-frame thatch huts in a compact garden, each cross-ventilated through screened louvered windows, with large walk-in showers and porches with hammocks. Three units have kitchens; all have fans and hot water. It has a small pool. A surcharge applies for credit cards.

$50-100

The **Cabinas Los Almendros** (tel. 510/2750-0235, www.cabinaslosalmendros.com, $40 s or $60 d rooms, $70 up to six people for apartments) is a modern structure with 10 rooms, four cabins, and three apartments around a courtyard with secure parking. The clean, spacious rooms are cross-ventilated and have both front and back entrances, double and single beds, ceiling fans, tile floors, Wi-Fi, and private bathrooms with hot water.

El Pizote Lodge (tel. 506/2750-0088, www.pizotelodge.com, $55 s/d standard,

$66–93 s/d bungalow, $93–96 s/d cabin low season; $63 standard, $79–109 bungalow, $106–108 cabin high season), inland of Playa Negra, is set in nicely landscaped grounds complete with giant hardwoods and sweeping lawns—a fine setting for eight small but clean and atmospheric rooms with four shared bathrooms with huge screened windows. There are also six bungalows and two houses. Four luxury bungalows have air-conditioning, refrigerators, and hot water. The lodge even has a swimming pool, volleyball court, and a pool table. The breeze-swept restaurant gets good reviews.

About 400 meters east of town, the Italian-run **Escape Caribeño** (tel./fax 506/2750-0103, www.escapecaribeno.com, $65–75 s, $70–80 d) has 11 attractive hardwood cabins with double beds (some also have bunks) with mosquito nets, plus clean bathrooms with hot water, minibars, fans, and hammocks on the porch. They're widely spaced amid landscaped gardens and reached by raised wooden walkways. It also has brick-and-stucco bungalows with kitchenettes, plus a wood-paneled house for four people ($65 per day, one-week minimum).

In a similar vein, although less appealing, is the **La Perla Negra** (tel. 506/2750-0111, www.perlanegra-beachresort.com, $40 s or $45 d low season, $80 s or $100 d high season, $120 suites year-round), on Playa Negra. It has 24 spacious rooms in a two-story, all-hardwood structure cross-ventilated with glassless screened windows, charming albeit minimally appointed bathrooms with large walk-in showers, and bare-bones furnishings. There's a lap pool, sundeck, and bar, plus tennis court and basketball. Rates include breakfast and tax.

I like the secluded and vibrant **Cashew Hill Jungle Lodge** (tel. 506/2750-0256, www.cashew hilllodge.co.cr, $90–110 s/d), on a hill south of the soccer field. Six simple cottages have heaps of charm thanks to lively Caribbean color schemes and other endearing artistic touches. They vary from one- to three-bedroom units, but all have screens, mosquito nets, broad decks, and hammocks, plus Wi-Fi. This offbeat charmer is the creation of Erich and Wende Strube, your delightful hosts.

$100-150

Samasati Nature Retreat (tel. 506/2756-8015 or U.S. tel. 800/563-9643, www.samasati.com, $98 s or $190 d guesthouse, $185 s or $270 d bungalows, including meals and tax) is a holistic retreat hidden amid 100 hectares of private rainforest on the mountainside one kilometer inland of Hone Creek. It specializes in yoga and other meditative practices, but anyone is welcome. Accommodations are in 10 handsome yet ascetically furnished Japanese-style log cabins with ocean and jungle vistas, all with verandas, loft bedrooms, and tiled walk-in showers. Larger units have mezzanine bedrooms with wraparound windows. There are also five simpler rooms in a guesthouse with shared bathrooms, plus three two-bedroom *casas* with living rooms and kitchens. Vegetarian meals (and seafood) are served buffet-style in a handsome lodge open to the elements. It has a whirlpool tub. You'll need a four-wheel-drive vehicle for the rugged climb up the mountain.

In 2009, the region gained its first deluxe boutique hotel, **Le Caméléon** (tel. 506/2582-0140, www.fashionhotels.info or www.le cameleon.cr). This chic retro-contemporary pad promises to draw fashionistas to town with its all-white vogue decor.

Food

Puerto Viejo is blessed with a cosmopolitan range of eateries, even gourmet cuisine.

For breakfast, I head to **Café Rico** (tel. 506/2750-0510, 6 A.M.–2 P.M. Fri.–Wed.), a laid-back place serving on a palm-fringed veranda; Roger, the English owner, serves huevos rancheros ($4), omelettes ($4), granola with yogurt and fruit ($3.50), pancakes, and sandwiches. I recommend the Annarosa special: fried potatoes with cheddar cheese, fried eggs, and bacon ($4). Competing in style and substance, **Bread and Chocolate** (tel. 506/2750-0723, 6:30 A.M.–6:30 P.M. Wed.–Sat., and 6:30 A.M.–2:30 P.M. Sun.) has killer cinnamon oatmeal pancakes ($4), crispy sautéed potatoes with jerk barbecue sauce, sandwiches, brownie sundaes, and more.

Alternately, consider **Pan Pay Panadería**

(tel. 506/2750-0081, 7 A.M.–5 P.M. daily), which serves omelettes and scramble breakfasts (from $2.50) and has fruit salads ($2) and fruit-filled pastries, croissants, breads, tortillas, and coffees. The **Caribbean Coffee & Chocolate Factory** (tel. 506/2750-0850, 7 A.M.–10 P.M. Sun.–Wed. and 7 A.M.–midnight Thurs.–Sat.) is a cool spot to enjoy home-baked muffins, macadamia cookies, multigrain breads, and veggie dishes, plus organic coffee and chocolate drinks. It has free Wi-Fi. And the **Musmanni** bakery chain was due to open an outlet here in 2009.

Justifiably popular by night, **Chile Rojo** (tel. 506/2750-0025, 9 A.M.–10 P.M. daily) has a simple open-air setting. The Asian-inspired menu packs in diners who know a good thing. I recommend the veggie samosa with tamarind chutney ($3.50), Thai fish and coconut soup ($6), and the delicious green curry with coconut milk and veggies ($9).

Restaurante Tamara (tel. 506/2750-0148, 11:30 A.M.–10 P.M. Thurs.–Tues., $5–10) has a shaded patio done up in Rastafarian colors. The menu runs to burgers and *típico* dishes such as fried fish with *patacones* (plantain), plus great *batidos* (milk shakes). For genuine Caribbean fare, head to **Jammin'** (tel. 506/8826-4332, 9 A.M.–9 P.M. daily), a small Rasta-styled *soda* with tree-trunk stools. I recommend the jerk chicken ($5) and roast fish ($3.50). It has tremendous rootsy Jamaican atmosphere.

I like the open-air, offbeat, Spanish-run **Salsa Brava** (tel. 506/2750-0241, noon–11 P.M. Tues.–Sun., $4–15), with rainbow-hued furniture. The menu includes tuna ceviche salad, Caesar salad with chicken teriyaki, and grilled garlic fish, plus sangria and ice cream. Portions are huge and the fare is surprisingly good. Nearby, the beachfront **Restaurante Parquecito** (tel. 506/2750-0748, noon–midnight daily, $5–10) offers a fabulous ambience, with pendulous surfboards. It's good for cheap *casados* and specializes in simple seafood. **Café Viejo** (tel. 506/2750-0817, 6–10 P.M. daily), the snazziest place in town, serves good Italian fare, including pizzas (from $3), pastas ($5), and a large dessert menu.

Stanford's (tel. 506/2750-0016, 9 P.M.– 2 A.M. Wed.–Sun.), with a fine beachside perch, has cleaned up its act of late and is now a lovely place to dine on ceviche ($5), garlic shrimp ($7), and other seafoods.

At night, a delightful Jamaican lady named **Bou Bou** sells jerk chicken from her streetside stand outside Johnny's Place. And "Miss Sam" bakes tarts and bread and offers meals at **Soda Miss Sam's.**

For ice creams, sundaes, and shakes, head to **Lechería Las Lapas** (no tel., 10 A.M.–10 P.M. daily).

There's a *feria agricola* (farmers market) every Saturday morning.

Information and Services

ATEC (tel./fax 506/2750-0191 www.ateccr.org, 8 A.M.–9 P.M. Mon.–Sat. and 10 A.M.–6 P.M. Sun.) is the informal node of local activity and acts as a tourist information bureau.

There's a **medical clinic** (tel. 506/2750-0079, or emergency tel. 506/8870-8029, 10 A.M.–7 P.M. Mon.–Fri. and weekends for emergencies). There are **dental clinics** 50 meters inland from the bus stop (tel. 506/2750-0303, or 506/2750-0389 for emergencies) and next to Bread & Chocolate café (tel. 506/8336-2339, 9 A.M.–noon and 1 –6 P.M. Mon.–Fri., and 9 A.M.–2 P.M. Sat.).

The **police station** (tel. 506/2750-0230) is next to Johnny's Place. There's a **bank** with ATM, plus at **post office** (tel. 506/2750-0404) and pharmacy in Centro Comercial Mané, which also has a **laundry** (8 A.M.–7 P.M. daily). **Café Rico** also has laundry service using biodegradable products and offers free coffee while you wait.

The ATEC office has public telephones (tel. 506/2750-0188) and Internet access.

Getting There

The bus fare from San José to Puerto Viejo is $8, and from Limón $2. Transportes Mepe (tel. 506/2257-8129) buses depart the Gran Caribe terminal in San José for Cahuita ($8) at 6 A.M., 10 A.M., 1:30 P.M., and 3:30 P.M. They continue to Puerto Viejo.

Return buses depart Puerto Viejo (tel.

© CHRISTOPHER P. BAKER

chilling at Playa Cocles

506/2750-0023) for San José at 7:30 A.M., 9 A.M., 11 A.M., and 4 P.M.; and for Limón hourly 6:45 A.M.–7:30 P.M. The Puerto Limón–Puerto Viejo buses are usually crowded; get to the station early.

Interbus (tel. 506/283-5573, www.interbus online.com) operates minibus shuttles from San José.

Getting Around
ATEC can arrange taxis.

Surf Rentals (tel. 506/8375-7328, surf rentals@gmail.com) rents beach cruiser bikes ($1 per hour, $5 daily) and scooters ($15 one hour, $48 per day). Each scooter is sponsored, with a portion of the rental fee donated for charity; for example "Drummer Boy" is named for a local boy who wants a drum set.

Poás Rent-a-Car (tel. 506/2750-0400) has an outlet here.

PLAYA COCLES TO PUNTA UVA
South of Puerto Viejo, the paved road runs via Punta Cocles and Punta Uva to Manzanillo, a fishing village at the end of the road, 13 kilometers southeast of Puerto Viejo. Coral-colored Playa Cocles runs southeast for four kilometers from Puerto Viejo to the rocky point of Punta Cocles, beyond which **Playa Chiquita** runs south four kilometers to Punta Uva, where caimans can be seen in the swampy estuary of the Río Uva. From here, a five-kilometer-long gray-sand beach curls gently southeast to Manzanillo. Coral reefs lie offshore, offering good snorkeling and diving.

There are no settlements (except the tiny hamlet of Punta Uva).

A Swiss couple offers tours and demos at their cocoa farm and chocolate "factory," **Chocoart** (tel. 506/2750-0075, chocoart@ racsa.co.cr, 8 A.M.–5 P.M. daily, $15 pp, by reservation only), at Playa Chiquita. You'll learn all about cacao production, from the bean to the chocolate bar, on their hilly farm.

Fascinated by butterflies? **Mariposario Punta Uva** (tel. 506/2750-0086, 7 A.M.–5 P.M. daily, $5 adults, children free), a netted butterfly garden and reproduction center in the hills above Punta Uva, has some 20 butterfly

© CHRISTOPHER P. BAKER

rastafarian relaxing at Punta Uva

species within its netted garden, and monkeys and other animals are easily seen on trails into the surrounding forest.

The dirt road to the butterfly garden ascends one kilometer to **La Ceiba Private Biological Reserve** (tel. 506/2750-0710, www.rp ceiba.com, open by appointment), an animal rescue center that works to rehabilitate wildlife for reintroduction into the forest. The delightful Spanish couple that runs it, Francisco and Angela, offer guided hikes ($30 pp four hours). The forest reserve and two-hectare garden are great for birding and animal sightings, and a lagoon is a poison-dart frog breeding ground good for a nocturnal "sex show" tour. La Ceiba rents three wooden cabins with kitchens, huge decks, and modern bathrooms; they're perfect for families.

Sports and Recreation

Seahorse Stables (tel. 506/2750-0468, www.horsebackridingincostarica.com, from $55), near Punta Cocles, offers horseback rides by reservation. Edwin Salem, the gracious Argentinian owner, arranges occasional polo matches on the beach. He also offers sailing lessons on his 18-foot Hobie Cat, as well as overnight turtle-watching tours ($150 including lodging), plus surfing trips.

Punta Uva Dive Center (tel. 506/2759-9191, www.puntauvadivecenter.com) has scuba trips to the reefs of Gandoca-Manzanillo, as does **Crocodive Caribe** (tel. 506/2750-2136), in La Terraza Cocles plaza.

Crazy Monkey Canopy Ride (tel. 800/317-4108, www.crazymonkeycanopytour.com), at Almonds & Corals Lodge Tent Camp (tel. 506/2271-3000, www.almondsandcorals.com), has zipline rides at 8 A.M. and 2 P.M. ($40).

Treat yourself to a decadent chocolate body rub and cacao butter massage at the **Pure Jungle Spa** (tel. 506/2750-0080), at La Costa de Papito.

Accommodations
UNDER $25
At **Cabinas El Tesoro** (tel. 506/2750-0128, www.puertoviejo.net/cabinaselteroro.htm, $11.50 pp dorm, $20–55 s/d private rooms) about one kilometer from Puerto Viejo, 11

simply furnished rooms have orthopedic mattresses, screened windows, fans, and private baths with hot water, plus hammocks on patios. There's also a his-and-hers surf dorm at the back, with a communal kitchen, toilets, and showers. Three more upscale rooms have earth-tone stucco, cross-ventilation, cable TV, refrigerators, and large walk-in showers; two have air-conditioning. It's well run by a friendly, in-the-know American, Charlie Wanger. There's free Internet, coffee, and parking, and free movies are shown nightly on a wide-screen television.

$25-50

La Casita (in Jamaica, tel. 876/974-2870, fax 876/974-2651, info@harmonyhall.com, $300/350 weekly low/high season) is a delightful albeit rustic log-and-thatch *casita* set in lush gardens, with forest all around. It's just you and the monkeys and geckos. A path leads to Playa Cocles, and a grocery store and restaurant are a short stroll.

In a similar vein, I like the German-run **El Tucán Lodge** (tel. 506/2750-0026, www.eltucanjunglelodge.com, $28 s, $40 d), a lovely spot to lay your head in the forest in stylishly simple wooden cabins on the edge of the Río Caño Negro, at Cocles.

$50-100

La Costa de Papito (tel. 506/2750-0704, www.lacostadepapito.com, $48–73 s/d low season, $54–78 s/d high season, including taxes), at Playa Cocles, is run by Eddie Ryan, a New York hotelier who has conjured 10 simple yet tastefully decorated bungalows at the jungle edge of a lush five-acre garden. Each has ceiling fan, leopard-skin sheets (!), exquisite tiled bathrooms, and shady porches with hammocks under thatch. Four smaller cabins have polished hardwoods and outside "rainforest" bathrooms. There's a laundry and massage, plus bicycle, surfboard, boogie board, and snorkel rentals. Hearty breakfasts are served on your porch and in a new restaurant. It has a full-service spa.

The Italian-run **Totem Hotel Resort &**

Restaurant (tel. 506/2750-0758, www.totemsite.com, $65 s or $80 d standard, $100 s/d suite) is a reasonable option on Playa Cocles. It has two types of accommodations in effusive gardens. Standards in a thatched, stone-and-timber two-story structure, although dark, have colorful decor and spacious gray-tile bathrooms. Suites boast huge lounges with terra-cotta floors and screened glassless walls opening to a walk-in landscaped pool with cascade. Two handicapped-accessible rooms were being added, along with six bungalows and six suites. There's an outdoor games room with Wi-Fi, a large thatched bar with TV, plus a surf shop. The Mediterranean restaurant doubles as an oyster bar by day.

I highly recommend ◖ **Aguas Claras** (tel. 506/2750-0131, www.aguasclaras-cr.com, $70 s/d one-bedroom, $130–160 two-bedroom, $220 three-bedroom), nearby, with five adorable *casas* on well-groomed grounds. Each is a different size, accommodating 2–6 people. Of a delightful Victorian style, they have gingerbread trim, bright tropical color schemes, ceiling fans, modern tiled bathrooms with hot water, large full kitchens, and shady verandas with rattan furnishings. Miss Holly's Kitchen is here.

The **Jardín Miraflores Lodge** (tel./fax 506/2750-0038, www.mirafloreslodge.com, $25–60 s/d), at Punta Cocles, appeals to nature lovers. Choose from double rooms with shared bathroom or private bathroom and balcony with hammock, and suites with king-size beds, private bathrooms, and living areas. Downstairs rooms have kitchenettes and king-size beds plus two sofa beds. Mosquito nets hang above the beds. It also has a basic six-bed dormitory with outside bathrooms for groups only ($10 per person). The wood and bamboo hotel is adorned with Latin American fabrics, masks, and art, and vases full of fresh tropical blooms. Upstairs, cool breezes flow through the rooms. Health-conscious meals are served in a rustic *rancho*. Tours are offered. Rates include a hearty breakfast.

Playa Chiquita Lodge (tel. 506/2750-

THE CARIBBEAN COAST

0062, www.playachiquitalodge.com, $55 s/d low season, $70 s/d high season), three kilometers south of Punta Cocles, is appealing for its jungle ambience. Eleven colorful and spacious "bungalows" offer murals, sunken bathrooms (no hot water), fans, and leather rocking chairs on a wide veranda. You can dine alfresco under thatch in the restaurant. The lodge arranges diving and snorkeling, boat trips, and bike and horse rentals.

The Italian-run **Pachamama B&B** (tel. 506/2759-9196, www.pachamamacaribe.com, $45–75 s/d low season, $55–75 high season) enjoys a marvelous riverside forest setting amid trees festooned with epiphytes. It has two one-bedroom bungalows featuring pastel color schemes including sponge-washed floors, simple furnishings, mosquito nets, pleasing tiled bathrooms with hot water, and hardwood decks. A spacious wooden one-bedroom house is a charmer. And a two-bedroom *casa* ($100) has a lively color scheme. The overall mood is endearing.

I like **Cariblue Bungalows** (tel. 506/2750-0035, www.cariblue.com, $95–110 s/d bungalows, $220 s/d house year-round), one kilometer south of Puerto Viejo, with 15 handsome, spacious hardwood *cabinas* amid shaded lawns. Some have king-size beds. All have colorful sponge-washed decor, bamboo ceilings with fans, private bathrooms with mosaic tiles, and sliding doors opening to delightful porches with hammock. There's boogie board and bike rentals, plus a gift shop, TV lounge, and a freeform pool with whirlpool tub and wet bar. An Italian seafood restaurant serves meals under thatch. Rates include tax and buffet breakfast.

Almost identical, **Azánia Bungalows** (tel. 506/2750-0540, www.azania-costarica.com, $70 s/d low season, $85 s/d high season), next to Cariblue, is another beautiful property on lush grounds. Eight thatched, hardwood cottages with large decks with hammocks are delightfully simple and have batik blinds on all-around screened windows, queen beds plus singles in a loft, and handsome bathrooms with colorful tiles, drop-down walk-in

showers with sauna seating, and huge windows. It rents bikes. The restaurant specializes in Argentinian fare.

Of similar standard, **Casa Camarona** (tel. 506/2750-0151, www.casacamarona.co.cr, $61.50 s/d low season, $66 s/d high season) is well-run by a Tico couple and offers 18 modestly furnished, air-conditioned wooden rooms with tile floors and hot water. It has an intimate breeze-swept restaurant, La Palapa, decorated in Jamaican style. There's also a gift store, beach bar, laundry, safe parking, bicycle and kayak rental, and tours. The facilities are wheelchair accessible.

At Punta Cocles, the upscale **Villas del Caribe** (tel. 506/2750-0202, www.villasdel caribe.com, $69 s/d standard, $79 s/d junior villa, $99 s/d villa low season; $79 s/d standard, $89 s/d junior villa, $109 s/d villa high season) has a superb location in the cusp of the bay. It has 12 colorfully furnished rooms in a two-story complex in landscaped gardens 50 meters from the beach. Fully equipped kitchen, hot water, and fans are standard. It has a restaurant and bar. The hotel is eco-conscious—even the soaps and toiletries are biodegradable. Rates include breakfast and tax.

Another Caribbean-cabin-style entity, **Hotel Kashá** (tel./fax 506/2750-0205, www.costarica-hotelkasha.com, $90 s, $110 d) offers all-inclusive packages in addition to rack rates. This place has 14 handsome hardwood bungalows set back from the road amid the forest. The units are spacious, with plenty of light, screened windows, ceiling fans, two double beds, and pleasant bathrooms with heated water and beautiful Italian ceramics. Some units are for two people; others are for four people. The hotel has a small *ranchito* restaurant and bar, plus a small pool with water cascade. Rates include tax and breakfast.

The relatively upscale **Hotel Punta Cocles** (tel. 506/2750-0337, www.hotelpunta cocles.com, $75 s/d low season, $80 s/d high season), about four kilometers south of Puerto Viejo, sprawls over covering 10 forested hectares well inland of the beach, accessed via a path. The hotel's 60 spacious, modern air-conditioned cabins (five with kitchenettes) appeal to Costa Rican families and have porches good for bird-watching. An open-air restaurant overlooks a swimming pool, and there's a whirlpool tub, game room, and TV lounge.

French-run **El Colibri Lodge** (tel. 506/2759-9036, www.elcolibrilodge.com, $50 s, $65 d), south of Punta Uva, has a lush jungle setting. Its four concrete cabins lack ventilation and get hot, but they boast hardwood floors, nice color schemes, and modern bathrooms with hot water. It has a gourmet restaurant, and trails lead to the beach. Monkeys hang out in the trees overhead, and an adjacent lagoon harbors caimans. The owners are a delight. Rates include breakfast.

OVER $100
The fanciest digs around are at the bargain-priced, French-owned **(Shawandha Lodge** (tel. 506/2750-0018, www.shawandhalodge.com, $95 s/d low season, $115 high season), one kilometer farther south at Playa Chiquita. It has 12 spacious, thatched, hardwood cabins, each marvelously furnished with simple yet beautiful modern decor, including four-poster beds, screened windows, and large verandas with hammocks. The bathrooms boast large walk-in showers with exquisite tile work. The restaurant is one of the best around, and there's a splendid open-air lounge with contempo decor. Rates include American breakfast.

Lovely, but overpriced, **Almonds & Corals Lodge Tent Camp** (tel. 506/2271-3000, www.almondsandcorals.com, $235 s or $300 d suite, $315 s or $400 d master suite), is three kilometers north of Manzanillo, with a lonesome forested setting a few leisurely steps from the beach. Each of 24 tent-huts is raised on a stilt platform and features two singles or one double bed, a locker, night lamps, table and chairs, plus mosquito nets and deck with hammock—a touch of Kenya come to the Caribbean. Very atmospheric! Separate junior suites and

suites are even nicer and verge on luxe. Each cabin has its own shower and toilet in separate washhouses. Raised walkways lead to the beach, pool, snack bar, and restaurant serving Costa Rican food. You can rent kayaks, bicycles, and snorkeling gear. It has four leaves in the Certified Sustainable Tourism program but in 2008 was accused by authorities of illegally clear-cutting protected forest for an expansion.

Eclectic in the extreme, **(Tree House Lodge** (tel. 506/750-0706, www.costaricatreehouse.com, $150–390 s/d depending on the unit), at Punta Uva, is a rustic yet upscale place with a fabulous Middle Earth feel. Having recently expanded, it now offers four individual and irresistible units with forest or beach setting. The original all-wood two-story Tree House is built in and around a huge tree, with separate elements connected by a steel suspension bridge. Two bedrooms share a bathroom; a spiral staircase leads to a loft bedroom with king-size bed. The Beach Suite features a Tolkien-style dome bathroom (owners claim it's the largest in the country) with stained-glass windows and huge Jacuzzi. *Fantastic!*

Food
Totem Hotel Resort & Restaurant (tel. 506/2750-0758, noon–10 P.M. daily) has great ambience, the advantage of beach views, plus great pizza, risotto, and Italian seafood. By day it's an oyster bar.

Speaking of Italian, the finest cuisine east of San José is to be savored south of Punta Cocles at **(La Pecora Nera** (tel. 506/2750-0490, pecoranera@racsa.co.cr, 5:30 P.M.–11 P.M. Tues.–Sun. high season only, $5–20), a genuine fine-dining experience in unpretentious surrounds at fair prices. Ilario Giannono, the young Italian owner, offers delicious bruschetta, spaghetti, pizzas, calzones, and a large selection of daily specials—all exquisitely executed. I recommend the mixed starters plate, a meal in itself. A wine cellar has been added. Credit cards are not accepted. Ilario also runs the adjoining **Il Gato Ci Cora** (noon–10 P.M. daily), serving salads, pizzas, and panini.

At Punta Uva, I love the **Punta Uva Lounge** (tel. 506/2659-9048, 11 A.M.–5 P.M. daily), with simple thatched dining areas in lawns opening to the beach; it serves sandwiches and simple rice and fish dishes, plus ice cream and cocktails.

Miss Holly's Kitchen (tel. 506/2750-0131, 8 A.M.–6 P.M.) has a gourmet café with Wi-Fi. It's a great breakfast spot for omelettes and fruit salads, and for lunchtime salads and sandwiches. Nearby **La Casa del Pan** is a lovely roadside café that doubles as a French bakery and pizzeria.

At Punta Cocles, you can stock up on food at the **El Duende Gourmet** deli and grocery, or at the fully stocked **Super Pirripí.**

Services

Café Internet Río Negro (tel. 506/2750-0801, 8 A.M.–8 P.M. Mon.–Sat.) serves fruit shakes, sandwiches, and Argentinian *empanadas.*

La Terraza Cocles plaza has a bookstore and Internet café.

Manzanillo and Vicinity

MANZANILLO

This lonesome hamlet sits at the end of the road, 13 kilometers south of Puerto Viejo. The populace has lived for generations in what is now the wildlife refuge, living off the sea and using the land to farm cacao until 1979, when the *Monilia* fungus wiped out the crop. Electricity arrived in 1989, four years after the first dirt road linked it to the rest of the world. The hamlet has become a darling of the off-beat, alternative-travel set.

From Manzanillo, a five-kilometer coastal trail leads to the fishing hamlet of **Punta Mona** (Monkey Point) and the heart of Gandoca-Manzanillo National Park.

Sports and Recreation

A local cooperative, **Guias MANT** (tel. 506/2759-9064), offers birding, fishing, hiking, horseback riding, and snorkeling excursions.

Aquamor (tel. 506/2759-9012, www.greencoast.com/aquamor.htm, 7 A.M.–6 P.M. daily) is a full-service dive shop offering dives ($35–95), PADI certification course ($350), snorkeling ($8–35), kayak trips (from $35), and a dolphin observation safari ($40).

Manzanillo Tarpon Expeditions (tel. 506/2759-9118 or U.S. tel. 406/586-5084, www.tarponville.com) has sportfishing packages.

Accommodations and Food

No camping on the beach is permitted. You can camp under palms at **Camping Manzanillo** (tel. 506/2759-9008, $5 pp).

Cabinas Maxi (tel. 506/2759-9086 or 2759-9042, $25 s/d standard, $35 s/d with refrigerator and TV), adjoining Restaurant/Bar Maxi, has six modern, clean, simple concrete *cabinas* with TV, fans, bamboo furnishings, and private bathrooms. Similar alternatives include **Cabinas Manzanillo** (tel. 506/2759-9033).

Pangaea (tel. 506/2759-9204, pangaea@racsa.co.cr, $25 s, $35 d including breakfast), 100 meters inland of the beach, has two simple yet pleasing, well-lit rooms with tin roofs, screened windows, fans, mosquito nets, hammocks on porches, and private bathrooms with hot water. It also has a beach house with kitchen for four people ($60).

By far the nicest digs are at the new, Dutch-run **Cabinas Faya Lobi** (tel. 506/2759-9167, www.cabynasfayalobi.com, $25 s/d), a modern two-story building with black stone highlights. It has four cross-ventilated rooms with stone floors and quaint bathrooms with hot water and mosaics. They share a simple kitchen and an open-air lounge with hammocks.

For your own house rental, I recommend

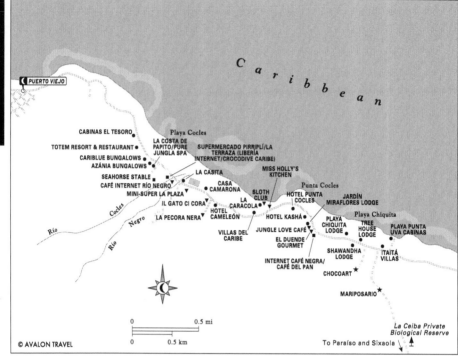

Caribbean

PUERTO VIEJO

CABINAS EL TESORO
Playa Cocles
LA COSTA DE
TOTEM RESORT & RESTAURANT   PAPITO/PURE
JUNGLA SPA   SUPERMERCADO PIRRIPLÍ/LA
CARIBLUE BUNGALOWS   TERRAZA (LIBERIA
INTERNET/CROCODIVE CARIBE)
AZÁNIA BUNGALOWS
LA CASITA   MISS HOLLY'S
KITCHEN
SEAHORSE STABLE
CAFÉ INTERNET RÍO NEGRO   CASA
CAMARONA   Punta Cocles
MINI-SÚPER LA PLAZA   SLOTH   HOTEL PUNTA   JARDÍN
LA   CLUB   COCLES   MIRAFLORES LODGE
IL GATO CI CORA   CARACOLA
HOTEL   Playa Chiquita
LA PECORA NERA   CAMELEÓN   HOTEL KASHÁ   PLAYA
CHIQUITA   TREE   PLAYA PUNTA
VILLAS DEL   JUNGLE LOVE CAFÉ   LODGE   HOUSE   UVA CABINAS
CARIBE   LODGE
EL DUENDE
GOURMET   SHAWANDHA   ITAITÁ
LODGE   VILLAS
INTERNET CAFÉ NEGRA/
CAFÉ DEL PAN   CHOCOART

MARIPOSARIO

Río   Cocles   Negro   Río

0   0.5 mi
0   0.5 km

© AVALON TRAVEL

La Ceiba Private
Biological Reserve
To Paraíso and Sixaola

the all-wood, beachfront **Dolphin Lodge** (in North America tel. 406/586-5084, www.vrbo.com/18442, $175–200), east of the river outside Manzanillo and inside the reserve. It's a two-story, three-bedroom, three-bathroom beach house with kitchen. No smokers are permitted. A caretaker and his family prepare meals.

Restaurant/Bar Maxi (tel. 506/2759-9086, restmaxis@racsa.co.cr, 11:30 A.M.–10 P.M. daily, $5–15) serves *típico* dishes and seafood, such as *pargo rojo* (red snapper) and lobster. Bar Maxi is one of the liveliest spots on the Caribbean. The gloomy disco-bar downstairs is enlivened by the slap of dominoes and the blast of Jimmy Cliff and Bob Marley, and the dancing spills out onto the sandy road. The upstairs bar has a breezy terrace and gets packed to the gills on weekends and holidays, even in the middle of the day. Service can be slow and indifferent, alas.

Getting There

Buses depart Puerto Limón for Manzanillo (two hours) via Cahuita and Puerto Viejo on an irregular (but more or less hourly) basis 6 A.M.–8 P.M. daily.

GANDOCA-MANZANILLO NATIONAL WILDLIFE REFUGE

The 9,446-hectare Refugio Nacional de Vida Silvestre Gandoca-Manzanillo protects a beautiful, brown-sand, palm-fringed, nine-kilometer-long, crescent-shaped beach where four species of turtles—most abundantly, leatherback turtles—come ashore to lay their eggs (Jan.–Apr. is best). Some 4,436 hectares of the park extend out to sea. The ocean has riptides and is not safe for swimming. The reserve—which is 65 percent tropical rainforest—also protects rare swamp habitats, including the only mangrove

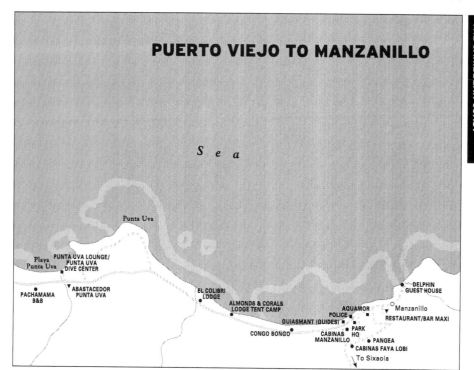

PUERTO VIEJO TO MANZANILLO

Sea

Punta Uva

Playa Punta Uva

PUNTA UVA LOUNGE/
PUNTA UVA
DIVE CENTER

PACHAMAMA B&B

ABASTACEDOR
PUNTA UVA

EL COLIBRI
LODGE

ALMONDS & CORALS
LODGE TENT CAMP

GUIASMANT (GUIDES)

CONGO BONGO

AQUAMOR
POLICE

Manzanillo
RESTAURANT/BAR MAXI

DELPHIN
GUEST HOUSE

PARK
HQ

CABINAS
MANZANILLO

PANGEA

CABINAS FAYA LOBI

To Sixaola

forest on Costa Rica's Caribbean shores, two jolillo palm swamps, a 300-hectare cativo forest, and a live coral reef.

The large freshwater **Gandoca Lagoon,** one kilometer south of Gandoca village, has two openings into the sea. The estuary, full of red mangrove trees, is a complex world braided by small brackish streams and snakelike creeks. The mangroves shelter both a giant oyster bed and a nursery for lobster and the swift and powerful tarpon. Manatees and a rare estuarine dolphin—the *tucuxí*—swim and breed here, as do crocodiles and caimans. The park is home to at least 358 species of birds (including toucans, red-lored Amazon parakeets, and hawk-eagles) as well as margays, ocelots, pacas, and sloths.

The hamlets of Punta Uva, Manzanillo (the northern gateway), Punta Mona, and Gandoca (the southern gateway) form part of the refuge. Because local communities live within the park, it is a mixed-management reserve; the locals' needs are integrated into park-management policies. **Punta Mona Center for Sustainable Living and Education** (tel. 506/2614-5735 or 506/8391-2116, http://puntamona.org) is an organic farm and environmental center. It teaches traditional and sustainable farming techniques and other environmentally sound practices. It accepts volunteers, and internships are available. Kayaking, guided hikes, and yoga retreats are offered. It's open to day visits Tuesday, Thursday, and Saturday ($40 pp including boat transfers, guided tour, and kayaking).

ANAI (Asociación Nacional de Asuntos Indígenas, tel. 506/2224-3570, www.anai cr.org) works to protect the forest and to evolve a sustainable livelihood through reforestation

© CHRISTOPHER P. BAKER

hikers at Gandoca-Manzanillo Wildlife Refuge

and other earth-friendly methods; it offers "Talamanca Field Adventures" trips throughout the southeast. The **Costa Rican Association of Community-Based Rural Tourism** (ACTUAR, tel. 506/2248-9470, www.actuar costarica.com) offers eco-minded tours, plus homestay accommodation with locals.

Turtle Patrol

Volunteers are needed for the **Marine Turtle Conservation Project,** which conducts research and protects the turtles from predators and poachers. Contact **ANAI** (tel. 506/2224-3570, www.anaicr.org) or **ATEC** (tel./fax 506/2750-0191 www.ateccr.org) to see how you can help.

Exploring the Park

The park is easily explored simply by walking the beaches; trails also wind through the flat, lowland rainforest fringing the coast. A coastal track leads south from the east side of Manzanillo village to Gandoca village (two hours), where you can walk the beach one kilometer south to Gandoca Lagoon. Beyond the lagoon, a trail winds through the jungle,

ending at the Río Sixaola and the Panamá border. A guide is recommended.

You can hire a guide and boat in Sixaola to take you downriver to the mangrove swamps at the river mouth (dangerous currents and reefs prevent access from the ocean).

The **MINAE ranger station** (tel. 506/2759-9001, 8 A.M.–4 P.M. daily) is at the entrance to Manzanillo village; the MINAE headquarters (tel. 506/2759-9100), at Gandoca, is 0.5 kilometer inland from the beach. Entrance costs $6 but there is rarely anyone to collect the fee.

Accommodations and Food

Camping is permitted in the park, but there are no facilities.

The nearest accommodations are in the villages of Manzanillo and Gandoca, on the northern and southern entrances to the reserve, respectively.

The various accommodations at Gandoca are often closed in low season and include the breeze-swept **Cabinas Orquideas** (tel. 506/2754-2392), run by a friendly elderly couple. They have 18 rooms. Four upstairs

THE *TUCUXÍ* DOLPHIN

The *tucuxí* dolphin (*Sotalia fluviatilis*) is a rare species whose existence hereabouts, though known to local anglers for generations, only recently filtered out from the swamps of Manzanillo to the broader world. The little-known species is found in freshwater rivers, estuaries, and adjacent coastal areas of South America and has recently been found as far north as Laguna Leimus, in Nicaragua. Pods of *tucuxí* (pronounced "tooKOO-shee") interact with pods of bottle-nosed dolphins, and interspecies mating has been observed.

The **Talamanca Dolphin Foundation** (tel. 506/2759-9118; in the U.S., 3150 Graf St. #8, Bozeman, MT 59715, tel./fax 406/586-5084; www.dolphinlink.org) is a nonprofit organization that conducts research into the dolphins and offers guided boating tours.

rooms have bunks and shared bath with cold water only for $12 per person ($20 with meals). Others have private bathrooms ($25 pp, or $30 with meals). The best bet in Gandoca is **Cabinas Kaniki** (tel. 506/2754-1071, info@alberguekaniki.com, $17 pp), with three small dorm rooms with bunks and lots of light and cold-water bathrooms. You can also camp on lawns. Two cabins were to be added. Meals are served. It rents sea kayaks and has horseback rides, plus birding, hiking, and dolphin tours.

Sportfishers opt for **Tarponville** (tel. 506/2759-9118 or U.S. tel. 406/586-5084, www.tarponville.com, $100 pp including meals, or from $1,880 five-day angling package, $825 non-angler), a handsome, two-story wooden lodge inside the reserve. It offers sportfishing packages from five days. Simply furnished rooms have ceiling fans. Rates include meals.

Punta Mona Center for Sustainable Living and Education (tel. 506/2614-5735 or 506/8391-2116, http://puntamona.org, $40 pp including meals) has cabins.

Getting There

You can drive to Gandoca village via a 15-kilometer dirt road that leads north from the Bribrí–Sixaola road; the turnoff is signed about three kilometers west of Sixaola. Keep left at the crossroads 1.5 kilometers down the road. If you get caught short of money, there's a roadside 24-hour **ATM** at Finca Sixaola, midway to Gandoca.

Río Sixaola Region

BRIBRÍ AND VICINITY

From Hone Creek, Highway 36 winds inland through the foothills of the Talamancas and descends to **Bribrí,** a small town 60 kilometers south of Puerto Limón, and the administrative center for the region. It is surrounded by banana plantations spread out in a flat valley backed by tiers of far-off mountain. The indigenous influence is noticeable.

The paved road ends in Bribrí, but a dirt road leads west through the gorge of the Río Sixaola and the village of **Bratsi,** where the vistas open up across the Valle de Talamanca surrounded by soaring mountains—a region known as **Alta Talamanca.** The United Fruit Company once reigned supreme in the valley, and the history of the region is a sad tale (many of the tribes who opposed destruction of their forests at the turn of the 20th century were hunted and jailed). You'll need a four-wheel-drive vehicle.

Talamanca Indigenous Reserves

The **Reserva Indígena Talamanca-Bribrí** and **Reserva Indígena Talamanca-Cabecar** are incorporated into La Amistad International Peace Park, on the slopes of the Talamanca mountains. The parks were established to protect the traditional lifestyle of the indigenous people, though the communities and their land remain under constant threat from loggers and squatters.

The Cabecar native peoples have no villages, as they prefer to live apart. Though the people speak Spanish and wear Western clothing, their philosophy that all living things are the work of Sibo, their god of creation, has traditionally pitted the native peoples against pioneers. Government proposals to build a trans-Talamanca highway and a hydroelectric dam are being fought by the local tribes. The communities supplement their income by selling crafts, and organically grown cacao.

The "capital" of the Talamanca-Bribrí reserve is the hamlet of **Shiroles,** setting for **Finca Educativa Indígena** (tel. 506/8373-4181), an administrative center for the Bribrí people.

The Cabecar are now turning to ecotourism as a means of preserving their culture. **Amubri,** eight kilometers west of Bratsi, is the "capital" and gateway to the reserve. If you go, enter with a sense of humility and respect. Do not treat the community members as a tourist oddity: You have as much to learn from the indigenous communities as to share.

Beyond Bribrí, a moderate 30-minute hike off the Bratsi road leads to the 20-meter **Volio waterfall,** popular with local tour guides; it has a pool good for swimming.

The **Reserva Indígena Yorkin** (tel. 506/8375-3372, www.greencoast.com/yorkin.htm) welcomes tourists and leads hikes. Artisans of the **Estibrawpa Women's Group** display their traditional (rather crude) crafts. The reserve is accessed by canoe up the Río Yorkin from Bambú. The two-day, one-night trip includes lodging, transport, and meals ($50 pp, $25 extra day). However, it is extremely basic (no towels, nor even toilet paper) and reports of the experience are mixed. The **Costa Rican Association of Community-Based Rural Tourism** (ACTUAR, tel. 506/2248-9470, www.actuarcostarica.com) offers tours.

Accommodations and Food

In Shiroles, **Finca Educativa Indígena** ($10

pp) has a rustic 12-bedroom lodge. At Buena Vista, northeast of Shiroles, **ACODEFO** (Asociación de Conservación y Desarrollo Forestal de Talamanca, tel. 506/2751-0020, acodefo@hotmail.com, $40 pp) has a basic, two-story, A-frame wooden lodge with six rooms, private bathrooms, and solar-generated power. Rates include three meals and a guided excursion to the reserves. **Reserva Indígena Yorkin** has a lodge for 15 people.

Information and Services

Banco Nacional (10 A.M.–noon and 1–3:45 P.M. Mon.–Fri.) in Bribrí has a $100 limit. It gets crowded and can take half a day to get money changed.

There's a **Red Cross** (tel. 506/2758-0125) evacuation center for emergencies. The **police station** (tel. 506/2758-1865) is opposite the Red Cross.

Getting There

The San José–Limón bus passes through Bribrí en route to Sixaola ($3.50 to Sixaola). Buses depart Limón from opposite Radio Casino on Avenida 4 eight times daily (5 A.M.–6 P.M.).

Buses depart Bribrí for Shiroles at 8 A.M., noon, and 5:30 P.M. daily.

If driving from Puerto Viejo, you can take a dirt road that crosses the mountains, linking Punta Uva to Paraíso, about 10 kilometers west of Sixaola.

SIXAOLA: CROSSING INTO PANAMÁ

Sixaola, 34 kilometers southeast of Bribrí, is on the north bank of the 200-meter-wide, fast-flowing Río Sixaola. The only visitors to this dour border town (it's not a place to get stuck overnight) are typically crossing the river into Panamá en route to Boca del Toro (the equally dour Panamanian village of Guabito is on the south bank of the river). You can walk or drive across the border. Remember to advance your watch by one hour as you enter Panamá.

The Costa Rican Customs and Immigration offices (tel. 506/2754-2044; open 7 A.M.–5 P.M.)

are on the west end of the bridge that links the two towns. The Panamanian office (tel. 507/759-7952), on the east end of the bridge, is open 8 A.M.–6 P.M.

The basic **Hotel el Imperio** (tel. 506/2754-2289) is on the left as you come into Sixaola. Its sole room costs $8. There are a few other grim cabins, and a fistful of uninspired eateries.

Buses depart Sixaola for San José at 5 A.M., 7:30 A.M., 9:30 A.M., and 2:30 P.M. daily; and for Limón at 5 A.M., 8 A.M., 10 A.M., 1 P.M., 3 P.M., and 5 P.M. daily.

There's a Texaco **gas station** about 10 kilometers east of Bribrí. You'll be stopped and possibly searched at the *comando* (police checkpoint, tel. 506/2754-2160) as you enter Sixaola.

SAN JOSÉ

San José, the nation's capital, squats on the floor of the Meseta Central, a fertile upland basin 1,150 meters (3,773 feet) above sea level in the heart of Costa Rica. Surrounded by mountains, it's a magnificent setting. The city's central position makes it an ideal base for forays into the countryside, applying the hub-and-spoke system of travel—almost every part of the country is within a four-hour drive.

San José—or "Chepe," as Ticos call it—dominates national life. Two-thirds of the nation's urban population lives in greater (or metropolitan) San José, whose population of 1.3 million represents 30 percent of the nation's total. San José is congested, bustling, and noisy. Its commercial center is dominated by hotels, offices, ugly modern high-rises, and shops. Though the city is not without its share of homeless people and beggars, there are few of the ghoulish *tugurios* (slums) that scar the hillsides of so many other Latin American cities. The modest working-class *barrios* (neighborhoods) are mostly clean and well ordered, while the tranquil residential districts such as Sabana Sur, San Pedro, and Rohrmoser are blessed with gracious houses with green lawns and high metal fences.

The city's chaos of architectural styles is part Spanish, part Moorish, and many streets in the older neighborhoods are still lined with one- or two-story houses made of wood or even adobe, with ornamental grillwork. What few older structures remain are of modest interest, however: The city is almost wholly lacking the grand colonial structures of, say, Havana or Mexico City. If it's colonial quaintness you're seeking, skip San José.

© CHRISTOPHER P. BAKER

HIGHLIGHTS

Museo del Oro Precolumbino: The highlight of the Museos Banco Central de Costa Rica, this splendid collection of pre-Columbian gold and jade displays a cornucopia of indigenous ornaments and artifacts. Also here is an excellent numismatic museum (page 80).

Teatro Nacional: San José's architectural pride and joy gleams after a recent restoration. View by day, then don your duds for a evening classical performance in season (page 80).

Museo de Jade: The world's largest collection of pre-Columbian jade ornamentation is exhibited in creative displays in a recently opened new facility (page 84).

Parque Nacional: A breath of fresh air in the crowded city, this leafy park is the setting for the Monumento Nacional (page 85).

Mercado Central: Tuck your wallet safely away to explore this tight-packed warren of stalls and stores selling everything from pig's heads to saddles. This is a great place to eat for pennies in true Tico fashion (page 87).

SAN JOSÉ

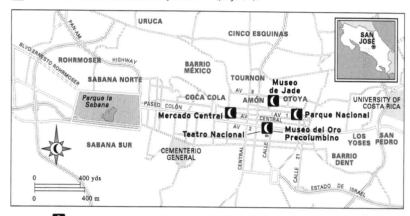

LOOK FOR **(** TO FIND RECOMMENDED SIGHTS, ACTIVITIES, DINING, AND LODGING.

Nonetheless, the city offers several first-rate museums and galleries. Despite its working-class tenor, the city is large enough and its middle-class component cosmopolitan enough in outlook to support a vital cultural milieu. And the city has scores of accommodations for every budget, including backpackers' hostels and one of the world's preeminent boutique hotels. The restaurant scene is impressive, with dozens of globe-spanning eateries, including some exciting nouvelle options. And night owls will appreciate San José's vivacious nightlife, from modest casinos to raging discos with Latin music hot enough to cook the pork.

PLANNING YOUR TIME

The vast majority of visitors to the country spend one or two days in the capital city, whose bona fide tourist attractions can be counted on two hands. After a day or two, it is time to move on.

You'll appreciate basing yourself in a leafy residential district to escape the noise and bustle of downtown, where the major sights of interest are located. Your checklist of must-sees downtown should include **Teatro Nacional,** San José'slate 19th-century belle-epoque theater, and the modest **Catedral Metropólitana,** as well as the **Fidel Tristan Museo de Jade**

SAN JOSÉ

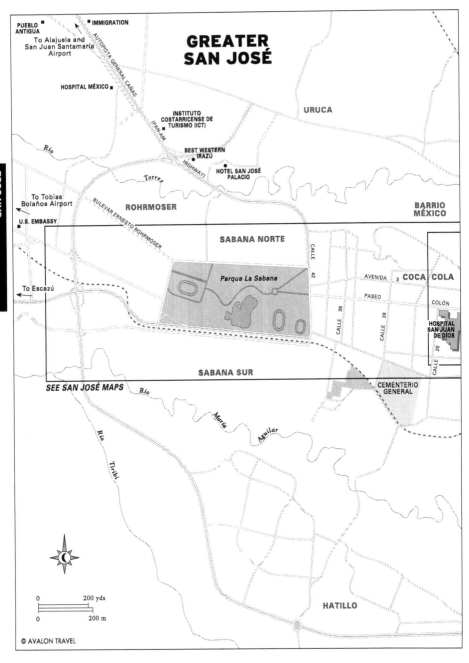

PUEBLO
ANTIGUA

IMMIGRATION

To Alajuela and
San Juan Santamaría
Airport

AUTOPISTA GENERAL CAÑAS

GREATER
SAN JOSÉ

HOSPITAL MÉXICO

URUCA

INSTITUTO
COSTARRICENSE DE
TURISMO (ICT)

(PAN-AM

Río

BEST WESTERN
IRAZÚ

Torres

HIGHWAY)

HOTEL SAN JOSÉ
PALACIO

To Tobías
Bolaños Airport

BULEVAR ERNESTO ROHRMOSER

ROHRMOSER

BARRIO
MÉXICO

U.S. EMBASSY

SABANA NORTE

CALLE 42

AVENIDA 3

COCA COLA

To Escazú

Parque La Sabana

PASEO

COLÓN

CALLE 36

CALLE 28

HOSPITAL
SAN JUAN
DE DIOS

CALLE 20

SABANA SUR

SEE SAN JOSÉ MAPS

Río

CEMENTERIO
GENERAL

María

Aguilar

Río

Tiribí

200 yds

200 m

HATILLO

© AVALON TRAVEL

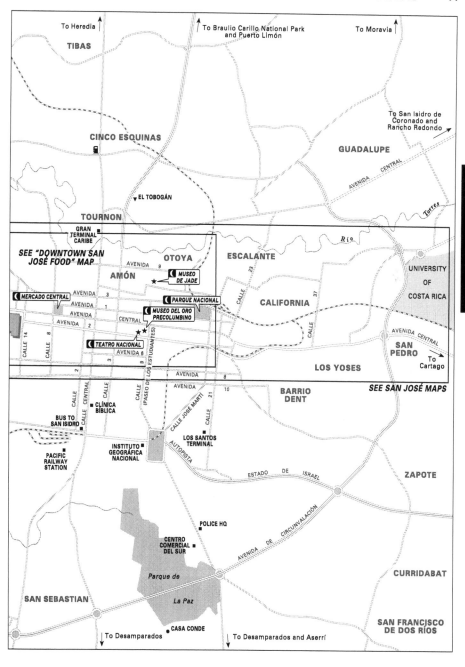

To Heredia

To Braulio Carillo National Park
and Puerto Limón

To Moravia

TIBAS

To San Isidro de
Coronado and
Rancho Redondo

CINCO ESQUINAS

GUADALUPE

AVENIDA   CENTRAL

SAN JOSÉ

EL TOBOGÁN

Torres

TOURNON

Río

GRAN
TERMINAL
CARIBE

*SEE "DOWNTOWN SAN
JOSÉ FOOD" MAP*

AVENIDA   9

OTOYA

ESCALANTE

AMÓN

MUSEO
DE JADE

**UNIVERSITY
OF
COSTA RICA**

MERCADO CENTRAL

AVENIDA   3

PARQUE NACIONAL

CALIFORNIA

CALLE   37

CALLE   23

AVENIDA   1

AVENIDA   2

CENTRAL

MUSEO DEL ORO
PRECOLUMBINO

AVENIDA   CENTRAL

CALLE   14

CALLE   8

TEATRO NACIONAL

AVENIDA   6

**SAN
PEDRO**

To
Cartago

AVENIDA   9

CALLE   2

CALLE   3

LOS YOSES

AVENIDA   8

SEE SAN JOSÉ MAPS

AVENIDA   8

CALLE   (PASEO DE LOS ESTUDIANTES)

AVENIDA   10

CALLE   21

**BARRIO
DENT**

CLÍNICA
BÍBLICA

CALLE   CENTRAL

CALLE   1

CALLE   JOSÉ MARTÍ

BUS TO
SAN ISIDRO

LOS SANTOS
TERMINAL

AUTOPISTA

PACIFIC
RAILWAY
STATION

INSTITUTO
GEOGRÁFICA
NACIONAL

ZAPOTE

ESTADO   DE   ISRAEL

AVENIDA   DE   CIRCUNVALACIÓN

POLICE HQ

CENTRO
COMERCIAL
DEL SUR

CURRIDABAT

Parque de

La Paz

SAN SEBASTIAN

**SAN FRANCISCO
DE DOS RÍOS**

To Desamparados

CASA CONDE

To Desamparados and Aserrí

and **Museo de Oro Precolumbino,** which honor the nation's pre-Columbian legacy with fine displays. The **Centro Nacional de Cultura,** also downtown, pays tribute to the works of contemporary artists, as does the **Contemporary Art Museum,** near Sabana Parque. If you enjoy walking, the historic **Barrio Amón** district makes for a pleasant stroll. By night, **El Pueblo,** a shopping and entertainment complex north of downtown, will prove fulfilling.

San José's outer-perimeter sights are few. An exception is **Pueblo Antiguo,** where the nation's almost extinct traditional lifestyle is honored in yesteryear re-creations.

SAFETY CONCERNS

Avoid driving in San José. Despite the city's grid system of one-way streets, finding your way around can be immensely frustrating. San José is ideal for walking: Downtown is compact, with everything of interest within a few blocks of the center. Watch out for potholes, tilted flagstones, and gaping sewer holes. And be wary when crossing streets—Tico drivers give no mercy to those still in the road when the light turns to green. Don't take your eyes off the traffic for a moment. Stand well away from the curb, especially on corners, where buses often mount the curb.

San José has a high crime rate. Be especially wary in and around the "Coca-Cola" bus terminal (avoid the area altogether at night) and the red-light district south of Avenida 2 (especially between Calles Central and 10) and the sleazy zone northwest of the Mercado Central. Be cautious in parks. And give a wide berth to Barrio Lomas, in the extreme west of Pavas; this is the city's desperately poor slum area and the domain of violent gangs. Also avoid Parque Nacional at night. Don't use buses at night, and be alert if you use them by day.

HISTORY

Until little more than 200 years ago, San José was no more than a few muddy lanes around which clustered a bevy of ramshackle hovels. The village first gained stature in 1737 when a thatched hermitage was built to draw together the residents then scattered throughout the valley. The new settlement was christened Villa Nueva de la Boca del Monte del Valle de Abra, later shortened to San José in honor of the local patron saint.

San José quickly grew to equal Cartago (the colonial capital city founded in 1564 by Juan Vásquez de Coronado) in size and developed a lucrative monopoly on the tobacco and nascent coffee trades, whose profits funded civic buildings. By the close of the 18th century, San José had a cathedral, a mint, a town council building, and military quarters.

When the surprise news of independence from Spain arrived by mail in October 1821, the councils of the four cities (Alajuela, Cartago, Heredia, and San José) met to determine their fate, and a constitution—the Pacto de Concordia—was signed. Alas, says historian Carlos Monge Alfaro, early Costa Rica was not a unified province but a "group of villages separated by narrow regionalisms." A bloody struggle for regional control soon ensued.

On April 5, 1823, the two sides clashed in the Ochomogo Hills. The victorious republican forces stormed and captured Cartago. San José thus became the nation's capital city. Its growing prominence, however, soon engendered resentment and discontent. In March 1835, in a conciliatory gesture, San José's city fathers offered to rotate the national capital among the four cities every four years. Unfortunately, the other cities had a bee in their collective bonnet. In September 1835, they formed a league, chose a president, and on September 26 attacked San José in an effort to topple the government. The Josefinos won what came to be known as La Guerra de la Liga (The War of the League), and the city has remained the nation's capital ever since.

By the mid-1800s the coffee boom was bringing prosperity, culture, and refinement to the once-humble backwater. San José developed a substantial middle class eager to spend its newfound wealth for the social good. Mud roads were bricked over and the streets illuminated by kerosene lamps. Tramways were built.

The city was the third in the world to install public electric lighting. Public telephones appeared here well ahead of most cities in Europe and North America. By the turn of the 20th century, tree-lined parks and plazas, libraries, museums, the Teatro Nacional, and grand neoclassical mansions and middle-class homes graced the city. Homes and public buildings, too, adopted the French-inspired look of New Orleans and Martinique.

Uncontrolled rapid growth in recent years has spread the city's tentacles until the suburban districts have begun to blur into the larger complex.

Sights

ORIENTATION

Streets *(calles)* run north to south; avenues *(avenidas)* run east to west. Downtown San José is centered on Calle Central and Avenida Central (which is closed to traffic between Calles Central and 11), though the main thoroughfare is Avenida 2. To the north of Avenida Central, *avenidas* ascend in odd numbers (Avenida 1, Avenida 3, and so on); to the south they descend in even numbers (Avenida 2, Avenida 4, etc.). West of Calle Central, *calles* ascend in even numbers (Calle 2, Calle 4, etc.); to the east they ascend in odd numbers (Calle 1, Calle 3, and so on).

West of downtown, Paseo Colón runs 2.5 kilometers to Parque Sabana (Paseo Colón is closed to traffic Sundays). East of downtown, Avenida 2 merges into Avenida Central, which runs through the Los Yoses and San Pedro districts en route to Cartago.

Josefinos (as San José residents like to be called) rarely refer to street addresses by *avenida* and *calle*. Very few streets have street numbers, there are no post codes, and an amazing number of Josefinos have no idea what street they live on! Costa Ricans use landmarks, not street addresses, to find their way around. They usually refer to a distance in meters *(metros)* from a particular landmark. A typical address might be "200 meters east and 425 meters south of the gas station, near the church in San Pedro."

These landmarks have passed into local parlance, so that Josefinos will immediately know where is meant by "100 meters north and 300 meters west of Auto Mercado," for example, although many reference landmarks disappeared years ago. For example, the Coca-Cola factory near Avenida Central and Calle 14 long ago disappeared, but the reference is still to "Coca-Cola."

The initial phase of a plan to introduce regular street numbers was begun in spring 2000. Progress, however, has been slow. Addresses are still written by the nearest street junction. Thus, the Bar Esmeralda, on Avenida 2 midway between Calles 5 and 7, gives its address as "Avenida 2, Calles 5/7." In telephone directories and advertisements, *calle* may be abbreviated as "c," and *avenida* as "a." Many streets have no signs. And although officially buildings have numbers, they're rarely posted and almost never used. Thus, there's no telling which side of the street the building you're seeking is on.

Distances are expressed in *cien metros* (100 meters), which usually refers to one block. *Cinquenta metros* (50 meters) is used to mean half a block.

PLAZA DE LA CULTURA

San José's unofficial focal point is the Plaza de la Cultura, bordered by Calles 3/5 and Avenidas Central/2. Musicians, jugglers, and marimba bands entertain the crowds. Tourists gather on the southwest corner to absorb the colorful atmosphere while enjoying a beer and food on the open-air terrace of the venerable Gran Hotel, fronted by a little plaza named **Parque Mora Fernández.**

Note, too, the historic **Cine Diversiones** (Calle 5, Avenidas Central/2), with a beautiful metal-filigree facade.

SAN JOSÉ

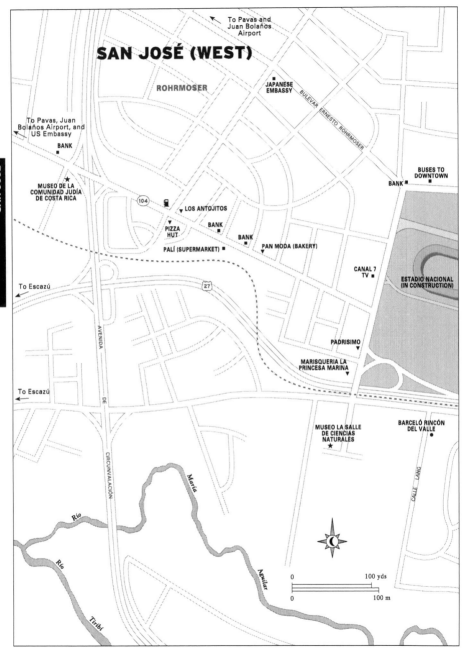

SAN JOSÉ (WEST)

To Pavas and
Juan Bolaños
Airport

ROHRMOSER

JAPANESE
EMBASSY

BULEVAR ERNESTO ROHRMOSER

To Pavas, Juan
Bolaños Airport, and
US Embassy

BANK ■

MUSEO DE LA
COMUNIDAD JUDÍA
DE COSTA RICA ★

BUSES TO
DOWNTOWN

BANK ■

104

LOS ANTOJITOS ▼

PIZZA
HUT ■

BANK ■

BANK ■

PAN MODA (BAKERY) ▼

PALÍ (SUPERMARKET) ■

CANAL 7
TV ■

ESTADIO NACIONAL
(IN CONSTRUCTION)

To Escazú

27

AVENIDA

PADRISIMO ▼

MARISQUERIA LA
PRINCESA MARINA ▼

To Escazú

DE

MUSEO LA SALLE
DE CIENCIAS
NATURALES ★

BARCELÓ RINCÓN
DEL VALLE ●

CIRCUNVALACIÓN

CALLE LANG

María

Río

Río

Aguilar

0   100 yds

0   100 m

Tiribí

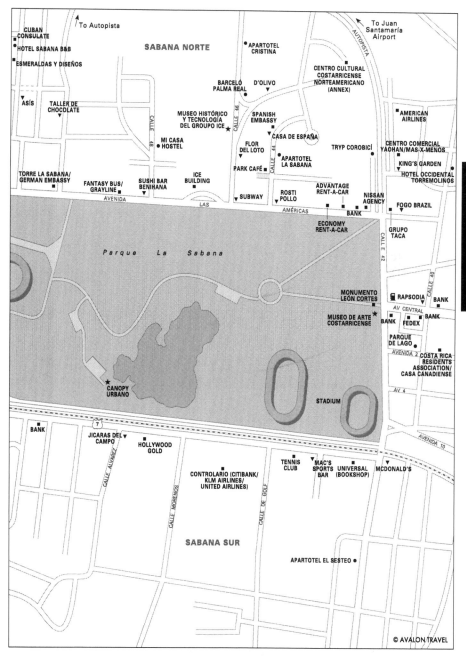

SAN JOSÉ

To Autopista

To Juan
Santamaría
Airport

CUBAN
CONSULATE

HOTEL SABANA B&B

ESMERALDAS Y DISEÑOS

SABANA NORTE

APARTOTEL
CRISTINA

CENTRO CULTURAL
COSTARRICENSE
NORTEAMERICANO
(ANNEX)

ASÍS

TALLER DE
CHOCOLATE

BARCELÓ
PALMA REAL

D'OLIVO

CALLE 46

AMERICAN
AIRLINES

MUSEO HISTÓRICO
Y TECNOLOGÍA
DEL GROUPO ICE

SPANISH
EMBASSY

MI CASA
HOSTEL

CASA DE ESPAÑA

FLOR
DEL LOTO

CALLE 44

CENTRO COMERCIAL
YAOHAN/MAS-X-MENOS

TRYP COROBICÍ

KING'S GARDEN

TORRE LA SABANA/
GERMAN EMBASSY

FANTASY BUS/
GRAYLINE

SUSHI BAR
BENIHANA

APARTOTEL
LA SABANA

PARK CAFÉ

HOTEL OCCIDENTAL
TORREMOLINOS

ICE
BUILDING

AVENIDA

LAS

SUBWAY

ROSTI
POLLO

ADVANTAGE
RENT-A-CAR

AMÉRICAS

BANK

NISSAN
AGENCY

FOGO BRAZIL

ECONOMY
RENT-A-CAR

CALLE 42

GRUPO
TACA

Parque   La   Sabana

MONUMENTO
LEÓN CORTES

RAPSODIA

BANK

CALLE 10

AV CENTRAL

MUSEO DE ARTE
COSTARRICENSE

BANK

FEDEX

BANK

PARQUE
DE LAGO

CANOPY
URBANO

AVENIDA 2

COSTA RICA
RESIDENTS
ASSOCIATION/
CASA CANADIENSE

AV 4

STADIUM

BANK

AVENIDA 10

JICARAS DEL
CAMPO

HOLLYWOOD
GOLD

TENNIS
CLUB

MAC'S
SPORTS
BAR

UNIVERSAL
(BOOKSHOP)

MCDONALD'S

CALLE ALVAREZ

CONTROLARIO (CITIBANK/
KLM AIRLINES/
UNITED AIRLINES)

CALLE MORENO

CALLE DE GOLF

SABANA SUR

APARTOTEL EL SESTEO

© AVALON TRAVEL

SAN JOSÉ

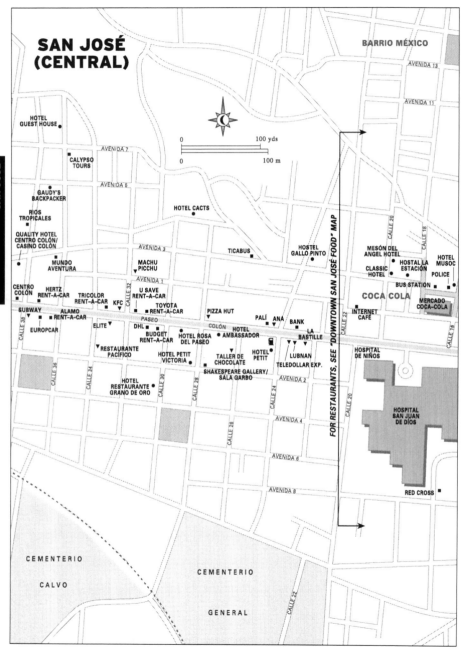

SAN JOSÉ (CENTRAL)

BARRIO MÉXICO

AVENIDA 13

AVENIDA 11

HOTEL GUEST HOUSE

AVENIDA 7

CALYPSO TOURS

AVENIDA 5

GAUDY'S BACKPACKER

RIOS TROPICALES

HOTEL CACTS

QUALITY HOTEL CENTRO COLÓN/ CASINO COLÓN

AVENIDA 3

TICABUS

HOSTEL GALLO PINTO

MESÓN DEL ANGEL HOTEL

HOTEL MUSOC

MUNDO AVENTURA

MACHU PICCHU

CLASSIC HOTEL

HOSTAL LA ESTACIÓN

POLICE

AVENIDA 1

CALLE 20

CALLE 18

CENTRO COLÓN

HERTZ RENT-A-CAR

U SAVE RENT-A-CAR

COCA COLA

BUS STATION

TRICOLOR RENT-A-CAR

KFC

TOYOTA RENT-A-CAR

PIZZA HUT

PALÍ ANA

BANK

INTERNET CAFÉ

MERCADO COCA-COLA

CALLE 32

SUBWAY

ALAMO RENT-A-CAR

PASEO

COLÓN

HOTEL

LA BASTILLE

EUROPCAR

ELITE

DHL

BUDGET RENT-A-CAR

HOTEL ROSA DEL PASEO

AMBASSADOR

LUBNAN

HOSPITAL DE NIÑOS

CALLE 38

RESTAURANTE PACÍFICO

HOTEL PETIT VICTORIA

TALLER DE CHOCOLATE

HOTEL PETIT

TELEDOLLAR EXP.

HOTEL RESTAURANTE GRANO DE ORO

SHAKESPEARE GALLERY/ SALA GARBO

AVENIDA 2

CALLE 36

CALLE 34

CALLE 30

CALLE 28

CALLE 24

AVENIDA 4

HOSPITAL SAN JUAN DE DIOS

CALLE 20

CALLE 22

CALLE 16

AVENIDA 6

CALLE 22

AVENIDA 8

RED CROSS

CEMENTERIO

CALVO

CEMENTERIO

GENERAL

CALLE 22

FOR RESTAURANTS, SEE "DOWNTOWN SAN JOSÉ FOOD" MAP

0   100 yds

0   100 m

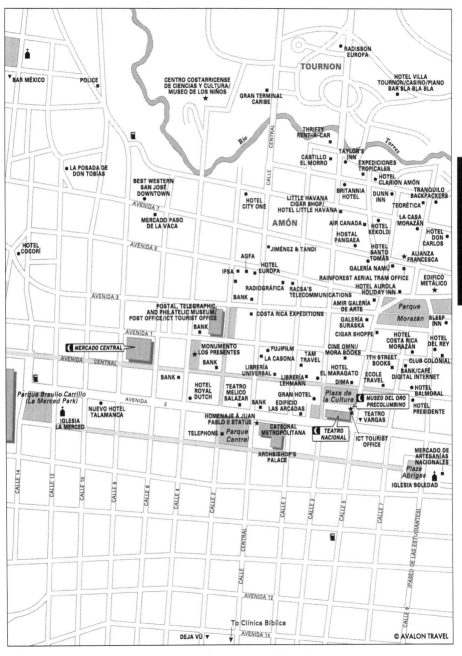

SAN JOSÉ

TOURNON

RADISSON EUROPA

BAR MÉXICO

POLICE

CENTRO COSTARRICENSE
DE CIENCIAS Y CULTURA/
MUSEO DE LOS NIÑOS

GRAN TERMINAL CARIBE

HOTEL VILLA
TOURNON/CASINO/PIANO
BAR BLA BLA BLA

Río

CENTRAL

Torres

THRIFTY RENT-A-CAR

TAYLOR'S INN

CASTILLO EL MORRO

EXPEDICIONES TROPICALES

LA POSADA DE DON TOBÍAS

BEST WESTERN
SAN JOSÉ
DOWNTOWN

HOTEL CLARION AMÓN

BRITANNIA HOTEL

DUNN INN

TRANQUILO BACKPACKERS

AVENIDA 7

HOTEL CITY ONE

LITTLE HAVANA
CIGAR SHOP/
HOTEL LITTLE HAVANA

TEORÉTICA

LA CASA MORAZÁN

MERCADO PASO
DE LA VACA

AMÓN

AIR CANADA

HOTEL KEKOLDI

HOTEL DON CARLOS

AVENIDA 9

HOSTAL PANGAEA

HOTEL
COCORÍ

JIMÉNEZ & TANDI

HOTEL SANTO TOMÁS

ALIANZA FRANCESCA

AGFA

HOTEL EUROPA

GALERÍA NAMÚ

EDIFICO METÁLICO

IFSA

RADIOGRÁFICA

RACSA'S TELECOMMUNICATIONS

RAINFOREST AERIAL TRAM OFFICE

HOTEL AUROLA HOLIDAY INN

AVENIDA 3

BANK

AMIR GALERÍA DE ARTE

Parque
Morazán

POSTAL, TELEGRAPHIC
AND PHILATELIC MUSEUM/
POST OFFICE/ICT TOURIST OFFICE

COSTA RICA EXPEDITIONS

GALERÍA SURASKA

SLEEP INN

AVENIDA 1

BANK

CIGAR SHOPPE

HOTEL COSTA RICA MORAZÁN

HOTEL DEL REY

MERCADO CENTRAL

MONUMENTO
LOS PRESENTES

FUJIFILM

CINE OMNI/
MORA BOOKS

7TH STREET BOOKS

CLUB COLONIAL

AVENIDA CENTRAL

BANK

LA CASONA

TAM TRAVEL

HOTEL EL MARAGATO

ECOLE TRAVEL

BANK/CAFÉ
DIGITAL INTERNET

BANK

LIBRERÍA UNIVERSAL

LIBRERÍA LEHMANN

DIMA

HOTEL BALMORAL

Parque Braulio Carrillo
(La Merced Park)

HOTEL
ROYAL DUTCH

TEATRO
MELICO
SALAZAR

GRAN HOTEL

Plaza de
la Cultura

MUSEO DEL ORO
PRECOLUMBINO

HOTEL PRESIDENTE

AVENIDA 2

NUEVO HOTEL
TALAMANCA

BANK

EDIFICIO
LAS ARCADAS

TEATRO VARGAS

IGLESIA
LA MERCED

HOMENAJE Á JUAN
PABLO II STATUE

TEATRO NACIONAL

TELEPHONE

Parque
Central

CATEDRAL
METROPOLITANA

ICT TOURIST
OFFICE

ARCHBISHOP'S
PALACE

MERCADO DE
ARTESANÍAS
NACIONALES

Plaza
Abrigas

IGLESIA SOLEDAD

CALLE 14

CALLE 12

CALLE 10

CALLE 8

CALLE 6

CALLE 4

CALLE 2

CALLE CENTRAL

CALLE 1

CALLE 3

CALLE 5

CALLE 7

CALLE 9

PASEO DE LAS ESTUDIANTES

AVENIDA 12

To Clínica Bíblica

DEJA VÙ

AVENIDA 14

© AVALON TRAVEL

SAN JOSÉ

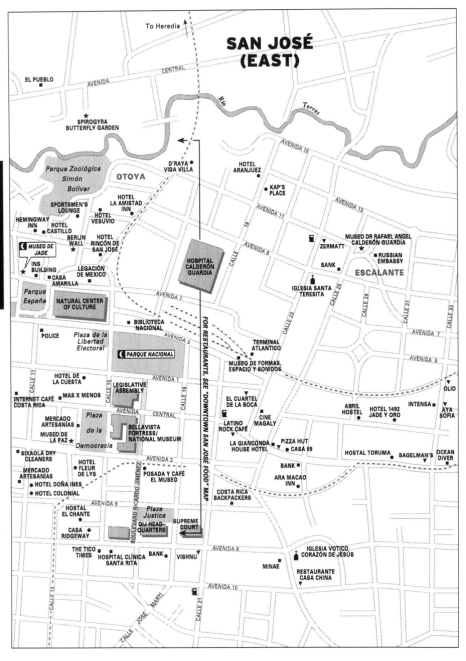

SAN JOSÉ (EAST)

To Heredia

EL PUEBLO

AVENIDA

CENTRAL

Río

Torres

AVENIDA 15

SPIROGYRA BUTTERFLY GARDEN

D'RAYA VIDA VILLA

HOTEL ARANJUEZ

KAP'S PLACE

AVENIDA 13

Parque Zoológica Simón Bolívar

OTOYA

HOTEL LA AMISTAD INN

AVENIDA 11

SPORTSMEN'S LOUNGE

HEMINGWAY INN

HOTEL CASTILLO

HOTEL VESUVIO

AVENIDA 9

ZERMATT

MUSEO DR RAFAEL ÁNGEL CALDERÓN GUARDIA

BERLIN WALL

HOTEL RINCÓN DE SAN JOSÉ

RUSSIAN EMBASSY

MUSEO DE JADE

INS BUILDING

LEGACIÓN DE MEXICO

BANK

ESCALANTE

CASA AMARILLA

HOSPITAL CALDERÓN GUARDIA

IGLESIA SANTA TERESITA

Parque España

NATURAL CENTER OF CULTURE

AVENIDA 7

CALLE 29

CALLE 31

CALLE 33

BIBLIOTECA NACIONAL

AVENIDA 7

POLICE

Plaza de la Libertad Electoral

AVENIDA 3

AVENIDA 5

TERMINAL ATLÁNTICO

PARQUE NACIONAL

OLIO

HOTEL DE LA CUESTA

AVENIDA 1

MUSEO DE FORMAS, ESPACIO Y SONIDOS

CALLE 11

MAS X MENOS

LEGISLATIVE ASSEMBLY

EL CUARTEL DE LA BOCA

ABRIL HOSTEL

HOTEL 1492 JADE Y ORO

INTENSA

AYA SOFIA

INTERNET CAFÉ COSTA RICA

CALLE 15

AVENIDA

CENTRAL

CINE MAGALY

MERCADO ARTESANÍAS

Plaza de la

LATINO ROCK CAFÉ

LA GIANCONDA HOUSE HOTEL

PIZZA HUT

CASA 69

MUSEO DE LA PAZ

Democracia

BELLAVISTA FORTRESS/ NATIONAL MUSEUM

HOSTAL TORUMA

BAGELMAN'S

OCEAN DIVER

SIXAOLA DRY CLEANERS

AVENIDA 2

BANK

MERCADO ARTESANÍAS

HOTEL FLEUR DE LYS

POSADA Y CAFÉ EL MUSEO

ARA MACAO INN

HOTEL DOÑA INES

HOTEL COLONIAL

COSTA RICA BACKPACKERS

AVENIDA 6

HOSTAL EL CHANTE

Plaza Justica

CASA RIDGEWAY

OIJ HEAD-QUARTERS

SUPREME COURT

THE TICO TIMES

HOSPITAL CLÍNICA SANTA RITA

BANK

VISHNU

AVENIDA 8

IGLESIA VOTICO CORAZÓN DE JESÚS

MINAE

RESTAURANTE CASA CHINA

AVENIDA 10

CALLE 13

CALLE 21

FOR RESTAURANTS, SEE "DOWNTOWN SAN JOSÉ FOOD" MAP

BOULEVARD RICARDO JIMENEZ

SAN JOSÉ

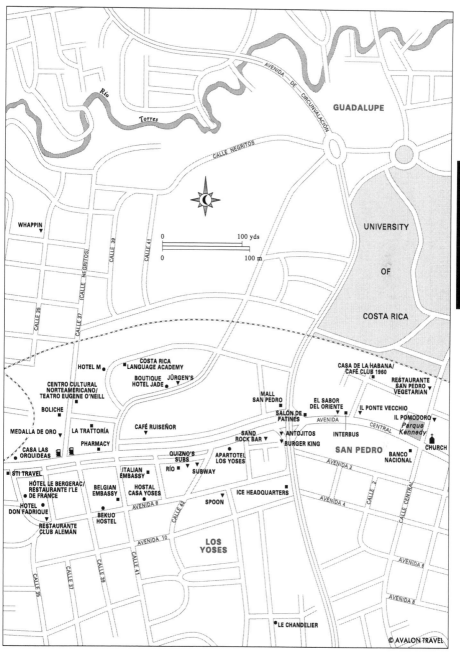

GUADALUPE

AVENIDA — DE — CIRCUNVALACIÓN

Río Torres

CALLE NEGRITOS

UNIVERSITY

OF

COSTA RICA

0   100 yds
0   100 m

WHAPPIN

CALLE 39
CALLE 41
CALLE 37 (CALLE NEGRITOS)
CALLE 35

HOTEL M
COSTA RICA LANGUAGE ACADEMY
BOUTIQUE HOTEL JADE   JÜRGEN'S
CENTRO CULTURAL NORTEAMERICANO/ TEATRO EUGENE O'NEILL
BOLICHE
MEDALLA DE ORO   LA TRATTORÍA   CAFÉ RUISEÑOR
CASA LAS ORQUIDEAS   PHARMACY

CASA DE LA HABANA/ CAFÉ CLUB 1960
RESTAURANTE SAN PEDRO VEGETARIAN
MALL SAN PEDRO
EL SABOR DEL ORIENTE   IL PONTE VECCHIO
SALÓN DE PATINES   IL POMODORO
AVENIDA   Parque
CENTRAL   Kennedy
SAND ROCK BAR   ANTOJITOS   INTERBUS
BURGER KING   CHURCH

SAN PEDRO   BANCO NACIONAL

STI TRAVEL
QUIZNO'S SUBS   APARTOTEL LOS YOSES
ITALIAN EMBASSY   RÍO   SUBWAY
HÓTEL LE BERGERAC/ RESTAURANTE I'LE DE FRANCE
BELGIAN EMBASSY   HOSTAL CASA YOSES
HOTEL DON FADRIQUE
BEKUO HOSTEL
RESTAURANTE CLUB ALEMÁN
AVENIDA 8
SPOON
ICE HEADQUARTERS

AVENIDA 2
AVENIDA 4

CALLE 43
CALLE 2
CALLE CENTRAL

AVENIDA 10

LOS YOSES

CALLE 35
CALLE 37
CALLE 39
CALLE 41

AVENIDA 6
AVENIDA 8

LE CHANDELIER

© AVALON TRAVEL

entrance to Museo del Oro Precolumbino

🄲 Museo del Oro Precolumbino

The world-class Pre-Columbian Gold Museum (tel. 506/2243-4202, 2243-4216 for tickets, www.museosdelbancocentral .org, 9:30 A.M.–5 P.M. daily, $7), in the triple-tiered former bank vaults beneath the plaza (the entrance is on Calle 5), is the highlight of the Museos Banco Central de Costa Rica, run by the state-owned Banco Central. The more than 2,000 glittering pre-Columbian gold artifacts displayed weigh in at over 22,000 troy ounces. Highlights include displays on early metallurgy and a gold-adorned, life-size *cacique* (chieftain), plus there's a large collection of pre-Columbian metates and more. A collection of old coins is displayed in the adjoining **Museo Numismática** (Numismatic Museum), while a small exhibit hall features works from the bank's art collection.

A self-guided audiotape tour costs $2. Guided tours are given with one week's notice ($35, 1–15 people). Bring identification for entry.

🄲 Teatro Nacional

The nation's architectural showpiece, the National Theater (Avenida 2, Calles 3/5, tel. 506/2221-9417, www.teatronacional.go.cr, 9 A.M.–4 P.M. Mon.–Sat., $5), on the south side of Plaza de la Cultura, is justifiably a source of national pride. The theater was conceived in 1890, when a European opera company featuring the prima donna Adelina Patti toured Central America but was unable to perform in Costa Rica because there was no suitable theater. Jilted, the ruling *cafeteleros* (coffee barons) voted a tax on coffee exports to fund construction of a theater, and craftsmen from all over Europe were imported. It was inaugurated on October 21, 1897, to a performance of *Faust* by the Paris Opera.

Outside, the classical Renaissance facade is topped by statues (they're replicas; the originals are inside) symbolizing Dance, Music, and Fame; note the figures of Beethoven and Spanish dramatist Calderón de la Barca to each side of the entrance. Inside, the vestibule, done in pink marble, rivals the best of ancient Rome,

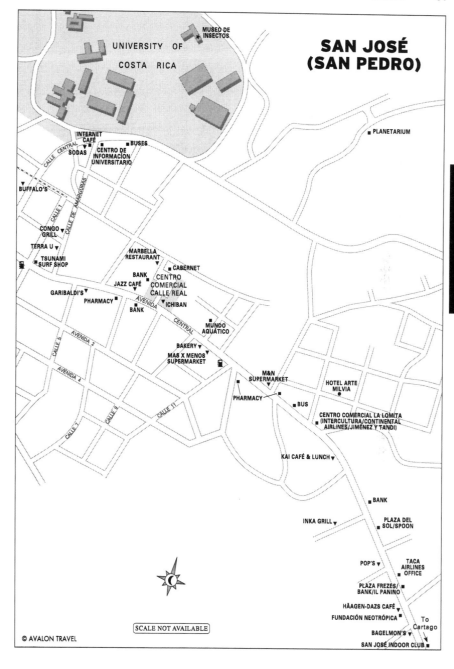

SAN JOSÉ
(SAN PEDRO)

UNIVERSITY OF COSTA RICA

MUSEO DE INSECTOS

PLANETARIUM

INTERNET CAFÉ
BUSES
SODAS
CENTRO DE INFORMACIÓN UNIVERSITARIO

CALLE CENTRAL

BUFFALO'S

CALLE 1

CALLE DE AMARGURAS

CONGO GRILL
TERRA U
TSUNAMI SURF SHOP

MARBELLA RESTAURANT
CABERNET
BANK
JAZZ CAFÉ
CENTRO COMERCIAL CALLE REAL
GARIBALDI'S
PHARMACY
AVENIDA
ICHIBAN
BANK
CENTRAL
MUNDO AQUÁTICO

AVENIDA 2
CALLE 5

AVENIDA 4

BAKERY
MAS X MENOS SUPERMARKET

CALLE 7
CALLE 9
CALLE 11

M&N SUPERMARKET
HOTEL ARTE MILVIA

PHARMACY
BUS
CENTRO COMERCIAL LA LOMITA (INTERCULTURA/CONTINENTAL AIRLINES/JIMÉNEZ Y TANDI)

KAI CAFÉ & LUNCH

BANK

INKA GRILL
PLAZA DEL SOL/SPOON

POP'S
TACA AIRLINES OFFICE

PLAZA FREZES/ BANK/IL PANINO

HÄAGEN-DAZS CAFÉ
FUNDACIÓN NEOTRÓPICA

To Cartago

BAGELMON'S
SAN JOSÉ INDOOR CLUB

SAN JOSÉ

SCALE NOT AVAILABLE

© AVALON TRAVEL

Plaza de la Cultura and Teatro Nacional

with allegorical figures of Comedy and Tragedy, stunning murals depicting themes in Costa Rican life and commerce, and a triptych ceiling supported by six-meter-tall marble columns topped with bronze capitals; a ceiling mural to the rear by Italian artist Milanés Villa shows an allegorical coffee and banana harvest.

Art and good taste are lavishly displayed on the marble staircase, with its gold-laminated ornaments sparkling beneath bronze chandeliers and in the upstairs foyer. A grandiose rotunda painted in Milan in 1897 by Arturo Fontana highlights the three-story auditorium, designed in a perfect horseshoe and seating 1,040 in divine splendor. The auditorium floor was designed to be raised to stage level by a manual winch so the theater could be used as a ballroom.

Guided tours are offered.

PARQUE CENTRAL

This small, palm-shaded park, laid out in 1880 between Calles Central/2 and Avenidas 2/4, is San José's main plaza. The unassuming park has a fountain, a bronze statue, hardwood

sculptures, and a large domed structure where the municipal band plays concerts on Sunday. The bandstand rests over the **Carmen Lyra Children's Library,** named for a Costa Rican writer famous for her children's stories.

Across Avenida 2, the **Teatro Melico Salazar** (tel. 506/2233-1500 or 2222-5424, open by appointment, free), dating to the 1920s and named for a famous Costa Rican tenor, is a study in understated period detail.

The area immediately southwest of the square is best avoided for safety reasons.

Catedral Metropólitana

Dominating the east side of Parque Central is the city's modest, Corinthian-columned Metropolitan Cathedral (tel. 506/2221-3826, 6 A.M.–noon and 3–6 P.M. Mon.–Sat., and 6 A.M.–9 P.M. Sun.), with a Greek Orthodox–style blue domed roof. The original cathedral was toppled by an earthquake in 1821; the current structure dates from 1871. The interior is unremarkable, barring its lofty barrel-arched ceiling supported by fluted columns. Outside, at the corner of Avenida Central, is

facade of Catedral Metropólitana

© CHRISTOPHER P. BAKER

the **Homenaje a Juan Pablo II,** the Homage to Pope John Paul II statue inaugurated in September 2006.

Tucked in the cathedral's shadow to the south is the **Curía** or Archbishop's Palace, dating from 1887.

PARQUES ESPAÑA AND MORAZÁN

Parque Morazán is tucked between Calles 5/9 and Avenidas 3/5. The park's four quadrants surround the domed **Temple of Music,** supposedly inspired by Le Trianon in Paris. The park has busts of various South American heroes.

Parque Morazán merges east into diminutive Parque España, a secluded place to rest your feet. Its tall and densely packed trees have been adopted by birds, and their chorus is particularly pleasing just before sunrise and sunset. Note the busts that form a pantheon of national figures. A life-size statue of a conquistador stands on the southwest corner. On the north side of the park you will see an old, ornately stuccoed, ocher-colored colonial building (dating from 1917), **Casa Amarilla,** which

once housed the Court of Justice and today is the Chancellery, or State Department (no entry). Alas, a giant ceiba tree planted out front in 1963 by President John F. Kennedy during his state visit was cut down in 2008. A huge chunk of the Berlin Wall is displayed in the northeast corner of the grounds.

The **Edificio Metálico,** between Parque Morazán and Parque España, is one of San José's more intriguing edifices. This ocher-colored prefabricated building is made entirely of metal. Designed by the French architect Victor Baltard, the structure was shipped piece by piece from Belgium in 1892 and welded together in situ. The facade is dressed with a bust of Minerva, the goddess of wisdom. The building is now a school.

The gleaming white **Legación de México** (Avenida 7, Calles 11/15), one block east of the park, is adorned with ceramic tiles.

Centro Nacional de Cultura

On the east side of Parque España is the erstwhile Fábrica Nacional de Licores (Liquor Factory), now housing the multifaceted

SAN JOSÉ

homage to Pope John Paul II outside the
Catedral Metrópolitana

National Center of Culture (CENAC, tel. 506/2221-2022, www.mcjdcr.go.cr/ministerio/cenac.html, 10:30 A.M.–5:30 P.M. Tues.–Sat., free admission). The building dates to 1887, and though it's drained of alcohol, relics of the distilling days linger. The ho-hum **Museo de Arte y Diseño Contemporáneo** (Museum of Contemporary Art and Design, tel. 506/2257-7202, www.madc.ac.cr) shows revolving displays by leading Costa Rican artists. Note the old sun clock and decorative stonework on the southeast side. The National Dance Company, National Theater Company, and Museum of Iberoamerican Culture are housed here.

◖ Museo de Jade

The fabulous Fidel Tristan Jade Museum (Calle 9 and Avenida 7, tel. 506/2287-6034, http://portal.ins-cr.com/Social/MuseoJade, 8 A.M.–3:30 P.M. Mon.–Fri., 9 A.M.–1 P.M. Sat., $7), adjoining the Instituto Nacional de Seguro (INS), displays the largest collection of jade in the Americas, including pre-Columbian

carved adzes and pendants, backlit to show off the beautiful translucence. The museum also displays pre-Columbian ceramics and gold miniatures organized by culture and region. It has excellent signage in English.

PLAZA DE LA DEMOCRACÍA

This square, between Avenidas Central/2 and Calles 13/15, was built in 1989 to receive visiting presidents attending the Hemispheric Summit. Dominating the plaza is the crenellated 1870 **Bellavista Fortress,** which today houses the National Museum. On the west side is a bronze statue of Don "Pepe" Figueres. The formerly unkempt, dreary plaza was being remodeled in early 2009. Two blocks south are the buildings of the "Judicial Circuit," including the Supreme Court and criminal investigation (OIJ) buildings. The National Museum and modernist **Supreme Court,** on Plaza Justicia, are linked by a pedestrian precinct, **Boulevard Ricardo Jiménez,** known colloquially as Camino de la Corte, with shade trees, wrought-iron lampposts, and benches.

Museo de la Paz

The tiny Museum for Peace (Avenida 2, Calle 13, tel. 506/2223-4664, www.arias.or.cr, 8 A.M.–noon and 1:30–4:30 P.M. Mon.–Fri., free) is 50 meters west of the plaza. Run by the Arias Foundation, it displays the Costa Rican president's Nobel Peace Prize and other awards.

Asamblea Legislativa

The Legislative Assembly (tel. 506/2243-2547, www.asamblea.go.cr) occupies three buildings on the north side of the plaza on Calle 15. The blue building—the **Castillo Azul**—to the east, was originally the Presidential Palace, built in 1911 by presidential candidate Máximo Fernández in anticipation of victory in the 1914 elections. He lost, then lent his home to president-elect Alfredo González Flores as his official residence. Later it served as the U.S. Diplomatic Mission. Behind it, the **Casa Rosada** (Pink House), dating from 1833, has two rooms with galleries of paintings and photographs of past Costa Rican presidents. The **Edificio Central**

Asamblea Legislativa building

(main building), built in 1937, houses the Congress, or legislative assembly.

Guided visits are offered 8 A.M.–4 P.M. Monday–Friday (tel. 506/2243-2545, ext. 2546, rruiz@congreso.aleg.go.cr). A dress code applies: no sandals or shorts (for men), nor miniskirts for women. Cameras are permitted, without flash.

Museo Nacional

A superb collection of pre-Columbian art (pottery, stone, and gold) and an eclectic mix of colonial-era art, furniture, costumes, and documents highlight the National Museum (Calle 17 and Avenidas Central/2, tel. 506/2257-1433, www.museocostarica.go.cr, 8:30 A.M.–4:30 P.M. Tues.–Sun., $4, $2 students), in the old Bellavista Fortress on the east side of Plaza de la Democracía. Separate exhibition halls deal with history, archaeology, geology, religion, and colonial life. Only a few exhibits are translated into English. The towers and walls of the fortress are pitted with bullet holes from the 1948 civil war. The museum surrounds a landscaped courtyard

featuring colonial-era cannons and ancient stone spheres.

Steps lead down to a netted butterfly garden, and in May 2008 it opened a passion flower garden.

◖ PARQUE NACIONAL

Recently renovated Parque Nacional, the largest and most impressive of the city's central parks, graces a hill that rises eastward between Calles 15/19 and Avenidas 1/3. At the park's center is the massive **Monumento Nacional** (National Monument), one of several statues commemorating the War of 1856. The statue depicts the spirits of the Central American nations defeating the American adventurer William Walker. The monument was made in the Rodin studios, in Paris. Avoid the park at night.

On the north side of the square, note the impressive Modernist **Biblioteca Nacional** (tel. 506/2257-4814), built in 1971.

The **Museo de Formas, Espacios y Sonidos** (Museum of Forms, Space and Sounds, Avenida 3, Calles 21/23), dedicated to plastic arts, architecture, and sounds and housed in the ornate former Atlantic Railway Station (built in 1907) immediately northeast of the park, closed in 2008 and its future is uncertain. To the rear are vintage rolling stock and an old steam locomotive, Locomotora 59 (or *Locomotora Negra*), imported from Philadelphia in 1939 for the Northern Railway Company. Ostensibly, the museum will move to an as-yet-unspecified location and the former station will become a reception hall for a new **Casa Presidencial** (www.casapres.go.cr) to house the president's office.

BARRIO AMÓN AND BARRIO OTOYA

Barrio Amón and Barrio Otoya, north of Parques Morazán and España, form an aristocratic residential neighborhood founded at the end of the 19th century by a French immigrant, Amón Fasileau Duplantier, who arrived in 1884 to work for a coffee enterprise owned by the Tournón family. The area, full of grand historic homes, is worth an exploratory walk. Of particular note is the **Castillo el Morro** (Avenida 11, Calle 3), an ornate, Moorish-style, turreted former home of Archbishop Don Carlos Humberto Rodriguez Quirós.

Avenida 9, between Calles 7 and 3, is lined with beautiful ceramic wall murals depicting traditional Costa Rican scenes. Check out the home with life-size figure of a *campesino* at Calle 11 #980.

TeoréTica (Calle 7, Avenidas 9/11, tel./fax 506/2233-4881, www.teoretica.org, 9 a.m.–6 p.m.Mon.–Fri., 10 a.m.–4 p.m. Sat.) is a local artists' foundation and gallery displaying revolving avant-garde exhibitions. It offers workshops.

Centro Costarricense de Ciencias y Cultura

The castle-like hilltop structure on the west side of Barrio Amón, at the north end of Calle 4, served as the city penitentiary from 1910 until 1979. Today it houses the Costa Rican Science and Cultural Center (tel. 506/2238-4929, www.museocr.com, 8 a.m.–4:30 p.m. Tues.–Fri., 9:30 a.m.–5 p.m. Sat.–Sun., $2

adults, $1.30 children), comprising a library and auditorium (note the fantastic sculptures outside), plus the **National Gallery** (not to be confused with the National Gallery of Contemporary Art), dedicated to contemporary art displayed in airy exhibition halls conjured from former jail cells. Also here is the **Museo de los Niños** (closed Mon., $1.50 adults, $1 children). The Children's Museum lets children reach out and touch science and technology, with exhibits that include a planetarium and rooms dedicated to astronomy, planet earth, Costa Rica, ecology, science, human beings, and communications.

Parque Zoológico

The 14-acre Simón Bolívar Zoo (Calle 7 and Avenida 11, tel. 506/2256-0012, www.fundazoo.org, 8 a.m.–3:30 p.m. Mon.–Fri., 9 a.m.–4:30 p.m. weekends and holidays, $3.50 adults, $2.50 children) has steadily improved, although conditions for many animals still fall short. The native species on display include spider and capuchin monkeys, amphibians and reptiles, most of the indigenous cats, and a small variety of birds, including toucans and tame macaws. A Nature Center has a video room, library, and work area for schoolchildren.

BARRIO TOURNÓN

This *barrio* (district) lies north of Barrio Amón, north of the Río Torres, and a hilly, 20-minute walk from the city center. Its main tourist draw is **Centro Comercial El Pueblo** (Avenida 0, tel. 506/2221-9434, info@ccelpueblocr.com, 11 a.m.–2 a.m. daily), an entertainment and shopping complex designed to resemble a Spanish colonial village. El Pueblo's warren of alleys harbors art galleries, craft stores, restaurants, and nightclubs. The Calle Blancos bus departs from Calles 1/3 and Avenida 5. Use a taxi by night. Taxis to and from El Pueblo often overcharge, so settle on a fee before getting into your cab. There's free parking and 24-hour security.

Worth a browse, too, is the **Spirogyra Butterfly Garden** (Avenida 0, tel./fax 506/2222-2937, www.infocostarica.com/

butterfly, 8 A.M.–4 P.M. daily, $6 adults, $5 students, $3 children), a small butterfly farm and botanical garden 50 meters east and 150 meters south of El Pueblo. More than 30 species flutter about in the netted garden. Hummingbirds abound! Bilingual tours are offered every half hour, or you can opt for a 30-minute self-guided tour; an educational video is shown.

WEST-CENTRAL DOWNTOWN
◖ Mercado Central
The Central Market (6 A.M.–8 P.M. Mon.–Sat.) between Avenidas Central/1 and Calles 6/8, is San José's most colorful market and heady on atmosphere. There are booths selling octopus, dorado, and shrimp; butchers' booths with oxtails and pigs' heads; flower stalls; saddle shops; and booths selling medicinal herbs guaranteed to cure everything from sterility to common colds. Pickpockets thrive in crowded places like this—watch your valuables.

Two nearby statues worth noting are the **Monumento Los Presentes** (Calle 4, Avenida Central), seven patinated statues of Costa Rican folk; and the bronze statue dedicated to Guanacastecan women, one block farther east.

Museo Postal, Telegráfico y Filatélico
Overlooking a grassy plaza, the exquisite **Edificio Postal** (Calle 2, Avenidas 1/3), the main post office, dates from 1911 in a dramatic eclectic style with Corinthian pilasters adorning the facade. The Postal, Telegraphic, and Philatelic Museum (tel. 506/2223-9766, ext. 205, 8 A.M.–5 P.M. Mon.–Fri., 150 colones; buy your ticket—a prepaid postcard—in the philately office downstairs), on the second floor, features old telephones, philatelic history displays, and postage stamps including Costa Rica's oldest stamp—dating from 1863. It hosts a stamp exchange the first Saturday of every month.

Parque Braulio Carrillo
Tiny Parque Braulio Carrillo, between Avenidas 2/4 and Calles 12/14, is also known as La Merced Park, because it faces **Iglesia La Merced,** completed in 1907 and gleaming

afresh after a lengthy restoration. The park is pinned by a monument honoring the astronomer Copernicus.

WEST OF DOWNTOWN
Cementerio General
When you've seen everything else, and before heading out of town, check out the Cementerio General (Avenida 10, Calles 20/36), the final resting place of Josefinos, with its many fanciful marble mausoleums of neoclassical design. The cemetery is particularly worth seeing on November 1 and 2, when vast numbers of people leave flowers at the tombs of their relatives.

Parque la Sabana
This huge park, one mile west of the city center, at the west end of Paseo Colón, used to be the national airfield. Today it's a focus for sports and recreation. A small lake on the south side is stocked with fish, and fishing is permitted. the park contains the **Canopy Urbano** (tel. 506/2215-2544, 9 A.M.–5 P.M., $20), a 10-platform zipline between treetops and over the lake! And a new **Estadio Nacional** soccer stadium, funded by the Chinese government, is to be built on the west side.

The Sabana-Cementerio bus, which leaves from Calle 7 and Avenida Central, will take you there.

The old terminal now houses the **Museo de Arte Costarricense** (Contemporary Art Museum, tel. 506/2222-7155, www.musarco.go.cr, 9 A.M.–5 P.M. Tues.–Fri., 10 A.M.–4 P.M. Sat.–Sun., $5 adults, $3 students, free Sun.), which faces Paseo Colón on the east side. The museum houses a permanent collection of important works by Costa Rica's leading artists, including a diverse collection of woodcuts, wooden sculptures, and 19th- and 20th-century paintings. Revolving exhibitions of contemporary artists are also shown. The Golden Hall (Salón Dorado), on the second floor, depicts the nation's history from pre-Columbian times through the 1940s; done in stucco and bronze patina, the resplendent mural was constructed by French sculptor Louis Feron. A highlight is the sculpture garden to the rear, combining magnificent contemporary and pre-Columbian pieces.

Museo La Salle de Ciencias Naturales (La Salle Museum of Natural Sciences, tel. 506/2232-1306, www.lasalle.edu.co/museo, 8 A.M.–4 P.M. Mon.–Sat., 9 A.M.–5 P.M. Sun., $2 adults, $1 children), in the Colegio La Salle on the southwest corner of Sabana Park, displays a comprehensive collection of Central American flora and fauna (mostly stuffed animals and mounted insects), plus geological specimens and other exhibits covering zoology, paleontology, archaeology, and entomology. Some of the stuffed beasts are a bit moth-eaten (others are so comic, you wonder if the taxidermist was drunk), but the overall collection is impressive. The foyer contains life-size dinosaurs (well, facsimiles). The Sabana-Estadio bus, which departs from the Catedral Metropólitana on Avenida 2, passes Colegio La Salle.

Towering over the north side of the park is the headquarters of **ICE** (Instituto Costarricense de Electricidad). Technicians on a busman's holiday might visit the **Museo Histórico y Tecnológico del Grupo ICE** (200 m north of ICE, tel. 506/2220-7656, 8 A.M.–4 P.M. Mon.–Fri., free), with various exhibits relating to electricity and telephones.

A short distance west, in Rohrmoser, the **Museo de la Comunidad Judía de Costa Rica** (tel. 506/2520-1013, ext. 129, www.geocities .com/museojudiodecostarica, 10 A.M.–2 P.M. by appointment) opened in 2007 and tells of the Jewish community in Costa Rica. It also has a Holocaust exhibit. It's inside the synagogue, behind huge metal gates. Entry is by prior application only; you will need to supply your passport details.

Pueblo Antiguo and Parque de Diversiones

This splendid 12-acre Disney-style attraction (tel. 506/2290-3035, www.parque diversiones.com/pueblo.htm, 9 A.M.–7 P.M. Fri.–Sun., free), 200 meters northeast of Hospital México, in La Uruca, is the Colonial Williamsburg of Costa Rica. It re-creates the

locales and dramatizes the events of Costa Rican history. Buildings in traditional architectural styles include a replica of the National Liquor Factory, Congressional Building, a church, a market, a fire station, and the Costa Rican Bank. The place comes alive with ox-carts, horse-drawn carriages, live music, folkloric dances, and actors dramatizing the past. The park has three sections: the capital city, coast, and country (with original adobe structures, including a sugar mill, coffee mill, and milking barn). There are crafts shops, and a restaurant serves typical Costa Rican cuisine. It hosts "Costa Rican Nights" with traditional entertainment 6:30–9:30 P.M. Friday and Saturday ($34 including historic show, $40 with transfers and dinner).

Pueblo Antiguo is part of a theme park *(parque de diversions)* that features roller coasters, bumper cars, and water slides.

SOUTH OF DOWNTOWN

Iglesia Soledad is a pretty, ocher-colored church fronting a tiny plaza at Avenida 4 and Calle 9, Paseo de los Estudiantes. Paseo runs south two kilometers to the **Parque de la Paz** (Peace Park), which is a favorite of Josefinos on weekends. It has a lake with boats, plus horseback rides, kite-flying, sports fields, and even horse-drawn carriage rides.

Desamparados, a working-class suburb on the southern outskirts of San José, has an impressive church that is a smaller copy of London's St. Paul's cathedral; and, on its north side, the **Museo de la Carreta** (Oxcart Museum, tel. 506/2259-7042, 8 A.M.–noon and 2–6 P.M. Tues.–Sun., $1) is in a venerable home displaying artifacts profiling the traditional peasant lifestyle, notably rustic oxcarts spanning the decades.

At **Fossil Land** (tel. 506/2276-6060, www.fossillandcr.com), two kilometers east of Patarrá, about three kilometers southeast of Desamparados, visitors can witness a fossil dig in the midst of mountains, although the place is more geared to activities such as rappelling, spelunking, ATV tours, and mountain biking.

EAST OF DOWNTOWN

The relatively upscale *barrios* of Los Yoses and San Pedro sprawl eastward for several kilometers but offer few attractions.

Immediately northeast of downtown, the suburb of Barrio Escalante hosts the **Museo Dr. Rafael Angel Calderón Guardia** (Avenida 11, Calles 25/27, tel. 506/2221-1239, www.mcjdcr.go.cr/patrimonio, 9 A.M.–5 P.M. Mon.–Sat., $0.50), celebrating the life of the former president (whose term was 1940–1944).

Iglesia Votico Corazón de Jesú (tel. 506/2222-6486), on Avenida 8 three blocks east of the Tribunales de Justicias, is a stunning contemporary Catholic church worth the visit to admire its stained glass.

University of Costa Rica

The university campus (tel. 506/2207-4000, www.ucr.ac.cr), in San Pedro, about two kilometers east of downtown, is a fine place to take in Costa Rica's youthful bohemianism. The School of Music (Facultad de Artes Musicales) basement houses the **Museo de Insectos** (tel. 506/2207-5647, www.miucr.ucr.ac.cr, 1–5 P.M. Mon.–Fri., $2 adults, $0.50 children), one of the largest collections of insects in the world. The Insect Museum features an immense variety of Costa Rican and Central American insects, including a spectacular display of butterflies. Knowledgeable guides are available, but call ahead. It was slated to move to a new location in the Centro de Investigación para la Protección de Cultivos (CIPROC), in the Escuela de Agronomía (Agronomy School).

The university **planetarium** (tel. 506/2202-6302, http://planetario.ucr.ac.cr) has three daily presentations on astronomy (in Spanish only, $3 adults, $2.50 students). English-language presentations can be requested in advance.

SAN JOSÉ

Entertainment and Recreation

Whatever your nocturnal craving, San José has something to please. The *Tico Times* and the "Viva" section of *La Nación* have listings of what's on in San José.

BARS

Tourist bars are concentrated in "Gringo Gulch" (Calles 5/9, Avenidas Central/3) but many are salacious, and muggings on the street are frequent. Bars in San Pedro are more bohemian, catering to the university crowd and upscale Ticos. Most of the other class acts are in the suburb **Escazú,** about seven kilometers west of town. Avoid the spit-and-sawdust workingmen's bars, with their many drunkards seeking a fight.

Downtown

Bar Morazán (Avenida 3, Calle 9, tel. 506/2221-9527, 11 A.M.–2:30 A.M. Mon.–Fri., 5 P.M.–3 A.M. Saturday) draws an eclectic crowd for its warm ambience—redbrick walls adorned with traffic signs. It has a jukebox and serves meals.

Catercorner, the slightly salacious **Key Largo** (Calle 7, Avenidas 1/3, tel. 506/2221-0277, 11 A.M.–3 A.M. daily) draws a Latin clientele with live music (Tuesday, Wednesday, and Friday is pop, Thursday is tropical music, and Saturday has the 1960s' greatest hits) and dancing. Local prostitutes have always been part of Key Largo and are still there since the owners of Hotel Del Rey took over.

Local bohemians prefer the laid-back **El Cuartel de la Boca del Monte** (Avenida 1, Calles 21/23, tel. 506/2221-0327, 11:30 A.M.–2 P.M. and 6 P.M.–2 A.M. Mon.–Fri. and 4 P.M.–2 A.M. Sat.–Sun., $4 men, free to women), a popular hangout for young Josefinos and the late-night, post-theater set. The brick-walled bar is famous for its 152 inventive cocktails, often served to wild ceremony and applause. It has live music on Monday, Wednesday, and Friday. It doesn't get in the groove until around 10 P.M.

The liveliest spot among gringos is the 24-hour **Blue Marlin Bar** (Calle 9, Avenida 1), in the Hotel Del Rey. Fishermen gather here to trawl for a good time while soliciting skippers' mates. It screens U.S. sports, as does the more upscale yet similarly inclined **Sportsmens Lodge** (Calle 13, Avenidas 9/11, tel. 506/2221-2533, www.sportsmenscr.com).

West of Downtown

The venerable and lively **Bar México** (Avenida 13, Calle 16, tel. 506/2221-8461, 10 A.M.–2 A.M. daily) serves excellent *bocas* and margaritas and has mariachi music. Music videos light up a giant screen, and there's live music on Friday and Saturday nights.

The **Shakespeare Bar** (Avenida 2, Calle 28, tel. 506/2258-6787, noon–midnight daily) brings a more intellectual crowd, drawn to the adjoining Teatro Laurence Olivier and Sala Garbo cinema. It has a piano bar and sometimes hosts live jazz. On Sabana Sur, **Mac's** (tel. 506/2231-3145, 9 A.M.–2 A.M. daily) is a TV bar popular with gringos. There's a pool table upstairs.

Rapsodia (Paseo Colón, Calle 40, tel. 506/2248-1720, www.rapsodialounge.com, 6 P.M.–1 A.M. Tues.–Thurs., until 2 A.M. Fri.–Sat.) is one of the chicest lounge bars in the city with its minimalist decor and retro lava lamp videos, although the dining here disappoints.

East of Downtown

Río (tel. 506/2225-8371, 5 P.M. until the last guest leaves, daily), on Avenida Central in Los Yoses, is a lively place with TVs showing music videos. A hip young crowd gathers, especially for occasional all-day musical events when the street outside is closed and the party spills out onto the road. It's often open until the last guest goes home. A short distance east, several club-bars congregate on the southwest side of the San Pedro traffic circle. Calles Central, 3 (also known as Calle de Amargura), and 5, north of Avenida Central in San Pedro, are lined with student bars. All get crowded, but otherwise offer nothing in decor.

Fancy a pint of Guinness? Then head to **Stan's Irish Pub** (tel. 506/2253-4360),

125 meters west of the Casa Presidencial, in the southeasterly district of Zapote. Owner Stanley Salas sells more than 60 beers from around the world.

Cigar Rooms

The classy **Casa del Habano** (Calle 4, Avenida 1, tel. 506/2253-4629, www.habanoscr.net, noon–2 A.M. Tues.–Sun.), in San Pedro, offers a VIP room with pool table, a café, mini-museum of cigars, plus a large collection of premium smokes. Nearby, **Jürgen's** (tel. 506/2283-2239, noon–2 P.M. and 6–10 P.M. Mon.–Fri., 6–11 P.M. Sat.) has a tasteful cigar lounge with leather seats.

Downtown at the risqué Hotel Little Havana is **The Cigar Bar** (tel. 506/2257-8624, www.hotellittlehavana.com, 24 hours), which aims for an upscale clientele. It offers female accompaniment, as the website makes plain.

Gentlemen's Nightclubs

San José has no shortage of gentlemen's strip clubs. Many are sleazy. Even the most respectable clubs are prone to ripping off patrons with exorbitant charges and strong-arm tactics. *Caveat emptor!*

DISCOS AND NIGHTCLUBS

The in-vogue spot at last visit was **El Tobogán** (tel. 506/2223-8920, 8 P.M.–2 A.M. Fri.–Sat., 4–9 P.M. Sun., $5), 200 meters north of *La República* office, off the Guápiles highway, where patrons dance beneath a huge *palenque* (thatched roof).

El Pueblo (9 P.M.–2 A.M. daily), in Barrio Tournón, boasts about a dozen bars and discos, featuring everything from salsa to Bolivian folk music. The most sophisticated disco is **Ebony 56** (tel. 506/2223-2195, 8 P.M.–4 A.M. Thurs.–Sun.), which revs things up with two dance floors and live bands on weekdays. Next door is **Twister** (tel. 506/2222-5749, 7 P.M.–4 A.M. Tues.–Sat.), with a choice of three dance floors playing salsa, rock, and Latin sounds. **Bongo's** (tel. 506/2222-5746, 5 P.M.–4 A.M. nightly) has Latin dancers on Tuesday and Wednesday.

East of downtown, multitiered **Planet Mall**

GAY SAN JOSÉ

ACCOMMODATIONS

A U.S. travel agency, Colours Destinations, operates **Colours Oasis Hotel** (tel. 506/2296-1880, toll-free from North America tel. 866/517-4390, www.coloursoasis.com, $59-169 low season, $79-219 high season), a small gay-owned colonial-style property in the quiet residential Rohrmoser district. It has exquisite contemporary decor. There's a pool, whirlpool tub, TV room, plus a café, restaurant, and bar.

In Barrio Amón is the gay-run and gay-friendly **Joluva Guesthouse** (Calle 3 bis, Avenidas 9/11, tel. 506/2223-7961, www.joluva.com). Other gay-friendly hotels include **Hotel Fleur de Lys, Hotel Kekoldi,** and **Hotel Santo Tomás.**

MEETING PLACES

Gay-friendly spots include **Café Mundo** (Avenida 9, Calle 15, tel. 506/2222-6190) and **Café La Esquina,** in Colours Oasis Hotel. The latter has gay theme parties monthly.

Joseph Itiel, author of *¡Pura Vida!: A Travel Guide to Gay & Lesbian Costa Rica*, strongly advises against "cruising" the parks, where "you can get yourself into real trouble." Transvestites hang out at night around Parque Morazán.

Gay saunas are particularly popular rendezvous, notably at **Hispalis** (Avenida 2, Calles 17/19, tel. 506/2256-9540, www.clubhispalis.com) and **Paris** (Calle 7, Avenida 7, tel. 506/2257-5272).

ENTERTAINMENT AND EVENTS

El Bochinche (Calle 11, Avenidas 10/12, tel. 506/2221-0500, www.bochinchesanjose.com), a two-story bar and restaurant with an art deco interior, is popular, as is **Puchos** (Avenida 8, Calle 11, tel. 506/2256-1147, www.puchosnightclub.com), with nude dancers nightly. The elegant **Deja Vu Disco** (Calle 2, Avenidas 14/16, tel. 506/2248-1500, www.clubohcr.com) caters to both men and women; don't go wandering alone around the run-down neighborhood. And **La Avispa** (Calle 1, Avenidas 8/10, tel. 506/2223-5343, www.laavispa.co.cr) caters to both gays and lesbians with a disco playing mostly techno and Latin music, plus a pool room, a bar, and a big-screen TV upstairs. Drag queens flock on show night.

(tel. 506/280-4693, 8 P.M.–2 A.M. Thurs.–Sat., $5–10) claims to be the largest disco in Central America, on the fifth and sixth floors of the Mall San Pedro.

Stylish **Club Tragaldabas** (tel. 506/8825-9611, www.clubtrabaldabas.com, 8 P.M.–4 A.M. Thurs.–Sat., $5), upstairs in Plaza Rohrmoser, packs in young sophisticates for sexy dancing into the wee hours. For rave-style partying, hit **Vértigo** (tel. 506/2257-8424, 8 P.M.–4 A.M. Mon.–Sat.), in Edificio Colón on Paseo Colón.

CINEMAS

More than a dozen movie houses show American and other foreign movies. (Movies with Spanish soundtracks are advertised as *hablado en Español.*) *La Nación* and the *Tico Times* list current movies. Most movie houses charge $2–6. **Sala Garbo** (Calle 28 and Avenida 2, tel. 506/2222-1034) shows avant-garde international movies. Other venues include **Cine Magaly** (Calle 23, Avenidas Central/1, tel. 506/2223-0085); **Cine Omni** (Calle 3, Avenidas Central/1 tel. 506/2221-7903); and the eight-cinema **Cineopolis** (tel. 506/2278-3631), in TerraMall, off the Cartago highway east of town.

THEATER

Theatergoing here is still light-years from Broadway, but San José has a score of professional theaters (many are tiny venues), including a viable fringe; many serve up burlesque. Book early. Tickets rarely cost more than $2. Performances normally run Thursday–Sunday and begin at 7:30 or 8 P.M. Most performances are in Spanish.

The **Little Theater Group** (tel. 506/8355-1623, www.littletheatregroup.org) presents

English-language musicals and comedies throughout the year at the Teatro Laurence Olivier (Avenida 2, Calle 28).

La Nación and the *Tico Times* list current productions.

LIVE MUSIC, DANCE, AND ART

Visiting big-time artists hit Costa Rica occasionally and typically perform at the Teatro Nacional, Teatro Melico Salazar, or Auditorio Nacional. Look for advertisements in the local newspapers.

Folklórica

The most colorful cabaret in town is the **Fantasía Folklórica,** which depicts the traditions, legends, and history of Costa Rica's seven provinces. The program blends traditional Costa Rican dances with avant-garde choreography and stunning stage backdrops. Shows are held at 8 P.M. every Tuesday at the Melico Salazar Theater (tel. 506/2222-5424).

Pueblo Antiguo (tel. 506/2231-2001, www.parquediversiones.com) hosts "Costa Rican Nights" with traditional entertainment at 7–10 P.M. Wednesday, Friday, and Saturday, with folkloric dancing ($40 with dinner).

Classical

The **National Symphony Orchestra** (tel. 506/2221-9417, www.osn.go.cr) performs at the Teatro Nacional (tickets tel. 506/2221-5341, www.teatronacional.go.cr) on Thursday and Friday (8 P.M.) and Sunday mornings (10:30 A.M.), April–December.

The **North American-Costa Rican Cultural Center** (tel. 506/2225-9433 or 800-2077-7500, www.cccncr.com) presents the "U.S. University Musicians Series," with concerts each month. The **National Lyric Opera Company** (tel. 506/2222-8571) presents operas June–mid-August in the Teatro Melico Salazar.

Jazz

The nascent jazz scene is now fairly robust. Venues include the **Shakespeare Gallery** (Calle 28, Avenida 2, tel. 506/2258-6787,

7 P.M.–midnight daily), but the big enchilada is the **Jazz Café** (Avenida Central, tel. 506/2253-8933, www.jazzcafecostarica.com, 6 P.M.–midnight daily, $5 pp cover) in a venerable redbrick building in San Pedro. It hosts big names from around the globe and has all the ambience one could hope for in a classic jazz club.

A pianist tickles the ivories nightly in the **Piano Bar Bla, Bla, Bla** in the Hotel Villa Tournon.

Dance Classes

Merecumbé (tel. 506/2224-3531, www .merecumbe.net) offers dance classes that include salsa and merengue. It has schools throughout San José and the highlands. **Prodanza** (tel. 506/2290-7969, http:// katabamibudokan.tripod.com/prodanza) offers classes spanning ballet to flamenco. And **Taller Nacional de Danza** (tel. 506/2227-3017, www.crtallernacionaldedanza.com) offers classes from belly dance to hip-hop!

Peñas

TeoréTica (Calle 7, Avenidas 9/11, tel./fax 506/2233-4881, www.teoretica.org), a local artists' foundation and gallery, hosts *tertulias* (get-togethers) every second Tuesday at 7 P.M.

CASINOS

Many major tourist hotels have a casino where the familiar sounds of roulette, craps, and blackjack continue until dawn. Rummy (a form of blackjack), canasta (a form of roulette, but with a basket containing balls replacing the roulette wheel), craps, and *tute* (a local variant of poker) are the casino games of choice. House rules and payoffs are stacked far more heavily in the house's favor than they are in the United States. As of 2008, hotel casinos are restricted to operating 6 P.M.–2 A.M.

The most upscale are **Club Colonial** (Avenida 1, Calles 9/11, tel. 506/2258-2807); **Horseshoe Casino** (Avenida 1, Calle 9, tel. 506/2233-4383); and the casinos in Aurola Holiday Inn, Hotel Clarion Amón Plaza, Barceló San José Palacio, Best Western Hotel Irazú, Centro Colón, and Radisson Europa Hotel.

© CHRISTOPHER P. BAKER

Motorcyclists parade down Avenida 2.

FESTIVALS

The **International Arts Festival** in November is launched with a street parade.

The **Oxcart Festival** (Festival de las Carretas), along Paseo Colón, in November, celebrates traditional rural life with a parade of dozens of oxcarts *(carretas)*.

The **Festival of Light** (Festival de la Luz; mid-December) is a Christmas parade along Calle 42 highlighted by floats trimmed with colorful Christmas lights (6–10 P.M.).

The annual running of the bulls occurs during Christmas and New Year's at the fairground in Zapote with a *tope* (horse parade) and bull riding and taunting. There's a special tourist-only section, with fireworks. It coincides with a massive *tope* each December 26, when as many as 3,000 men and women ride down Paseo Colón and downtown.

SPORTS AND RECREATION

Sabana Park has baseball diamonds, basketball courts, jogging and walking trails, soccer fields, tennis and volleyball courts, plus an Olympic-size swimming pool (open noon–2 P.M. daily, $3) and showers. Sabana's trails provide a peaceful environment for running.

The members-only **San José Indoor Club** (tel. 506/2225-9344, www.indoorclub.com), in Curridabat, has the best all-around facilities in the city.

Bowling

At **Boliche** (Calle 37, tel. 506/2253-5745, 11 A.M.–midnight daily), in Los Yoses, 10-pin bowling costs $10 per hour. And the **Costa Rica Tennis Club** (tel. 506/2232-1266, www.costaricatennisclub.com), in Sabana Sur, has eight lanes.

Gyms and Health Clubs

Most upscale hotels have spa facilities: the **Crowne Plaza Corobicí** (tel. 506/2232-8122) and **Hotel Palma Reál** (tel. 506/2290-5060) are noteworthy.

Skating

The **Salón Los Patines** (Avenida Central,

tel. 506/2224-6821, 7–10 P.M. Mon.–Fri., 1–3:30 P.M., 4–6:30 P.M., and 7–10 Sat.–Sun., $3), just east of the San Pedro roundabout, offers roller-skating.

Soccer
You can ask to join in a soccer game in Sabana Park. The San José team, Saprissa, plays at

Estadio Ricardo Saprissa (tel. 506/2235-3591 or 800-2727-7477), in Tibas.

Tennis
You'll find public courts in Sabana Park. Close by, members and guests can play at the **Tennis Club** (tel. 506/2232-1266, www.costaricatennisclub.com), on Sabana Sur.

Shopping

Shop hours are usually 8 A.M.–6 P.M. Monday–Saturday. Many places close at noon for a siesta; a few stay open until late evening.

BOOKS
American-owned **7th Street Books** (Calle 7 and Avenidas Central/1, tel. 506/2256-8251, marroca@racsa.co.cr) has the widest variety of books in English, emphasizing travel and nature, but also offering novels and nonfiction.

Librería Internacional (www.libreriainternacional.com), Costa Rica's answer to Barnes & Noble, has stores on Avenida Central (tel. 506/2257-2563), in Rohrmoser (tel. 506/2290-3331) and San Pedro (tel. 506/2253-9553), and outside town in Escazú (tel. 506/2201-8320). Arch-rival **LibroMax** (tel. 800/542-7662, www.libromax.com) has outlets in Mall San Pedro and Multiplaza (in Escazú); and **Librería Universal** has outlets at Avenida Central and Calles Central/1 (tel. 506/2222-2222) and on Sabana Sur at Calle 42 (tel. 506/2296-1010).

Mora Books (Avenida 1, Calles 3/5, tel./fax 506/2255-4135, www.morabooks.com, 11 A.M.–7 P.M. Mon.–Sat.), in the Omni Building, sells used books, plus magazines and maps.

COFFEE
Every souvenir store sells premium packaged coffee. Make sure the package is marked *puro,* otherwise the coffee may be laced with enough sugar to make even the most ardent sugar-lover turn green. You can also buy whole beans—albeit not the finest export quality—roasted

before your eyes at the Mercado Central. Ask for whole beans *(granos),* or you'll end up with superfine grounds. One pound of beans costs about $1.

The airport departure lounge has several well-stocked coffee stores.

ART, HANDICRAFTS, AND SOUVENIRS
San José is replete with arts and crafts, such as reproduction pre-Columbian gold jewelry, hammocks, wood carvings, Panamanian *molas,* and miniature oxcarts. **Mercado de Artesanías Nacionales** (Calle 11, Avenidas 4/6, closed Sun.), in Plaza Artigas, teems with colorful stalls. The plaza hosts an open-air art exhibition *(Pintura al aire libre)* every Saturday (10 A.M.–4 P.M.), March–July. And the **Mercado Central,** on Avenida 1, has a panoply of leather work and other artisans' stalls.

Specialty handicraft stores concentrate on Calle 5 between Avenida 1/5 and include **Suraska Gallery** (tel. 506/2222-0129), selling top-quality woodcarvings and furniture. And a handful of handicrafts stores cluster together on two levels at **La Casona** (Calle Central, Avenidas Central/1, 9:30 A.M.–6:30 P.M. Mon.–Sat. and 9 A.M.–5 P.M. Sun.). **Centro Comercial El Pueblo** also has many high-quality art galleries and crafts stores.

My favorite store is **Galería Namú** (Avenida 7, Calles 5/7, tel. 506/2256-3412, www.galerianamu.com), where the superb indigenous art and crafts include Boruca masks and weavings and jewelry from Panamá and elsewhere.

SHOPPING WITH A CONSCIENCE

Think twice before buying something exotic: The item may be banned by U.S. Customs and, if so, you could be fined. Even if legal to import, consider whether your purchase is an ecological sin. In short, shop with a conscience. Don't buy:

- Combs, jewelry, or other items made from tortoise shells.

- Coral or coral items. Costa Rica's coral reefs are being gradually destroyed. And every

shell taken from a beach is one less for the next person to enjoy.

- Jewelry, artwork, or decorated clothes made of feathers.

- Furs from jaguars, ocelots, and other animals in danger of extinction. Such furs are illegal.

- Tropical hardwood products, unless denoted as made from fallen timber.

East of downtown, the new **Fine Art Cellar Gallery** (tel. 506/2384-3544, www.fineartcellar.com) sells works by the nation's finest contemporary artists. Another excellent gallery is **Arte Contemporáneo Andrómeda** (Avenida 9, Calle 9, tel. 506/2223-3529).

CLOTHING

If you admire the traditional Tico look, check out the **Mercado Central** (Avenida 1, Calle 6), where you'll find embroidered *guayabero* shirts and blouses and cotton *campesino* hats. **La Choza Folklórica** (Avenida 3, Calle 1) specializes in replicas of national costumes. Shoemakers abound, many selling cowboy boots, including dandy two-tones; a bevy of high-quality shoemakers can be found on Avenida 3 between Calles 24 and 26.

The best place for upscale brand-name boutiques is **Mall San Pedro** (Avenida Central and *circunvalación,* San Pedro, tel. 506/2283-7540).

You can buy hiking gear, from fanny-packs to safari vests, at **Mundo Aventura** (Avenida 3, Calle 36, tel. 506/2221-6934, www.maventura.com).

JEWELRY

Artisan markets sell attractive ethnic-style earrings and bracelets. Much of what you'll see on the street is actually gold-washed, not solid gold. Most upscale hotel gift stores sell Colombian emeralds and semiprecious stones, 14-karat-gold earrings and brooches, and fabulous pre-Columbian re-creations: try **Esmeraldas y Diseños** (tel. 506/2231-4808) in Sabana Norte and **Esmeraldas y Creaciones** (tel. 506/2280-0808) in Los Yoses.

Galerías Metallo (tel. 506/2225-1570, www.studiometallo.com), in Barrio Escalante, has both a jewelry academy and showroom.

The **Gold Museum Shop** (tel. 506/2256-9125), beneath the Plaza de la Cultura, sells quality gold reproductions.

CIGARS

Costa Rica is a prime spot to buy Cuban cigars. (U.S. citizens should note that it is illegal to buy Cuban cigars, and even non–U.S. citizens can have them confiscated in transit home via the United States.) Costa Rica's own selections run the gamut from mediocre to superb, including some brands made of leaves aged with aromatic coffee beans.

Good bets are the **Tobacco Shop** (tel. 506/2223-0873) in Centro Comercial El Pueblo and, best of all, the **Casa del Habano** (Calle 4, Avenida 1, tel. 506/2253-4629, www.habanoscr.net) in San Pedro.

Accommodations

San José's accommodations run the gamut from budget hovels to charming boutique hotels and large name-brand options. San José is a noisy city; it is always wise to ask for a room away from the street. Hotels are arranged by price category, then by area.

UNDER $25
Downtown

Among budget dorm options, number one choice is ◖ **Costa Rica Backpackers** (Avenida 6, Calles 21/23, tel. 506/2221-6191, www.costaricabackpackers.com, $12 pp dorms, $26–28 private rooms), run by two friendly and savvy French guys, Stefan and Vincent. This splendid, spotless, secure backpackers' pad is in a large house with a small kidney-shaped swimming pool and garden with hammocks and swing chairs. It offers clean male, female, and mixed dorms with shared bathrooms, plus private rooms (one a lovely space with king-size bed), all with heaps of hot water. A huge TV lounge has leather sofas. It has cooking facilities, laundry, storage, and tour-planning room, as well as free 24-hour Internet and coffee. Movies are shown nightly. All dorms have lockers.

The same owners recently opened the more upscale **Costa Rica Guesthouse** (tel./fax 506/2223-7034, www.costa-rica-guesthouse.com) across the road, with 23 rooms perfect for couples.

Readers also rave about **Pangea Hostel** (Avenida 7, Calles 3/5, tel. 506/2221-1992, www.hostelpangea.com, $12 pp dorm, $28–35 private rooms), in a converted old home in Barrio Amón. And no wonder! Splashed with colorful murals throughout, this thoughtfully prepared hostel offers splendid services, from a kitchen, TV lounge, and pool table to a lovely pool with whirlpool tub and wet bar. It even has its own shuttle, and the open-air restaurant upstairs has a licensed bar with views. There are six clean dorms and 26 basically furnished private rooms, all with shared bathrooms with hot

water. It offers free storage, free Internet access, free international calls, and free breakfast.

Nearby, the no-frills, German-run **Tranquilo Backpackers** (Calle 7, Avenida 11, tel. 506/2222-2493, www.tranquilobackpackers.com, $10 pp dorms, $28 s/d private rooms) is another good option, although here furnishings are more bare-bones.

The best of several new hostels near the Coca-Cola bus terminal is ◖ **Hostel Gallo Pinto** (Calle 24, Avenida 3/5, tel. 506/2257-1618, www.gallopintocr.com, $12 pp dorm, $25 s/d room). This exquisite conversion of a gracious old home has four dorms with shared bath, and five private rooms with private bath, all delightfully furnished with art pieces and lovely color schemes. Rates include breakfast and free Internet, plus kitchen use. *Nice!*

Nearby, **La Posada de Don Tobías** (Calle 12, Avenidas 7/9, tel. 506/2258-3162, $12–20 s, $22–30 d), adjoining Terminal Atlántico Norte, is a clean, safe, well-run budget option with clean private rooms.

If you prefer a conventional hotel near the bus stations, the best bet is the **Hotel Cocorí** (Avenida 3, Calle 16, tel. 506/2233-0081, fax 506/2255-1058, $15 s, $25 d), with 26 rooms with simple but adequate furnishings, a TV lounge, restaurant, and laundry.

Backpacker alternatives include **Casa Ridgeway** (tel. 506/2233-6168, www.amigosparalapaz.org) and, across the street, the well-run **Abril Hostel** (Calle 29 #124, esq. Avenida 1, tel. 506/2233-6397, www.abrilhostel.com).

West of Downtown

A shining star among San José's hostels is ◖ **Mi Casa Hostel** (Calle 48, tel. 506/2231-470, www.micasahostel.com, $12 pp dorm, $26–30 s/d room including breakfast), a beautiful 1950s modernist home with a pool table and Internet in the exquisite stone-faced TV lounge, opening through a wall of glass to a stone patio and quaint garden. It has a communal kitchen and laundry. A superb mixed dorm upstairs gets heaps of light; a women's dorm is simpler. Four private rooms have foam mattresses and vary in size. It's 150 meters north and 50 meters west of ICE, in Sabana Norte.

I also recommend **Gaudy's Backpackers** (Avenida 5, Calle 36/38, tel. 506/2258-2937, www.backpacker.co.cr, from $10 pp dorm, $25 shared room, $28–30 private room), in a beautiful and spotless home in a peaceful residential area. You enter to a lofty-ceilinged TV lounge with sofas and pool table. It opens to a courtyard with hammocks. There are two co-ed dorms (one with eight bunk beds, another with 12 bunk beds) and 13 small private rooms. Guests get use of a full kitchen, and there's laundry service, plus free Internet.

The new, super-clean **Hostel Guest Home** (Calle 36, Avenidas 7/9, tel./fax 506/2223-6302, www.hostelguesthomecr.com, $7–23 s, $24–35 d) is another great option for backpackers.

East of Downtown

The **Hostal Toruma** (Avenida Central, Calles 29/31, tel. 506/2234-8186, www.hostel toruma.com, $12 pp dorm; $30 s/d shared bath; $35 s, $55 d private bath) is a beautiful old colonial-style structure with segregated dormitories accommodating 95 beds in 17 well-kept rooms, plus seven private rooms with shared baths. There are laundry facilities and a restaurant, plus Internet, cable TV, and parking. Rates include breakfast.

⟨ **Hostel Bekuo** (Avenida 8, Calles 39/41, tel. 506/2234-1091, www.hostelbekuo.com, $12 pp dorm, $30 s/d shared bath, $35–40 s/d private bath) is a conversion of a beautiful 1950s home with shiny hardwood floors, clean modern bathrooms, a breeze-swept lounge with pool table, and an Internet and TV lounge. Walls of glass open to a garden. It has male, female, and mixed dorms, plus private rooms.

One block east, and also a winner, **Hostal Casa Yoses** (Avenida 8, Calles 41/43, tel. 506/2234-5486, www.casayoses.com, $12 pp dorm, $18 s or $28 d shared bath, $32 s/d private bath) occupies a colonial mansion and has dorms and private rooms, plus heaps of services including games and Wi-Fi.

$25-50
Downtown
The **Hotel Talamanca** (Avenida 2, Calles 8/10, tel. 506/2233-5033, hoteltalamanca@ racsa.co.cr, $45 s/d, $50 suite) is an elegant option on the city's main drag. The 50 air-conditioned rooms and four junior suites (with hot tubs and minibars) are tastefully appointed and have TVs and telephones.

For something more eccentric, try **Hotel La Cuesta** (Avenida 1, Calles 11/13, tel. 506/2256-7946, www.pensiondelacuesta.com, $20 s, $28 d), a cozy charmer for those who like offbeat hotels. This 1930s house, full of antiques and potted plants, is owned by local artists Dierdre Hyde and Otto Apuy, whose artworks adorn the walls. There are nine rooms, plus a furnished apartment for up to six people. The shared baths are clean. There's a TV room and self-service laundry. Guests get use of the kitchen and Wi-Fi.

I like the **Hotel Colonial** (Calle 11, Avenidas 2/4, tel. 506/2223-0109, www.hotelcolonial cr.com, $42 s, $52 d low season, $50 s, $60 d high season), a lovely conversion of an old three-story mansion with high ceilings and carved hardwood beams. Rooms boast spacious bathrooms and picture windows opening to a courtyard with a pool.

Others to consider in this price range include the **Hotel Costa Rica Morazán** (Calle 7, Avenida 1, tel. 506/2222-4622, www.costa ricamorazan.com); the **Hotel Vesuvio** (Avenida 11, Calles 13/15, tel. 506/2221-7586, www.hotel vesuvio.com); the **Hotel & Casino Royal Dutch** (Avenida 2, Calle 4, tel. 506/2222-1414, www.hotelroyaldutchcr.com); the **Hemingway Inn** (Calle 9, Avenida 9, tel./fax 506/2221-1804, www.hemingwayinn.com); and the **Hotel El Maragato** (tel. 506/2222-7737, www.hotelel maragato.com), formerly the Hotel Gran Vía.

West of Downtown
The **Hotel Petit** (Calle 24, Paseo Colón, tel. 506/2233-0766, fax 506/2233-4794, $25 s, $35 d including full breakfast) has 15 simple rooms, all with hot showers. Rooms vary. Some are light and airy, others dingy; some

SAN JOSÉ

have electric stoves. There's a kitchen, laundry service, secure parking, and a cable TV in the lounge, plus a bar and café.

Mesón del Ángel Hotel (Calle 20, Avenidas 3/5, tel. 506/2222-3405, www.hotelmesondelangel.com, $49 s, $59 d) is a restored two-story, mid-20th-century home with natural stone highlights. The huge lounge with mirrored wall is graced by a hardwood floor and opens to a pleasing dining room and garden courtyard with outside lounging areas. The 21 rooms (some spacious and with floor-to-ceiling windows onto the courtyard) feature tall ceilings, modest but pleasing furnishings, cable TV, security box, and private bathroom. Rooms facing the street get traffic noise. It offers parking and Internet. Rates include breakfast and tax.

The rambling **Hotel Cacts** (Avenida 3 bis, Calles 28/30, tel. 506/2221-2928, www.hotelcacts.com, $40 s or $45 d standard, $50 s or $60 d superior including breakfast and tax) offers 33 nonsmoking rooms, all with telephone and cable TV, plus private bath with hot water. Some rooms in the new extension are a bit dark and have small bathrooms, although all are kept sparklingly clean. Meals are served refectory-style in a rooftop bar-restaurant. It offers a tour agency, airport pick-up, secure parking, and a swimming pool.

The high-rise **Hotel Ambassador** (Paseo Colón, Calles 26/28, tel. 506/2221-8155, www.hotelambassador.co.cr, $45 s or $50 d standard, $55 s or $60 d junior suite, $85 s or $90 d suite) offers a good location within a 20-minute walk of both the city center and Sabana Park. The 74 air-conditioned rooms are clean and spacious and have minibars, safes, and cable TVs. Amenities include a restaurant, a coffee shop, and a bar with dance floor. Rates include continental breakfast.

Also to consider in this category is the ho-hum **Hotel Petit Victoria** (Calle 28, Avenida 2, tel. 506/2255-8488, fax 506/2221-6372).

East of Downtown

Bamboo and rattan abounds in the **Ara Macao Inn** (Calle 27, Avenidas Central/2, tel.

506/2233-2742, www.aramacaoinn.com, $45 s, $55 d), a restored early-20th-century house in Barrio La California. The four sun-filled standards and seven triples have polished hardwood floors, ceiling fans, cable TV, and radios. Some are compact, pleasantly furnished apartments; triples have coffeemakers, refrigerators, and microwaves. Rates include tax and breakfast, served in a breeze-swept patio corridor.

Readers rave about **⟨ Kap's Place** (Calle 19, Avenidas 11/13, tel. 506/2221-1169, www.kapsplace.com, $25–80 s, $35–95 d), a clean, charming guesthouse with 23 rooms (including six hostel-type rooms; three with shared bathrooms) in various adjoining buildings, on a tranquil street in Barrio Aranjuez, a 20-minute walk from downtown. All rooms are decorated in lively colors and have cable TV and telephones, and there's free Internet and Wi-Fi access. Twelve rooms have full kitchens. Two small rooms are for one person only. A lovely covered patio garners sunlight and has hammocks. No meals are served, but guests have kitchen privileges, and there's a kids' playroom. Karla Arias, the erudite Tica owner, speaks fluent English and French. No unregistered guests are permitted.

Across the street, the rambling **Hotel Aranjuez** (Calle 19, Avenidas 11/13, tel. 506/2256-1825, www.hotelaranjuez.com, $23 s or $26 d with shared bath, $30 s or $40 d standard, $36 s or $47 d superior) has 23 eclectically decorated rooms rich with hardwoods and all with cable TV, phones, and hair dryers. It's formed of four contiguous houses, each with its own personality. Together, they operate like a hostel. It has Internet, and an airy garden lounge.

Of similar standard, **Boutique Hotel Casa Las Orquideas** (tel. 506/2283-0095, www.lasorquideashotel.com, $12 pp dorm, $50 s, $60 d), on Avenida Central in Los Yoses, is an attractive option done up in pea-green and tropical murals. The 11 rooms have tile floors and New Mexico–style bedspreads. Upstairs rooms have more light plus king-size beds. There's a small yet elegant restaurant, plus secure parking.

$50-100
Downtown

The adorable **Hotel Kekoldi** (Avenida 9, Calles 5/7, tel. 506/2240-0804, www.kekoldi.com, $51 s, $62 d standard, $73 s, $83 d superior low season; $57 s, $69 d standard, $79 s, $89 d superior high season), in a two-story 1950s house in Barrio Amón, offers 10 spacious rooms with hardwood floors, heaps of light, and lovely albeit modest furnishings in tropical pastels, plus cable TV, fans, and security box. Breakfasts are served in a beautiful garden in Japanese style.

Also worth considering is the small and homey **Hotel Doña Inés** (Calle 11, Avenidas 2/6, tel. 506/2222-7443, www.donaines.com, $40 s or $55 d low season; $45 s or $60 d high season), behind the Iglesia la Soledad. It's a good bet for its luxury bathrooms with full-size tubs, plus TVs, phones, and reproduction antique furnishings in the 20 carpeted bedrooms. It has a small and pleasant restaurant for breakfasts and dinner. Rates include breakfast and tax.

The **Gran Hotel** (Avenida 2, Calle 3, tel. 506/2221-4000, www.grandhotelcostarica.com, $85 s/d standard, $97 s/d superior, $135–179 suites), dating from 1899 and named a national landmark, recently emerged from a total remake that has reinvigorated this once-dowdy dowager. It has a basement casino, plus an elegant open-air restaurant merging into the hotel's 24-hour Café 1830. However, the 102 air-conditioned, modestly furnished rooms are still unexciting; all have telephones and cable TVs, plus bright art, and older tiled baths. Rooms facing the plaza can be noisy. The five junior suites are elegant.

Hotel Europa (Calle Central, Avenidas 3/5, tel. 506/2222-1222, www.hoteleuropacr.com, $50 s, $60 d) has 72 spacious, paneled, air-conditioned rooms, and two suites with more elegant tones. All have cable TVs, direct-dial telephones, and safes, although the hotel remains frumpy. Four larger "deluxe" rooms have wide balconies at no extra cost. Avoid lower-floor rooms facing onto the noisy street (quieter, inner-facing rooms are more expensive).

It has a small plunge pool, a reasonable restaurant, and efficient service. Rates include breakfast and tax.

The **Hotel Balmoral** (Avenida Central, Calles 7/9, tel. 506/2222-5022, www.balmoral.co.cr; $75 s, $95 d standard, $109 s/d premier, $139–155 s/d suites), a steps-to-everything option one block east of Plaza de la Cultura, offers 112 small, air-conditioned, carpeted rooms, plus four junior suites and four suites, all with cable TVs and safe-deposit boxes. A sauna and mini-gym, a restaurant and pleasing outdoor café, a casino, and tour desk and car rental agencies are on the ground floor. It has secure parking. Rates include breakfast. Opposite the Balmoral, and preferable following a snazzy makeover, the **Hotel Presidente** (tel. 506/2222-3022, www.hotel-presidente.com, $89 s/d, $131 s/d "spa" rooms, $125 s/d junior suites, $145 s/d suites) has also upgraded its 110 air-conditioned bedrooms, each with a direct-dial telephone, cable TV, and safe-deposit box. The spacious rooms now boast a lovely contemporary elegance and travertine-clad bathrooms. The hotel has a rooftop whirlpool and sauna, a casino, and bar, plus a wonderful street-front restaurant and café. Rates include breakfast and free Wi-Fi. Nice!

For old-world charm, consider the **Britannia Hotel** (Calle 3, Avenida 11, tel. 506/2223-6667, www.hotelbritanniacostarica.com, $65 s or $76 d standard, $80 s or $93 d deluxe, $93 s or $105 d junior suite low season; $77 s or $89 d standard, $93 s or $105 d deluxe, $106 s or $117 d junior suite high season), in a neoclassical Victorian-style mansion built in 1910 in Barrio Amón. The five deluxe rooms and four junior suites in the old house boast high ceilings, stained glass, arches, ceiling fans, mosaic tile floors, and English-style furniture. A new block has 14 standard rooms, all with cable TVs, telephones, safe-deposit boxes, a king-size or two twin beds, plus a private bathroom with tub. The boutique hotel features "tropical courtyards," a restaurant converted from the old cellar, a coffee shop, and room service.

Another historic charmer is the U.S.–run **Hotel Santo Tomás** (Avenida 7, Calles 3/5, tel.

506/2255-0448, www.hotelsantotomas.com, $80 s/d standard, $90 s/d superior, $110 s/d deluxe), an intimate bed-and-breakfast with 19 nonsmoking rooms in an elegant turn-of-the-20th-century plantation home with high vaulted ceiling and original hardwood and colonial tile floors. Rooms vary (some are huge), but all have cable TV and direct-dial phones, queen-size beds with orthopedic mattresses, antique reproduction furniture, throw rugs, and watercolors. There are three separate TV lounges and a full-service tour planning service, library, gift store, and Internet access. The hotel features the delightful Restaurant El Oasis, a solar-heated swimming pool, whirlpool tub, and water slide. Rates include breakfast.

Nearby, the homey, well-run **Hotel Don Carlos** (Calle 9 bis, Avenidas 7/9, tel. 506/2221-6707, www.doncarloshotel.com, $65 s or $75 d standard, $75 s or $85 d superior, $95 family room) occupies an aged colonial-style mansion replete with Sarchí oxcarts, magnificent wrought-iron work, stained-glass windows, stunning art, and bronze sculptures. It has 36 rooms and suites, including colonial-era rooms reached by a rambling courtyard. All rooms have cable TVs, safes, and hair dryers. It has a gift shop, free Internet service, a tour service, small gym, sundeck with water cascade and plunge pool, plus an espresso bar and a restaurant lit by an atrium skylight. Rates include continental breakfast.

Somewhat more dowdy, **La Casa Morazán** (Calle 7, Avenidas 7/9, tel. 506/2257-4187, www.casamorazan.com, $45 s or $55 d low season, $55 s or $65 d high season) is also set in a colonial mansion boasting antique furnishings and modern art, plus original (rather stained) tile floors. The 11 air-conditioned rooms all have cable TV, old-style telephones, large bathrooms, and 1950s furniture. Breakfast (included in rates) and lunch are served on a small patio.

Similarly gracious, the Swiss-owned **Hotel Fleur de Lys** (Calle 13, Avenidas 2/4, tel. 506/2223-1206, www.hotelfleurdelys.com, $79 s or $89 d standard, $104 s/d junior suite, $119–135 suite low season; $84 s or $94 d standard, $109 s/d junior suite, $124–139 suite high season). This restored mansion offers 31 individually styled rooms, each named for a species of flower. All have sponge-washed pastel walls, tasteful artwork, phones, cable TVs, hair dryers, and wrought-iron or wicker beds with crisp linens. A wood-paneled restaurant serves Italian cuisine, and live music is offered twice weekly in the bar. There's a tour desk and on-site parking. Rates include breakfast.

For more contemporary styling, try the modern **Hotel Villa Tournon** (tel. 506/2233-6622, www.costarica-hotelvillatournon.com, $75 s or $80 d standard, $90 s or $97 d superior), in Barrio Tournón, 200 meters from El Pueblo, and brimful of contemporary art and sculpture. The 80 mammoth air-conditioned rooms are graciously appointed in autumnal colors with wood furnishings and leather chairs. The restaurant, centered on a massive brick hearth, offers fireside dining, and there's a piano bar. Ask for rooms off the street. It has free Internet, secure parking, and a swimming pool.

City slickers might appreciate the hip Austrian-run **Hotel City One** (Avenida 9, Calles Central/2, tel. 506/2248-1778, www.hotelcityone.com, $60 s/d low season, $70 s/d high season), with its white, orange, and chocolate brown color schemes, modernist decor, and contemporary art. The lobby makes a good impression, but many of the 50 rooms furnished in simple 1950s retro vogue are dowdy and dark and somewhat spartan. The upstairs Caribbean restaurant and all-white lounge-bar have volcano views.

A complete opposite in decor, the **Raya Vida Villa** (tel. 506/2223-4168, www.rayavida.com, $80 s, $95 d) bed-and-breakfast is a lovely two-story antebellum-style mansion tucked in a cul-de-sac in Barrio Otoya, at the end of Avenida 11 and Calle 17. The live-in owner, Michael Long, rents four rooms, each delightfully done up in individual decor: the Pineapple Room, ideal for honeymooners, has a four-poster bed; the Mask Room features masks from around the world; another room has a king-size bed and limestone floor and opens to a shaded patio with fountain. There's an exquisite TV lounge and reading room with fireplace and chandeliers, although all rooms have cable TV plus fans. The place is secluded and peaceful and festooned with original artwork, including Toulouse-Lautrec and Salvador Dalí. Rates include full breakfast and airport pickup.

Sportsmens Lodge (Calle 13, Avenida 11, tel. 506/2221-2533 or 800/291-2798, www.sportsmenscr.com, $119–159 s/d), in the historic Barrio Otoya district, offers a tranquil setting a stone's throw from downtown. Centered on a colonial building, it has 22 rooms; most have classy antique furnishings and silent air-conditioning, including 10 elegant rooms in a new wing, while a Penthouse Suite ($250) is super-contemporary. It advertises adult TV channels, and draws heavily from the sportfishing crowd trawling for the girls who flock to the bar. Likewise, bed-and-bawd is the theme at the five-story, 104-room **Hotel Del Rey** (Avenida 1, Calle 9, tel. 506/2258-4880, www.hoteldelrey.com), appealing mainly to a male clientele making out with the professional gals in the bar. Hustlers outside the door are an annoyance. *Caveat emptor!*

If you don't mind institutional-style hotels, the centrally located **Sleep Inn** (Avenida 3, Calles 9/11, tel. 506/2222-0101, www.sleep innsanjose.com, $90–100 s/d) offers good value for the money. It's done up in earth tones, with charming contemporary furnishings and Internet connections, plus marble tops and king-size beds in junior suites; my mattress gave me a backache! It adjoins the Club Colonial Casino, but the restaurant (also in the casino) is gloomy and affected by the casino's smokers. Rates include local calls.

The 27-room, Dutch-run **Hotel Rincón de San José** (Avenida 9, Calles 13/15, tel. 506/2221-9702, www.hotelrincondesanjose .com, $52 s, $66 d), in a quiet part of Barrio Otoya, offers a pleasing ambience combining antique furnishings and a subdued elegance. It has a lovely skylit restaurant.

And the new-in-2007 **Hotel Inca Real** (Ave. 11, Calles 3/5, tel. 506/2223-8883, http:// gruporealinternacional.com, $45 s, $55 d)

offers a combination of gracious yesteryear-themed intimacy and comfort in its 33 rooms. Nothing outstanding here, but it's a perfectly adequate option.

Also-rans to consider include the **Hotel Posada de Museo** (Avenida 2, Calle 17, tel. 506/2258-1027, www.hotelposadadelmuseo .com), catercorner to the Museo Nacional; **Hotel Castillo B&B** (Avenida 9, Calle 9, tel. 506/2221-5141, www.hotelcastillo.biz), a cheap conversion of a 1900-era three-story colonial home; **Taylor's Inn** (Avenida 13, Calles 13/15, tel. 506/2257-4333, taylor@catours.co.cr), with nine nonsmoking rooms in a 1908 property; and **Dunn Inn** (Calle 5, Avenida 11, tel. 506/2222-3232, www.hoteldunninn.com), in a restored 19th-century home and operated by Texan Patrick Dunn.

West of Downtown

The slightly jaded **Hotel Rosa del Paseo** (Paseo Colón, Calles 28/30, tel. 506/2257-3213, http:// rosadelpaseo.com, $70 s or $80 d standard low season, $75 s or $85 d high season; $90 s or $100 d junior suite, $120 s or $140 d suite year-round) has 18 nicely decorated rooms plus one suite in a century-old residence on Paseo Colón. Architectural details combine parquet and tile floors, original artwork, and art-nouveau flourishes with "Victorian Caribbean." All rooms have cable TV, safes, and ceiling fans, plus white-tiled private bathrooms with hot water. A master suite has a large whirlpool tub, and there's a garden courtyard and secure parking. Rates include breakfast.

Focusing on a business clientele, the **Quality Hotel Centro Colón** (Avenida 3, Calle 38, tel. 506/2257-2580, www.hotelcentrocolon.com, $75–95 s/d standard, $85 s/d superior and business room, $90 junior suite) is in the Centro Colón complex. The 126 carpeted, air-conditioned rooms (including 42 suites) are "extra-large" and have king-size beds as well as cable TVs, safe-deposit boxes, hair dryers, and telephones. Some rooms have volcano views. An executive floor has a business center and business rooms have Wi-Fi, plus there's a restaurant, casino, and a nightclub/bar.

SAN JOSÉ

The delightful **Hotel Occidental Torremolinos** (Avenida 5, Calle 40, tel. 506/2222-5266, www.occidental-hoteles.com, $72 s/d standard, $85 s/d suite) is entered via a classically elegant lounge and bar opening to a lush garden with shade umbrellas and a pool. Its 80 rooms and 12 suites in contemporary style are modest in size but handsomely furnished, with lots of hardwoods. All have cable TVs, carpeting, clock radios, direct-dial telephones, and hair dryers. Suites have glassed-in balconies. It offers a pool and a whirlpool tub, plus a courtesy bus, car rental service, and a beautiful restaurant. Rates include breakfast.

In a similar vein is the stylish **C Barceló Palma Real** (tel. 506/2290-5060, www.hotelpalmareal.com, $105 s/d standard, $166 s/d executive, $182 s/d junior suite), in a quiet residential area 200 meters north of the ICE in Sabana Norte. This upscale, contemporary boutique hotel, full of marble and autumnal colors, draws a business clientele. It features 65 carpeted, tastefully decorated, air-conditioned rooms, with handsome wooden floors, orthopedic mattresses, and spacious travertine-lined bathrooms. Two suites have king-size beds and whirlpool bathtubs. There's a state-of-the-art gym, whirlpool tub, business center, bar, and elegant restaurant.

Looking for something more intimate? The small, family-run **Hotel Sabana B&B** (tel. 506/2296-3751, www.costaricabb.com, $65 s or $75 d low season, $70 s or $90 d high season), on the north side of Sabana, offers five simple yet cozy upstairs rooms with parquet floors, fans, cable TVs, and private baths with hot water. It also has one downstairs room for handicapped travelers, plus Internet and Wi-Fi, a tour desk, kitchenette, free tea and coffee, and a terrace and garden. Rates include airport pickup, breakfast, and tax.

The **Costa Rica Tennis Club & Hotel** (tel. 506/2232-1266, www.costaricatennisclub.com) offers a reasonable alternative, as does the nearby and contemporary themed **Barceló Rincón del Valle** (tel. 506/2231-4927, www.barcelo.com). Both are on the south side of Sabana Park.

For self-catering, the best options are **Apartotel La Sabana** (tel. 506/2220-2422, www.apartotel-lasabana.com), on the north side of Sabana Park; **Apartotel Cristina** (tel. 506/2220-0453, www.apartotelcristina.com) nearby, 300 meters north of ICE; and the **Apartotel El Sesteo** (tel. 506/2296-1805, www.sesteo.com), 200 meters south of McDonald's on Sabana Sur.

East of Downtown

The **Hotel Don Fadrique** (Calle 37, Avenida 8, tel. 506/2225-8186, www.hoteldonfadrique.com, $65 s, $75 d) claims 20 "luxuriously furnished rooms" and "lush tropical gardens." The rooms are decorated in tropical pastels (some have Guatemalan bedspreads), with original modern art on the walls. Each has parquet wood or tile floor, telephone, cable TV, safe-deposit box, and fan. Take an upstairs room, with heaps of light. There's a lounge with lush sofas, and a charming patio where you can enjoy breakfast, included in rates.

Nearby, **L'Hôtel Le Bergerac** (Calle 35, Avenida Central, tel. 506/2234-7850, www.bergerachotel.com, $80 s or $90 d standard, $105 s or $115 d superior, $125 s or $135 d deluxe) is a pretty colonial home in Los Yoses, with views south toward the Cordillera Talamanca. Exuding French influence, Le Bergerac is a full-service hotel with a deep maroon and gray color scheme and the feel of a bed-and-breakfast. Service is discreet. The hotel has 19 rooms in three buildings (five in the original home, reached via a sweeping spiral staircase), all with cable TVs, direct-dial telephones, Internet access, and safes, plus hardwood floors and classical furniture. Rooms vary in size, and some have bidets and their own patio gardens. It boasts a gourmet restaurant and has secure parking, a travel agency, and a conference room. Rates include full breakfast. It was for sale at last visit.

In a similar vein, the Italian-run **La Giaconda House Hotel** (tel. 506/2248-9422, www.costaricahousehotel.com) offers a viable alternative at similar rates. A stone's throw away, the **Casa 69** (tel. 506/2256-8879, www.casa69.com,

$40–65 s/d) is a graceful conversion of a centenary mansion and now offers tasteful furnishings and king-size beds in some rooms. It has a rooftop terrace. Both hotels opened in 2008. Traffic noise is an issue here!

In San Pedro, the modestly appealing **Hotel Arte Milvia** (tel. 506/2225-4543, www.hotel milvia.com, $59 s, $69 d) has three spacious, individually styled rooms in the restored turn-of-the-20th-century wooden home, plus six downstairs rooms in a contemporary add-on built around a tiny garden courtyard (noise from adjoining rooms can be a problem). All have king-size beds and tiny TVs; bathrooms feature hand-painted decorative tiles. There's a dining room, lounge with TV and VCR, and boutique. Lively pop-art works by owner Florencia Urbia, a well-known artist, adorn the walls. Rates include taxes and continental breakfast.

A more appealing option, the **Hotel 1492 Jade y Oro** (Avenida 1 #2985, Calles 31/33, tel. 506/2225-3752, www.hotel1492.com, $60 s or $70 d standard, $80 s/d deluxe, $90 s/d junior suite), in the quiet residential neighborhood of Barrio Escalante, is a beautiful colonial-style residence boasting 10 handsomely appointed rooms (three are junior suites) with hardwood floors, private bath, hot water, ceiling fan, telephone, and cable TV. Most rooms have windows that open to small gardens, and there's a patio garden done up in Tico fashion where a happy hour of wine and cheese is hosted nightly. The handsome lounge has a soaring ceiling and fireplace. Rates include Tico breakfast.

$100-150
Downtown

Dominating the downtown skyline is the sophisticated **Hotel Aurola Holiday Inn** (Avenida 5, Calle 5, tel. 506/2523-1000, www.aurola-holidayinn.com, $104 s/d standard, $140 executive, $200 s/d suite). The modern high-rise overlooking Parque Morazán offers 201 hermetically sealed, air-conditioned rooms featuring regal furnishings. The 11th floor is smoke-free, an executive floor caters to

business travelers, and one room is wheelchair accessible. Topping off the hotel's attractions is the *mirador* restaurant on the 17th floor, adjacent to the casino. The hotel contains a gym, sauna, and indoor pool.

For purely functional comfort, try the handsome albeit overpriced **Clarion Hotel Amón Plaza** (Avenida 11, Calle 3 bis, tel. 506/2523-4600, www.choicehotels.com, $120–165 s/d, $185–295 suites), in the historic Barrio Amón area. This modern, four-story, "neo-Victorian" hotel has 90 air-conditioned rooms, including 24 junior and six deluxe suites, all with subdued decor and the expected appointments. Facilities include a spa and solarium, casino, disco, and underground parking, plus elegant restaurant.

The business-oriented **Radisson Europa Hotel & Conference Center** (Calle 3, Avenida 15, tel. 506/2257-3257, www.radisson.com/san josecr, from $135 s/d) is a contemporary five-star hotel with 107 "superior" rooms, six executive suites, and one presidential suite, all with air-conditioning, 24-hour room service, direct-dial telephones, cable TVs, minibars, and safes.

If you're considering **Best Western San José Downtown** (tel. 506/2255-4766, www.bestwesterncostarica.com), note that it has an awful location on the edge of the city's roughest neighborhood.

West of Downtown

The ◖ **Hotel Restaurante Grano de Oro** (Calle 30, Avenida 2, tel. 506/2255-3322, www.hotelgranodeoro.com, $105–140 s/d rooms, $160–275 suite low season; $115–165 s/d rooms, $175–305 suite high season) is indisputably the city's finest hotel (and a great bargain). It's my hotel of preference whenever I stay in San José. The guestbook is a compendium of compliments. "What charm! What comfort!" "The best hotel we've stayed in—ever!" "We would love to keep it a secret, but we promise we won't." A member of the Small Distinctive Hotels of Costa Rica, the gracious turn-of-the-20th-century mansion, in a quiet residential neighborhood off Paseo Colón, proves that a fine house, like a jewel, is made complete by its setting. Congenial hosts Eldon

© CHRISTOPHER P. BAKER

Executive room at Hotel Restaurante Grano de Oro

and Lori Cooke have overseen the creation of a real home away from home that combines traditional old-world Costa Rican style with sophisticated elegance. A recent expansion has graced the hotel with a 21st-century staircase entry, a contemporary lobby, and a superlative restaurant that is now indisputably San José's finest. Orthopedic mattresses guarantee contented slumber in the 41 faultlessly decorated guest rooms (including five more stately rooms in a new wing). Upgraded in 2008, they're done up in a tasteful combination of regal greens and maroons or deep blues; black rattan and handcrafted iron furniture; and king-size canopied beds in some rooms. Gleaming hardwood floors add to the sense of refinement. Flat-screen cable TV and direct-dial telephones are standard. Extravagant bathrooms have also been modernized and boast torrents of piping-hot water. The sumptuous rooftop wood-paneled Vista de Oro suite has a plate-glass wall providing views of three volcanoes. There's a well-stocked gift shop and a rooftop solarium with two whirlpool tubs. No request is too much for the ever-smiling staff.

Nearby, and a total contrast, is the **Crowne Plaza Corobicí** (tel. 506/2232-8122, www.crowneplaza.com, $110 s/d standard, $140 junior suite, $331–501 suite), on the northeastern corner of Sabana Park. Its angled exterior is ungainly, but its soaring atrium with a surfeit of marble and tier upon tier of balconies festooned with ferns is impressive. The 200 spacious rooms and eight suites boast handsome furnishings and modern accoutrements. Suites have kitchenettes. It has a business center, nightclub, casino, 24-hour cafeteria, Internet café, plus Italian and Japanese restaurants.

Nearby, and bringing San José squarely into the 21st century, **Parque del Lago** (Paseo Colón, Calles 40/42, tel. 506/2257-8787, www.parquedellago.com, $130 s/d studio, $149 s/d superior, $160 s/d executive, $175 s/d junior suite) is a modern four-story hotel with 33 exquisitely decorated, air-conditioned rooms, plus six suites with kitchenettes, all with a hip contemporary vogue (and to-die-for mattresses) and white, orange, and dark hardwood color schemes. Cable TV, direct-dial phone with fax, minibar, coffeemaker, and hair dryer are standard. Suites have kitchenettes. There's a fabulous café/restaurant and bar, plus a spa, Internet room, and meeting rooms. Still, I consider it overpriced.

Dominating the advertising pages of local publications, the **Hotel Casa Roland** (tel. 506/2231-6571, www.casa-roland.com, $85 s or $95 d rooms, $145 s/d executive, $200 s/d suite) is off Rohrmoser Boulevard, in Pavas. Crammed full of original paintings and oversize murals, plus potted plants, this rambling entity is claustrophobic (many rooms have no windows). An adjoining restaurant, however, impresses.

The overpriced **Barceló San José Palacio** (tel. 506/2220-2034, www.barcelo.com, $177 s/d standard, $223 junior suite, $235 executive, $270 suites) has 254 carpeted, air-conditioned rooms, plus all the expected facilities for a hotel of its size. However, the hotel's location on the Autopista General Cañas two kilometers northwest of the city necessitates a taxi, and it charges for its three-times-a-day shuttle to San José.

Other good options in this range, including the Ramada Plaza Herradura and the Costa Rica Marriott Hotel and Resort, can be found in Ciudad Cariari, just outside town and close to the airport.

East of Downtown

A standout hotel is the members-only (yet walk-ins allowed) **Hotel M** (tel. 506/2253-8345 or U.S. tel. 800/304-1625, www.hotelmcosta rica.com, $150–250 s/d), 100 meters north and 200 meters west of Mall San Pedro, in Barrio Dent. A tasteful restoration of a huge modernist 1950s home has produced a luxury hotel with 10 individually styled rooms. It has a "Sports Viewing Room," bar, gym, 12-person whirlpool tub, and solarium. However, it aims for an uninhibited mature adult crowd and can get very risqué!

Around the corner, and also offering a classy contemporary theme, the low-rise **Boutique Hotel Jade** (tel. 506/2224-2445, www.hotel boutiquejade.com, $107 s or $117 d standard, $142 s or $152 d suite) has 30 spacious, air-conditioned, carpeted, executive-style rooms with rich and lively decor, handsome fittings, cable TVs, desks, phones, modems, minibars, vanity chairs and sofa, and spacious showers. Six are handicapped equipped, and there are some nonsmoking rooms. Junior suites are truly classy. Murals adorn the corridor walls. There's a small lounge, a rear garden with a beautiful swimming pool and fountain, and a café. The highlight, however, is the sophisticated Jürgen's Restaurant, and there's a cafeteria and a gift store.

Casa Conde Apartotel & Suites (tel. 506/2274-2326, www.grupocasaconde.com, $165 s/d standard to $320 s/d suites), just south of the Autopista, is handy for exploring south of the city.

Farther Afield

To the northwest, in Uruca, the **Best Western Irazú** (Autopista General Cañas, tel. 506/2290-9300, www.bestwestern.com, $132 s/d) has 350 rooms, including a nonsmoking floor. Most rooms have a balcony overlooking the pool or gardens, plus direct-dial telephones, cable TVs, irons and ironing boards, and air-conditioning. The hotel is popular with tour groups and features all the amenities of a deluxe property: tennis courts, sauna, swimming pool, restaurant, casino, plus shops. It's overpriced, and its out-of-the-way location has little to recommend it, although there's an hourly shuttle bus to downtown.

Food

Recommended restaurants are listed according to type and location. Many of the best restaurants can be found in the suburb of Escazú, within a 15-minute drive of San José.

BREAKFAST
Downtown
I always enjoy **La Criollita** (Avenida 7, Calles 7/9, tel. 506/2256-6511, 7 A.M.–8 P.M. Mon.–Fri., 7–11 A.M. Sat.), a clean and atmospheric favorite of the business crowd. It serves full American breakfasts ($5) plus Tico breakfasts ($4), as well as soups, salads, sandwiches, tempting entrées such as garlic shrimp ($8) and roast chicken ($5), plus natural juices. You can choose an airy, skylit indoor setting with contemporary decor, or a shaded patio.

West of Downtown
The ◖ **Restaurante Grano de Oro** (Calle 30, Avenidas 2/4, tel. 506/2255-3322,

7 A.M.–10 P.M. daily) is justifiably popular with both tourists and Tico families and businesspeople for intimate breakfasts on the outdoor patio. Try the superb gringo or Tico breakfasts. The Gringo—a large bowl of granola with bananas, and thick slices of freshly baked whole-wheat toast—should see you through the day.

East of Downtown
One of the best spots is **Bagelmen's** (Avenida 2, Calle 33, tel. 800/2212-1314, 7 A.M.–9 P.M. daily), in Barrio La California; it also has an outlet in eastern San Pedro. The ambience is pleasing, with dark wood paneling and wrought-iron chairs. It serves Reuben, tuna, smoked ham, and other sandwiches ($2–5), as well as bagels (onion, pumpernickel, etc.), muffins, brownies, and cinnamon rolls, plus breakfast specials, from *gallo pinto* to scrambled eggs.

Restaurante Grano de Oro

© CHRISTOPHER P. BAKER

SAN JOSÉ

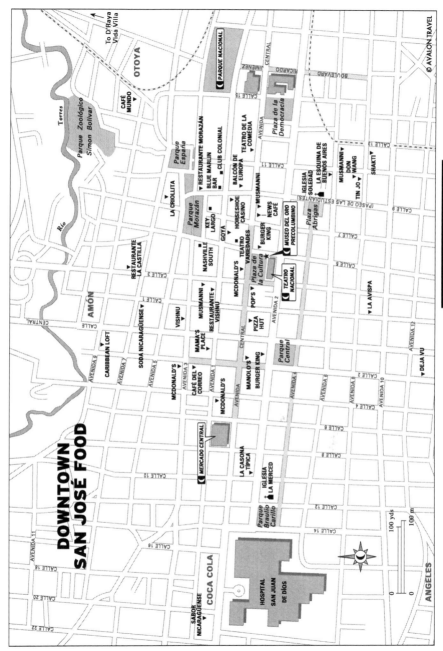

DOWNTOWN SAN JOSÉ FOOD

SAN JOSÉ

© AVALON TRAVEL

SODAS

Sodas—cheap snack bars serving typical Costa Rican fare—are a dime a dozen. They serve "working-class" fare, such as tripe soup, and chicken with rice-and-bean dishes. You can usually fill up for $2–4.

Downtown

The **Mercado Central** (Avenidas Central/1 and Calles 6/8) has dozens of inexpensive *sodas,* as does **Mercado La Coca Cola** (Avenidas 1/3, Calles 16/18), at the Coca-Cola bus station.

Manolo's (Avenida Central, Calles Central/2, tel. 506/2221-2041) is a lively 24-hour bistro with a menu that runs from salads to filet mignon. Try the *churros,* greasy Mexican doughnuts, best enjoyed at the patio open to the pedestrian street. Upstairs you can fill up on sandwiches, seafood, meat dishes, and other fare; the third story is a bit more elegant and double the price. It has a daily special for $2.50.

Another of my favorites is **Mama's Place** (Avenida 1, Calles Central/2, tel. 506/2223-2270, 7 A.M.–7 P.M. Mon.–Fri., 7 A.M.–4 P.M. Sat.), a mom-and-pop restaurant run by an Italian couple and serving huge portions heavy on the spaghetti. It serves *casados* ($4.50).

West of Downtown

I like **Sabor Nicaragüense** (Calle 20, Avenidas Central/1, tel. 506/2248-2547, and at Calle 1, Avenida 7, tel. 506/2223-1956, 7 A.M.–9 P.M. daily), a clean family diner with heaps of light and both inside and outside dining. It serves *gallo pinto,* enchiladas, and Nicaraguan specialties.

COSTA RICAN
Downtown

The Centro Comercial El Pueblo, in Barrio Tournón, has several restaurants known for traditional Costa Rican fare. **La Cocina de Leña** (tel. 506/2555-1360, 11:30 A.M.–10 P.M. Sun.–Thurs., 11 A.M.–11:30 P.M. Fri.–Sat., entrées $10) is touted as one of the best (although food and service don't always live up to expectations). Here, you'll dine by candlelight, surrounded by the warm ambience of a cozy rural

farmhouse. Dishes include creole chicken; *olla de carne* soup; and square tamales made with white cornmeal, mashed potatoes, and beef, pork, or chicken, wrapped tightly in a plantain leaf. The open-air **Lukas** (tel. 506/2257-7124), also in El Pueblo, is a steakhouse with a pleasing aesthetic that stays open until dawn. It serves an executive lunch (noon–3 P.M.) plus such dishes as mixed tacos and *picadillos* (small chopped-vegetable platter), fried pork, mixed meats, and grilled corvina in garlic butter prepared al dente over a large grill.

Budget hounds should head to **La Casona Típica** (Avenida 2, Calle 10, tel. 506/2248-0701, 6 A.M.–10 P.M. daily), done up like a traditional farmhouse. It serves great *casados* (from $4) and traditional Costa Rican fare.

The 24-hour **Café 1930** (tel. 506/2221-4000), the terrace café fronting the Gran Hotel, serves simple but filling Costa Rican fare—*arroz con pollo* (rice with chicken; $4) plus an excellent buffet (until 10 A.M.) and more—at a reasonable price. The hustle and bustle of the *plazuela* out front provides good theater. A pianist entertains.

West of Downtown

Jicaros del Campo (tel. 506/2520-1757, 11 A.M.–10 P.M. daily), on Sabana Sur, recreates a country farmhouse and serves *típico* cuisine, include a lunch buffet ($5). Try the tongue in tomato sauce ($12).

East of Downtown

Whappin' (Calle 35, Avenida 13, tel. 506/2283-1480, 11:30 A.M.–3 P.M. and 6–10 P.M. Mon.–Sat.), in Barrio Escalante, serves up delicious Caribbean cooking in no-frills surrounds. Many dishes are cooked in coconut milk, such as *rondon* stew, and even classic chicken, rice, and beans.

NOUVELLE
Downtown

Also on a Caribbean theme, **Caribbean Loft** (Avenida 9, Calles Central/2, tel. 506/2248-1778, 6–10 P.M. daily), in the Hotel City One, serves Caribbean fusion cuisine such as plantain ceviche, shrimp soup with rum and coconut ($5), and chicken in coconut sauce ($10). It has a huge cocktail list, and the magnesium-white decor transports you to a groovy Soho nightspot.

Alas, the world-class **Bakéa** closed in 2008.

West of Downtown

Don't leave town without eating at least once at the **(Restaurante Grano de Oro** (Calle 30, Avenidas 2/4, tel. 506/2255-3322, 7 A.M.–10 P.M. daily), where chef Francis Canal has successfully merged Costa Rican ingredients into an exciting fusion menu. Opened in 2007, this supremely elegant twin-level, wood-paneled restaurant has elevated dining in San José to new levels. The menu features such dishes as poached mahi mahi with leeks, tenderloin in green peppercorn sauce, a superb salmon soufflé, and sweet curry chicken sprinkled with coconut. Prices are exceedingly fair. So, too, the specialty cocktails and an array of desserts (you *must* try the sublime Pie Grano de Oro). The gracious interior has huge windows open to the shady dining patio surrounded by lush palms and stained-glass windows. And you can even dine at the island bar, with high chairs on the patio side. Upstairs, elegant banquet rooms accommodate groups.

Nearby, the **Iconos Café Bar** (tel. 506/2257-8787, 5 A.M.–10 P.M. daily) at Hotel Parque del Lago, is a chic option where the sophisticated decor is matched by superlative dishes that include ceviche, tilapia in olive oil with white wine and herb sauce ($15), and cheesecake.

(Park Café (Calle 44, tel. 506/2290-6324, noon A.M.–3 P.M. and 7–9:30 P.M. daily), off Sabana Norte, ranks among the finest restaurants in the country. Set in an antique store with courtyard garden, its contemporary styling (not to mention the setting) is bold and exciting. Michelin-starred English chef Richard Neat (with his wife Louise) conjures up divine tapas and globe-spanning dishes. Lunch might include a roasted tuna filet with ginger chutney and artichoke salad under the shade of the flowering orchid tree, while candlelit dinner might be ballotine of foie gras with grilled sweet corn.

East of Downtown

I like the marvelous aesthetic at **Jürgen's** (tel. 506/2283-2239, noon–2 P.M. and 6–10 P.M. Mon.–Fri., 6–10 P.M. Sat., $5–25), in the Boutique Hotel Jade in San Pedro. It serves such nouvelle treats as gazpacho, mussels Rockefeller, toast Winston (beef with white wine sauce, mushrooms, and cheese with salad), shrimp gratin with camembert and jelly, and tilapia with mustard. A bar and cigar lounge offer postprandial pleasure. It has a dress code and exemplary service.

CONTINENTAL
Downtown

The streetfront **News Café** (tel. 506/2222-3022, 6 A.M.–11 P.M. daily) of the Hotel Presidente has lost much of its cozy charm following a recent remodel, but is an airy place to watch the street life. Its wide-ranging menu runs from soups, salads, and sandwiches to calamari rings ($4), fajitas ($6), burgers (from $5), and even rib eye steak ($13) and garlic tilapia ($8.50). It has lunch specials and scrumptious desserts. Across the street, the **El Patio del Balmoral,** in the Hotel Balmoral, is a carbon copy.

East of Downtown

Restaurante Club Alemán (Avenida 8, Calles 35/37, tel. 506/2225-0366, fax 506/2225-2016, www.clubaleman.org, 11 A.M.–3 P.M. and 5–11 P.M. Tues.–Sat., 11 A.M.–6 P.M. Sun., $6.50–9) is a clean and elegant place with a typical German menu: Bismarck herring, sauerkraut and sauerbraten, pork Cordon Bleu, and peach melba.

SPANISH AND SOUTH AMERICAN
Downtown

The atmospheric **Goya** (Avenida 1, Calles 5/7, tel. 506/2221-3887, 11:30 A.M.–11 P.M. Mon.–Fri., noon–9 P.M. Sat.) provides generous *bocas* as well as excellent Spanish cuisine, including a splendid paella plus rabbit in wine, at moderate prices (entrées begin at about $6). It has live entertainment nightly.

One of my favorite gems is **(La Esquina**

de Buenos Aires (Calle 11, Avenida 4, tel. 506/2223-1909, laesquina@ice.co.cr, 11:30 A.M.–3 P.M. and 6–10:30 P.M. Mon.–Fri., 12:30–11 P.M. Sat., noon–10 P.M. Sun., $5–20), a genuine Argentinian restaurant with tremendous atmosphere. The wide-ranging menu of gourmet dishes is supported by a vast wine list heavy with malbecs. The onion soup is excellent, and I enjoyed a filet of sole in blue cheese with boiled potatoes ($9).

Meat eaters will salivate at **Fogo do Brasil** (Avenida las Amémericas, Calles 40/42, tel. 506/2248-2526, venast@fogobrasi.co.cr, 11:30 A.M.–10:30 P.M. daily, $6–25), a classy Brazilian steakhouse where waiters dressed as Argentinian *gauchos* serve charcoal roasted meats. It also has a pasta bar and excellent buffet and the wide-ranging menu even has sushi. And the caipirinhas are great! It offers free hotel shuttles.

West of Downtown

The **Café España** (Calle 44, tel. 506/2290-8526, noon–8 P.M. Mon.–Sat.), in Edificio Casa de España, on Sabana Norte, offers tapas in an elegant bar setting. Prices are fair at $2–9.

Another of my favorite restaurants is ◖ **Machu Picchu** (Calle 32, Avenidas 1/3, tel. 506/2222-7384, 11 A.M.–3 P.M. and 6–10 P.M. Mon.–Sat.), with delicious authentic Peruvian seafood and *spicy* sauces! Try the superb ceviches ($2.50–5) or the *picante de mariscos* (seafood casserole with onions, garlic, olives, and cheese), enjoyed in a suitably nautical ambience. The menu is moderately priced (some potato entrées are less than $4; garlic octopus is $6). The pisco sours are powerful.

East of Downtown

Chef Emilio Machado works wonders at **Marbella Restaurant** (Centro Comercial de la Calle Real, tel. 506/2224-9452, 11:30 A.M.–3 P.M. and 6:30–10:30 P.M. Tues.–Thurs., until 11 P.M. Fri., noon–3:30 P.M. and 6:30–11:30 P.M. Sat., noon–5 P.M. Sun., $5–15), in San Pedro. The large selection of seafood dishes includes paella Marbella (shellfish and sea bass) and paella Valenciana (chicken

and seafood). The paella Madrilena (rabbit, chicken, and pork) is particularly good.

FRENCH AND MEDITERRANEAN
Downtown

The Italianate **Gourmet Restaurant** (Avenida 2, Calle 3, tel. 506/2221-4000, noon–3 A.M. daily, $11–28), on the ground floor of the Gran Hotel, is a lovely space for enjoying Mediterranean seafood.

West of Downtown

The elegant **La Bastille** (Paseo Colón, Calle 22, tel. 506/2255-4994, www.la-bastille -restaurante.com, noon–2 P.M. and 6–10 P.M. Mon.–Fri., 6–10 P.M. Sat., $6–30) is the oldest French restaurant in San José. Chef Hans Pulfer produces superb French cuisine.

East of Downtown

Cognoscenti craving classical French head to the **L'Ile de France** (tel. 506/2234-7850, 6 A.M.–10 P.M. Mon.–Sat.), at L'Hôtel Le Bergerac, serving entrées such as *pâté de lapin au poivre* (rabbit with green peppercorns and cognac), vichysoisse, salon in cream of watercress, and sea bass in thyme sauce. Desserts include profiteroles, and there's a large wine collection.

Nearby is **Le Chandelier** (tel. 506/2225-3980, www.lechandeliercr.com, 11:30 A.M.–2:30 P.M. and 6:30–11 P.M. Mon.–Fri., and 6:30–11 P.M. Sat., $5–25), in a restored Mediterranean-style mansion 400 meters south of the ICE building in San Pedro. It has 10 separate dining areas, including a sculpture garden. Chef Claude Dubuis conjures up imaginative cuisine, stunning sauces, and his own version of typical Costa Rican fare: roasted heart of palm, cream of *pejivalle* soup, gratin of corvina with avocado. The restaurant is adorned with murals and the owner's art.

Exuding romantic ambience with its dark wainscoting and soft lighting, the bistro-style **Olio** (Calle 33, Avenida 3/5, tel. 506/2281-0541, 11:30 A.M.–1 A.M. Mon., 4 P.M.–midnight Sat., $5–12), 200 meters north of Bagelmon's in Barrio Escalante, specializes in

Spanish tapas and Mediterranean fare, such as a Greek *mezza* plate. Meat lovers should try the *arrollado siciliano*—a filet of steak stuffed with sun-dried tomatoes, spinach, and mozzarella. It has a large wine list.

ITALIAN
Downtown
The **Balcón de Europa** (Calle 9, Avenidas Central/1, tel. 506/2221-4841, 11:30 A.M.– 10 P.M. Sun.–Fri., below $10) is a revered culinary shrine where the late chef Franco Piatti was a local institution who presented moderately priced cuisine from central Italy in an appropriately warm, welcoming setting with wood-paneled walls festooned with historic photos and framed proverbs. New chef Jean Pierre has tilted the menu towards French-Italian.

West of Downtown
The elegant **L'Olivo** (tel. 506/2220-9440, noon–3 P.M. and 6:30–10:30 P.M. Mon.–Sat., $4–15), next to Hotel Palma Real on Sabana Norte, serves pastas and seafood.

East of Downtown
Il Ponte Vecchio (tel. 506/2283-1810, noon–2 P.M. and 6–10:30 P.M. Mon.–Sat., $5– 15), 200 meters west of San Pedro church, serves moderately priced, tasty cuisine cooked with imported Italian ingredients such as sun-dried tomatoes, porcini mushrooms, and basil. Pastas are homemade by chef Antonio D'Alaimo.

A more down-home ambience can be enjoyed at **Il Pomodoro** (Calle Central, tel. 506/2224-0966, 11:30 A.M.–11 P.M. Sun.– Mon. and Thurs., 11 A.M.–midnight Fri.–Sat.), 100 meters north of San Pedro church; it's a popular hangout for university types who favor the pizzas ($4–8).

MIDDLE EASTERN
For a taste of the Levantine, head to **Lubnan** (Paseo Colón, Calles 22/24, tel. 506/2257- 6071, 11 A.M.–3 P.M. and 6–11 P.M. Tues.– Sat., 11 A.M.–4 P.M. Sun.), serving noteworthy Middle Eastern specialties such as shish kebob, falafel, *michi malfuf* (stuffed cabbage), and

kafta naie (marinated ground beef); most entrées cost less than $10. Middle Eastern music plays, waiters wear fezzes, and a hookah is passed around!

East of downtown, **Aya Sofia** (Calle 31, tel. 506/2224-5050, 7 A.M.–7 P.M. Mon.–Sat.), in Barrio Escalante, is a Turkish bistro serving hummus, goat cheese marinated with olives and herbs ($3), and sandwiches. It has belly dancing.

MEXICAN
One of the best options is **Los Antojitos** (11:30 A.M.–11 P.M. Mon.–Thurs., 11 A.M.–midnight Fri.–Sat., 11 A.M.–10 P.M. Sun.), inexpensive yet classy, and popular with Ticos. Meals start at $4 and a grilled tenderloin costs $10. It has four outlets in San José: west of Sabana Park, in Rohrmoser (tel. 506/2231-5564); east of downtown in Los Yoses (tel. 506/2225-9525); in Centro Comerciál del Sur, in San Pedro (tel. 506/2227-4160); and north of town on the road to Tibas (tel. 506/2235-3961).

ASIAN
Downtown
My favorite Asian restaurant is **Tin Jo** (Calle 11, Avenidas 6/8, tel. 506/2221-7605, 11:30 A.M.–3 P.M. and 5:30–10 P.M. Mon.– Thurs. and Sun., 11:30 A.M.–11 P.M. Fri.–Sat.). The decor is quaintly colonial Costa Rican, but the food is distinctly Asian: tasty Mandarin and Szechuan specialties, plus Thai, Indian, Indonesian, and Japanese food at moderate prices. It even has sushi, satay ($4), samosas ($3), and curries ($6).

Next door, **Don Wang** (tel. 506/2223-6484, 10:30 A.M.–3:30 P.M. and 5:30–10:30 P.M. Mon.–Thurs., until 11 P.M. Fri., 10:30 A.M.– 11 P.M. Sat., 10 A.M.–10 P.M. Sun.) serves generous, reasonably priced portions, although the quality isn't up to par with Tin Jo. It offers Taiwanese dishes and dim sum. Seafood dishes are a particular bargain ($4–6); it also has *platos fuertes* (set meals) for $3.

West of Downtown
The **Flor del Loto** (Calle 46, tel. 506/2232- 4652, 11 A.M.–3 P.M., 6–11 P.M. Mon.–Fri.,

11 A.M.–11 P.M. Sat., 11 A.M.–9:30 P.M. Sun., $7), in Sabana Norte, is the place if you like your Chinese food hot and spicy. Mouth-searing specialties include *mo-shu-yock* (Shi Chuen–style pork) and *ma po tofu* (vegetables, bamboo shoots, and tofu stir-fried in sizzling hot-pepper oil).

Another acclaimed option is **King's Garden** (tel. 506/2255-3838, 11 A.M.–1 A.M. daily), adjoining the Centro Comercial Yaohan. The head chef is from Hong Kong; the menu features many favorites from the city, as well as Cantonese and Szechuan dishes. A set dinner for two costs about $14.

Restaurante Pacífico (Calle 24, Paseo Colón/Avenida 2, tel. 506/2257-9523, 11:30 A.M.–3 P.M. and 5:30–10:30 P.M. Mon.–Sat., 5–9 P.M. Sun.) is a small family-run Japanese restaurant with a sushi bar. It has a homey atmosphere.

East of Downtown

The **Restaurante Casa China** (Calle 25, Avenidas 8/10, tel. 506/2257-8392, 9 A.M.–11 P.M. daily) is the real McCoy and the head-quarters for the Asociación China de Costa Rica. This no-frills, refectory-style eatery serves real Chinese dishes for $4–12. You could be in Shanghai! It even has ping-pong and theatrical performances.

For sushi, head to **Ichiban** (tel. 506/2291-5220, noon–3 P.M. and 6:30–11 P.M. Mon.–Fri., noon–10 P.M. Sat.–Sun., $5–15), in Centro Comercial Calle Real, on Avenida Central, in San Pedro. Try the Ichiban roll: fried noodles with crab, eel, avocado, and cream cheese.

SEAFOOD AND STEAKS
Downtown

I recommend **Restaurant El Oasis** (Avenida 7, Calles 3/5, tel. 506/2255-0448, 4–11 P.M. Tues.–Sat., noon–7 P.M. Sun., $5–20), in the Hotel Santo Tomás, a real charmer with a co-lonial tiled bar, elegant place settings, ceiling fans, and a courtyard garden with waterfall. It serves shrimp cocktails, salads, filet mignon, sea bass with garlic and white wine, pastas, and desserts such as banana flambé.

West of Downtown

For a cheap meal, check out **Marisquería La Princesa Marina** (tel. 506/2296-7667, 11 A.M.–10:30 P.M. Mon.–Sat., 11 A.M.–9 P.M. Sun., $1–9), on Sabana Oeste. This canteen-like seafood spot is a favorite of Ticos at lunch. It serves from a wide menu and wins no gour-met prizes, but at least you fill up.

Another great spot is **La Fuente de Los Mariscos** (tel. 506/2231-0631, 11:15 A.M.–10:30 P.M. daily, $4–12), in Centro Comercial San José adjacent to the Hotel Irazú in La Uruca, with seafood at moderate prices.

VEGETARIAN
Downtown

The superb ◖ **Restaurante Vishnu** (Avenida 1, Calles 1/3, tel. 506/2250-6063, vishnu@racsa.co.cr, 7 A.M.–9 P.M. Mon.–Sat., 9 A.M.–7 P.M. Sun.) serves health-food break-fasts, lunches, and dinners. Meals are generous in size and low in price (a *casado* costs $4); the menu includes veggie lasagna, veggie burgers, and fruit salads. Vishnu has 10 other outlets around town, including at Calle 14, Avenida Central/2, and at Calle 1, Avenida 4.

Restaurant Eco-Shakti (Avenida 8, Calles 11/13, tel. 2222-4475, 7:30 A.M.–7 P.M. Mon.–Fri., 8 A.M.–6 P.M. Sat.) serves veggies dishes, from black bean soup to soy burgers and yo-gurt shakes.

East of Downtown

The small, simple, inexpensive **Restaurante Vegetariano San Pedro** (tel. 506/2224-1163, 10 A.M.–6 P.M. Mon.–Fri.), on Calle Central 200 meters north of San Pedro church, has a *casado* with juice ($2), plus soy burgers, salads, and pastas.

CAFÉS AND PASTRY SHOPS
Downtown

One of the best coffee shops in town is the **Café Teatro** (tel. 506/2221-1329 ext. 250, 9 A.M.–5 P.M. Mon.–Fri., 9 A.M.–4 P.M. Sat.) inside the foyer of Teatro Nacional. A lovely neoclassical Parisian ambience is comple-mented by tempting sandwiches, snacks, and desserts. Across the plaza, the **Café Teando** (tel. 506/2221-4000, 24 hours) in the foyer of the Gran Hotel competes with hip contemporary decor.

The **Café del Correo** (tel. 506/2257-3670, 9 A.M.–7 P.M. Mon.–Fri., 10 A.M.–5 P.M. Sat.), in the post office overlooking Avenida Central, is another little gem. Soft lighting and jazz provide a romantic background for enjoying lattes, espressos, mochas, and pastries such as cheesecakes and strawberry tarts.

The artsy, Argentinian-run **Café de la Posada** (Avenida 2, Calle 17, tel. 506/2258-1027, 9 A.M.–7 P.M. Mon.–Thurs., 9 A.M.–11 P.M. Fri.–Sun.) appeals to a bohemian crowd. It offers jazz and classical music and serves espressos and cappuccinos, plus quiches, omelettes, sandwiches (all from $1.50), Argentinian *empanadas,* and tempting desserts.

The bohemian **Café Mundo** (Avenida 9, Calle 15, tel. 506/2222-6190, 11 A.M.–11 P.M. Mon.–Fri., noon–2:30 P.M. and 5 P.M.–midnight Sat.) is popular with businessfolk. This handsome remake of a colonial mansion has open patios and several indoor rooms. Its eclectic menu spans tempura veggies ($5.50), chicken satay ($5.50), Caesar salad (from $3.50), pastas, pizzas, surf and turf (from $8), desserts such as tiramisu, plus cappuccino ($1.75). Portions are generous.

Spoon (www.spooncr.com) has burgeoned over the past decade from a small takeout bakery into a chain with outlets throughout the city, including Avenida Central, Calle 5/7 (tel. 506/2255-2480) and Mall Pedro in Los Yoses (tel. 506/2283-4538). In addition to desserts, Spoon serves sandwiches, salads, lasagna, soups, *empanadas* (pastries stuffed with chicken and other meats), and *lapices,* the Costa Rican equivalent of submarine sandwiches, all at bargain prices. **Musmanni** (tel. 506/2296-5750, www.musmanni.net) is a national *pastelería* chain selling pastries and fresh breads.

West of Downtown
Chocoholics should sniff out the **Taller de Chocolate** (Calle 26, Paseo Colón/Avenida 2, tel. 506/2231-4840, and 100 meters

north of Torre La Sabana, on Sabana Norte, 10 A.M.–6 P.M. Mon.–Fri., 10 A.M.–3 P.M. Sat.). It sells delicious homemade chocolates, plus cappuccinos and espressos.

One block west, a gorgeous 1950s modernist home hosts **Asís** (tel. 506/2232-2657, noon–6 P.M. Mon.–Fri.), a marvelously upscale venue for pastries, teas, and coffees, plus pastas, pizzas, and *casado* lunches ($4).

East of Downtown
In Los Yoses I like **Café Ruiseñor** (Avenida Central, Calles 41/43, tel. 506/2225-2562, 7 A.M.–7:30 P.M. Mon.–Fri., 10 A.M.–6 P.M. Sat.), a classy, trendy spot serving a range of coffee drinks including lattes ($1.75), plus soups, salads, sandwiches, and entrées such as curried chicken, sea bass with herbs and white wine, pepper steak, as well as desserts such as banana splits, German apple tart, and parfaits.

Ice cream fans should head to **Häagen-Dazs Café** (Avenida Central, tel. 506/2280-5245, 10 A.M.–10 P.M. Sun.–Thurs., 10 A.M.–11 P.M. Fri.–Sat.), in San Pedro. This clean, contemporary parlor serves everyone's favorite ice cream, from cones to special sundaes. It also has espressos and cappuccinos. Nearby, and new in 2008, the **Kai Café and Lunch** (Avenida Central, tel. 506/2281-0955, 9 A.M.–9 P.M. Mon.–Sat., 10 A.M.–8 P.M. Sun.) offers a beautiful contemporary elegance, with leather sofas and walls of glass. It serves sandwiches, paninis, salads, and scrumptious desserts.

MARKETS
Within the warren of the **Mercado Central** (Calles 6/8, Avenidas Central/1, closed Sun.) and adjoining **Mercado Borbón** (Calle 8, Avenidas 3/5) are stands selling poultry, flowers, meat, fish, medicinal herbs, fresh produce, and coffee. The **Mercado Paso de la Vaca** (Avenida 7, Calle 6) is a clean produce market selling everything from fresh herbs to meats; take a taxi and be careful walking around this area.

Cabernet (in the Centro Comercial Real #16, tel. 506/2281-2481, mseaward@racsa.co.cr), off Avenida Central in San Pedro, sells all things wine-related and is well stocked with wines.

Information and Services

TOURIST INFORMATION

ICT operates a tourist information office booth at the airport (tel. 506/2443-2883). Its main tourist information office (tel. 506/2222-1090, ictplazacultura@icc.co.cr), beneath the Plaza de la Cultura on Calle 5, is open 9 A.M.–1 P.M. and 2–5 P.M. Mon.–Sat.; its outlet in the post office (Calle 2, Avenidas 1/3) was temporarily closed at last visit.

TRAVEL AGENCIES

There are dozens of English-speaking travel agencies in San José. They can arrange city tours, one- and multi-day excursions, beach resort vacations, air transportation, and more. Above all I recommend U.S.-run **Costa Rica Expeditions** (Avenida 3, Calle Central, tel. 506/2257-0766, www.costaricaexpeditions.com). **STI Travel** (Avenida Central, Calle 35, tel. 506/2283-8200, www.stitravel.com), in Los Yoses, specializes in cheap airfares.

NEWSPAPERS AND MAGAZINES

Most major hotel gift stores sell popular international newspapers and periodicals, as does **7th Street Books** (Calle 7, Avenidas Central/1). **La Casa de las Revistas** has outlets at Calle Central, Avenidas 4/6 (tel. 506/2222-0987), and Calle 7, Avenidas 1/3 (tel. 506/2256-5092), selling a wide range of Spanish- and English-language magazines.

LIBRARIES

The **Biblioteca Nacional** (National Library, Avenida 3, Calles 15/17, tel. 506/2257-4814, 8 A.M.–4 P.M. Mon.–Fri.) has more than 100,000 volumes.

You may be able to access the **Biblioteca Universidad de Costa Rica** (tel. 506/2253-6152), at the university in San Pedro; and the **Mark Twain Library** (Calle Negritos, tel. 506/2225-9433 or 800/2077-7500, www.cccncr.com/biblioteca.html, 9 A.M.–7 P.M.

Mon.–Fri., 9 A.M.–noon Sat.), in the Centro Cultural Norteamericano in Los Yoses.

MONEY

San José has dozens of banks. Most have a separate foreign exchange counter, will give cash advances against your Visa card (and in some cases, your MasterCard), and have ATM machines that issue cash advances against credit cards. Outside banking hours, head to **Teledolar Casa de Cambio** (Paseo Colón, Calle 24, tel. 506/2248-1718, 8:30 A.M.–4 P.M. Mon.–Sat., 8:30 A.M.–2 P.M. Sun.), which changes foreign currency.

Credomatic (Calle Central, Avenidas 3/5, tel. 506/2295-9000, www.credomatic.com) will assist you with card replacement for Visa and MasterCard.

POST AND COMMUNICATIONS
Mail

The main post office, or **Correo Central** (Calle 2, Avenidas 1/3, tel. 506/2223-9766, www.correos.go.cr, 8 A.M.–5 P.M. Mon.–Fri. 7:30 A.M.–noon Sat.), has a 24-hour stamp machine. You can also buy stamps and post your mail at the front desks of upscale hotels.

To collect incoming mail at the Correo Central, go to window 17 through the entrance nearest Avenida 1. You'll need to show your passport. There's a small charge (about $0.25) per letter.

FedEx (Paseo Colón, Calle 40, tel. 506/2255-4567) and **DHL** (Paseo Colón, Calles 30/32, tel. 506/2209-6000) offer courier service.

Telephones

There are public telephones throughout the city. **KitCom** (Calle 3, Avenidas 1/3, tel. 506/2258-0303, www.kitcom.net), on the second floor of the OTEC Building, 175 meters north of the Plaza de la Cultura, has a complete telecommunications office.

Alternately, use the **ICE** offices on Sabana

© CHRISTOPHER P. BAKER

Casa Amarilla and INS building

Norte or south of the San Pedro roundabout; or RACSA's **Telecommunications Center** (Avenida 5, Calle Central/1, tel. 506/2287-0515, 7:30 A.M.–4:30 P.M. Mon.–Fri., and 9 A.M.–1 P.M. Sat.).

Internet Access

Most hotels have Internet access for guests, and there are Internet cafés throughout the city.

Downtown, one of the best Internet cafés is the **CyberCafé** (Avenida 2, Calles 1/3, tel. 506/2233-3310, 7 A.M.–9 P.M. daily), in the basement of Las Arcadas, 50 meters west of the Teatro Nacional. It also has a pleasant outdoor dining area and a travel desk.

Internet Café Costa Rica has outlets at Avenida Central, Calle 2 (tel. 506/2255-0540, 9 A.M.–10 P.M. daily); at Avenida Central, Calle 3 (tel. 506/2255-1154, 9 A.M.–10 P.M. daily); west of downtown in Centro Colón (tel. 506/2233-3179, 8 A.M.–9 P.M. Mon.–Sat.); and east of downtown at Avenida Central, Calle Central (tel. 506/2224-7382, 24 hours), in San Pedro.

LAUNDRIES

Most laundries *(lavanderías)* offer a wash-and-dry service (about $4 per load). Downtown, try **Sixaola** (Avenida 2, Calles 7/9, tel. 506/2240-7667), which has outlets throughout San José. The **CyberCafé** (Avenida 2, Calles 1/3, tel. 506/2233-3310, 7 A.M.–9 P.M. daily) has a self-service laundry ($5 wash and dry per tub).

PHOTOGRAPHY

The major photographic outlet is **Dima** (Avenida Central, Calles 3/5, tel. 506/2222-3969), which also offers repair service.

MEDICAL SERVICES

The privately run **Hospital Clínica Bíblica** (tel. 506/2522-1000 or 2257-5252) is the best hospital in town and accepts U.S. Medicare.

The public **Hospital Dr. Calderón Guardia** (tel. 506/2257-7922) and **Hospital México** (tel. 506/2242-6700) are alternatives, as is the public **Hospital San Juan de Díos** (Paseo Colón, Calle 16, tel. 506/2257-6282), the most centrally located medical facility. They provide free emergency health care on the Social Security system. The **Children's Hospital** (Hospital Nacional de Niños, Paseo Colón, tel. 506/2222-0122) cares for children. Women are served by the **Hospital de la Mujer** (Calle Central, Avenida 22, tel. 506/2257-9111).

TOILETS

There are clean public toilets beneath the Plaza de la Cultura.

Getting There and Around

GETTING THERE
By Air
Juan Santamaría International Airport (tel. 506/2437-2626, www.alterra.co.cr) is on the outskirts of Alajuela, 17 kilometers west of San José.

A tourist information booth (tel. 506/2443-2883, 9 A.M.–5 P.M. Mon.–Fri.) is in the baggage claim area, and another immediately beyond Customs. There's a bank in the departure terminal. Taxis accept dollars, but you'll need local currency for public transport into San José. (At press time, the **departure tax** for travelers leaving Costa Rica was $26, payable in dollars or colones equivalent. You pay at the booth to the right inside the departure lounge prior to checking in. To avoid long lines, pay your departure tax when you arrive in Costa Rica.)

Pavas Airport (Tobías Bolaños, tel. 506/2232-2820), about four kilometers west of town, is used for domestic flights, including small charter planes and air-taxis. Bus 14B runs from Avenida 1, Calles 16/18, and stops in Pavas, a short walk from the airport.

By Train
Train service runs between San Pedro and Pavas, five times daily Monday–Friday and three times daily Saturday and Sunday, departing the **Pacific Railway Station** (Avenida 20, Calle Central/7, tel. 506/2257-6161).

By Car
Westbound from downtown San José, Paseo Colón feeds right onto the Pan-American Highway (Hwy. 1, or Autopista General Cañas), which leads to the Pacific coast, Guanacaste, and Nicaragua. A tollbooth just east of the airport charges 60 colones ($0.25) per vehicle for westbound traffic only.

Calle 3 leads north from downtown and becomes the Guápiles Highway (Hwy. 32) for Puerto Limón and the Caribbean and Northern Zone. Avenida 2 leads east via San Pedro to Cartago and the southern section of the Pan-American Highway (Hwy. 2), bound for Panamá; there's a tollbooth (60 colones) about three kilometers east of the suburb of San Pedro.

By Bus
San José has no central terminal. Buses for Puerto Limón and the Caribbean depart from the **Gran Terminál Caribe** on Calle Central, Avenidas 15/17. Most buses to other destinations leave from the area referred to as **Coca-Cola** (the zone is centered on Avenida 3, Calles 16/18, but encompasses many surrounding streets; there's a 24-hour **police station,** tel. 506/2257-3096). Other buses leave from the bus company office or a streetside bus stop *(parada)*. Many street departure points are unmarked, so ask locals.

A Safe Passage/Viaje Seguro (tel. 506/8365-9678, www.costaricabustickets.com) will make your bus reservations and buy your tickets for you in advance. Tickets cost $15 single, $25 a pair to anywhere in the nation. It also offers airport transfers.

The ICT publishes a listing of current bus schedules, including the bus company and telephone numbers.

GETTING AROUND
Getting to and from the Airport
TAXIS
Taxi Aeropuerto (tel. 506/2222-6865, www.taxiaeropuerto.com) operates taxis between the airport and downtown and accepts 24-hour reservations; they're orange (local San José taxis are red). The legally sanctioned fare into downtown San José adjusts according to gasoline prices and at press time was $23 by day and night ($5 to Alajuela); you pay in advance at an official booth immediately outside the arrivals lounge and are given a ticket.

BUSES
Public buses run by **Tuasa** (tel. 506/2222-5325) operate between downtown San José (Avenida 2, Calles 12/14) and Alajuela every five minutes via the airport, 5 A.M.–10 P.M., and then every 30 minutes 10 P.M.–5 A.M. The fare is 250 colones ($0.50). The driver will make change, but you'll need small bills or coins. The journey takes about 30 minutes. Luggage space is limited.

SHUTTLES
Interbus (tel. 506/2283-5573, www.interbusonline.com) offers a 24-hour airport shuttle for $6 per person by reservation. **Grayline** (tel. 506/2220-2126, www.graylinecostarica.com) operates an "Airline Express" linking the airport and downtown San José every 30 minutes ($10). Some hotels offer free shuttles.
   Costa Rica Van Go (tel. 506/2441-7837, www.costaricavango.com) offers private airport transfers.

CAR RENTAL
Several car-rental companies have offices immediately beyond Customs; additional offices are within one kilometer east of the airport, in Río Segundo de Alajuela. If you plan on spending a few days in San José before heading off to explore the country, you'll be better off using taxis and local buses. Make your reservations *before* departing home.

Park & Fly (tel. 506/2441-3134, www.parkandflycr.com) offers 24/7 shuttle service between its parking facility and the airport.

By Car
There are about 50 car-rental agencies in San José, concentrated along Paseo Colón. However, don't even think about using a rental car for travel *within* San José. Too many headaches! Most places are quickly and easily reached by taxi, by bus, or on foot. Note that Paseo Colón (normally with two-way traffic) is one-way only—eastbound—weekdays 6:30–8:30 A.M.

   A peripheral highway *(circunvalación)* passes around the south and east sides of San José.

   Private parking lots offer secure 24-hour parking; you must leave your ignition key with the attendant. Never park in a no-parking zone, marked Control por Grúa (Controlled by tow truck). Regulations are efficiently enforced.

   Break-ins and theft are common (rental cars are especially vulnerable). Never leave anything of value in your car, even in the trunk.

By Bus
San José has an excellent network of privately owned local bus services. Most buses operate 5 A.M.–10 P.M., with frequency of service determined by demand. Downtown and suburban San José buses operate every few minutes. Buses to suburbs often fill up, so it's best to board at their principal downtown *parada,* designated by a sign, Parada de Autobuses, showing the route name and number.

   A sign in the windshield tells the route number and destination. Fares are marked by the doors and are collected when you board. Drivers provide change and tend to be honest. Buses cost 75 colones ($0.15) downtown and under 100 colones elsewhere within the metropolitan area.

   From the west, the most convenient bus into town is the Sabana-Cementerio service (route 2), which runs counterclockwise between Sabana Sur and downtown along Avenida 10, then back along Avenida 3 (past the "Coca-Cola" bus station) and

SAN JOSÉ

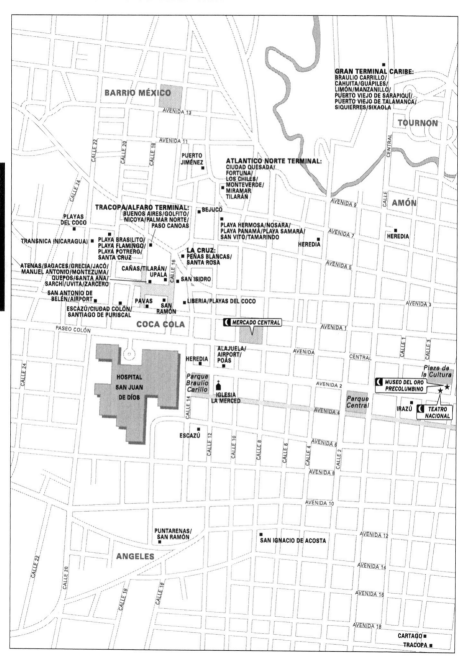

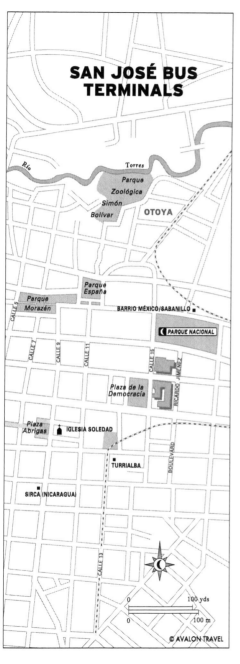

Paseo Colón. The Cementerio-Estadio service (route 7) runs in the opposite direction along Paseo Colón and Avenida 2 and back along Avenida 12. Both take about 40 minutes to complete the circle.

Buses to Los Yoses and San Pedro run east along Avenida 2 and, beyond Calle 29, along Avenida Central. Buses to Coronado begin at Calle 3, Avenidas 5/7; to Guadalupe at Avenida 3, Calles Central/1; to Moravia from Avenida 3, Calles 3/5; and to Pavas from Avenida 1, Calle 18.

Be wary of pickpockets on buses.

By Train

A great way to beat the cross-town traffic is to hop on the **Tren Interurbano** commuter train that links Pavas (on the west side of town) with San Pedro (on the east side). Trains operate five times daily in each direction (5 A.M.–6 P.M. Mon.–Fri., 150 colones, or $0.25 cents), stopping at or near the U.S. Embassy, La Salle (south side of Parque La Sabana), and Universidad de Costa Rica (University of Costa Rica).

As of May 2009, San José is also linked by train to the nearby town of Heredia.

By Taxi

Licensed taxis are red (taxis exclusively serving the airport are orange); if it's any other color, it's a "pirate" taxi operating illegally. You can travel anywhere within the city for less than $6 (the base fare is $0.85).

By law taxi drivers (who must display a business card with name, license plate, and other details) must use their meters *(marias)* for journeys of less than 12 kilometers. Always demand that the taxi driver use his meter, otherwise you're going to get ripped off. Some taxi drivers get commissions from certain hotels: They may tell you that the place you're seeking is closed or full and will try to persuade you to go to a hotel they recommend. Don't fall for this! If the cabbie insists, get out and take another cab.

You do not normally tip taxi drivers in Costa Rica, but give your taxi driver any small change.

Finding a taxi is usually not a problem, except during rush hour and when it's raining. One of the best places is Parque Central, where they line up on Avenida 2, and in front of the Gran Hotel and Teatro Nacional two blocks east. Otherwise, call **Coopetaxi** (tel. 506/2235-9966) or **Coopetico** (tel. 506/2224-7979).

There are reports of taxi drivers making sexual advances toward single women; this is more likely to happen with pirate taxis, which you should always avoid. Few taxis have seat belts! The belts are usually there; it's the connecting latches that are missing. And if an on-call taxi draws up to your hotel against the flow of traffic, as often happens, you'd be wise to seek another taxi.

By Tour

Californian Kevin Wilks's **Tico Walks** (tel. 506/2234-8575, www.ticowalks.com, $10 per person) offers 2.5-hour educational tours of downtown San José, beginning at the Teatro Nacional on Tuesday, Thursday, Saturday, and Sunday at 10 P.M.

A fun way to explore is with **Segway Costa Rica** (tel. 506/2232-4822, www.segwaycosta rica.com), which currently has a two-hour tour of Parque Sabana ($69). Expect more options to be added.

www.moon.com

DESTINATIONS | ACTIVITIES | BLOGS | MAPS | BOOKS

MOON.COM is all new, and ready to help plan your next trip! Filled with fresh trip ideas and strategies, author interviews, informative blogs, a detailed map library, and descriptions of all the Moon guidebooks, Moon.com is all you need to get out and explore the world—or even places in your own backyard. As always, when you travel with Moon, expect an experience that is uncommon and truly unique.

MAP SYMBOLS

▦	Expressway	▐	Highlight	✗	Airfield	⌁	Golf Course
	Primary Road	○	City/Town	✗	Airport	▣	Parking Area
	Secondary Road	◉	State Capital	▲	Mountain	▰	Archaeological Site
	Unpaved Road	⊛	National Capital	✛	Unique Natural Feature	⬧	Church
	Trail	★	Point of Interest				
	Ferry	•	Accommodation	⌇	Waterfall	⬢	Gas Station
	Railroad	▼	Restaurant/Bar	⬧	Park	◌	Glacier
	Pedestrian Walkway	▪	Other Location	⬢	Trailhead	⬰	Mangrove
	Stairs	⋀	Campground	✘	Skiing Area	▨	Reef
						▭	Swamp

CONVERSION TABLES

°C = (°F - 32) / 1.8
°F = (°C x 1.8) + 32
1 inch = 2.54 centimeters (cm)
1 foot = 0.304 meters (m)
1 yard = 0.914 meters
1 mile = 1.6093 kilometers (km)
1 km = 0.6214 miles
1 fathom = 1.8288 m
1 chain = 20.1168 m
1 furlong = 201.168 m
1 acre = 0.4047 hectares
1 sq km = 100 hectares
1 sq mile = 2.59 square km
1 ounce = 28.35 grams
1 pound = 0.4536 kilograms
1 short ton = 0.90718 metric ton
1 short ton = 2,000 pounds
1 long ton = 1.016 metric tons
1 long ton = 2,240 pounds
1 metric ton = 1,000 kilograms
1 quart = 0.94635 liters
1 US gallon = 3.7854 liters
1 Imperial gallon = 4.5459 liters
1 nautical mile = 1.852 km

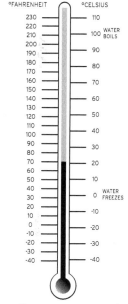

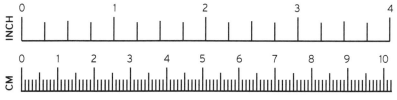

MOON COSTA RICA'S CARIBBEAN COAST

Avalon Travel
a member of the Perseus Books Group
1700 Fourth Street
Berkeley, CA 94710, USA
www.moon.com

Editors: Sabrina Young, Michelle Cadden
Series Manager: Kathryn Ettinger
Copy Editor: Valerie Sellers Blanton
Graphics Coordinator: Kathryn Osgood
Production Coordinators: Darren Alessi,
 Amber Pirker
Cover Designer: Kathryn Osgood
Map Editor: Albert Angulo
Cartographers: Chris Markiewicz, Kat Bennett

ISBN: 978-1-59880-497-3

Front cover photo: "Costa Rica island" © Luis Seco,
dreamstime.com

Title page: © Christopher P. Baker

Printed in the United States

ABOUT THE AUTHOR

Christopher P. Baker

Since 1983, Christopher P. Baker has made his living as a professional travel writer, photographer, lecturer, and tour guide, and is acclaimed for his specialist knowledge of Cuba and Costa Rica, about which he has written 10 books. He has contributed to more than 150 publications worldwide including *Caribbean Travel & Life, Elle, Maxim, National Geographic Traveler, The Robb Report,* and the *Los Angeles Times.* He has been profiled in *USA Today,* and appears frequently on radio and television talk shows and as a guest lecturer aboard cruise ships. Christopher currently escorts cruise-tours to Costa Rica and Panama on behalf of National Geographic Expeditions, and has been privileged to address such organizations as the National Press Club, the World Affairs Council, and the National Geographic Society's *Live... From National Geographic.*

Christopher was born and raised in Yorkshire, England. He received a BA in geography at University College, London, and master's degrees in Latin American studies from Liverpool University and in education from the Institute of Education, London University. He began his writing career in 1978 as Contributing Editor on Latin America for *Land & Liberty,* a London-based political journal. In 1980 he received a Scripps-Howard Foundation Scholarship in Journalism to attend the University of California, Berkeley.

Christopher is the author of more than 20 books, including *Moon Costa Rica, Moon Cuba* and *Mi Moto Fidel: Motorcycling Through Castro's Cuba,* winner of two national book awards. In 2008, he was named the prestigious Lowell Thomas Travel Journalist of the Year by the Society of American Travel Writers Foundation. His other awards include the 1995 Benjamin Franklin Best Travel Guide Award (for *Moon Costa Rica*) and the Caribbean Tourism Organization's 2005 Travel Journalist of the Year. You can learn more about Christopher's work on his website, www.christopherbaker.com.